vah
n (Gurnard's Head)
nor

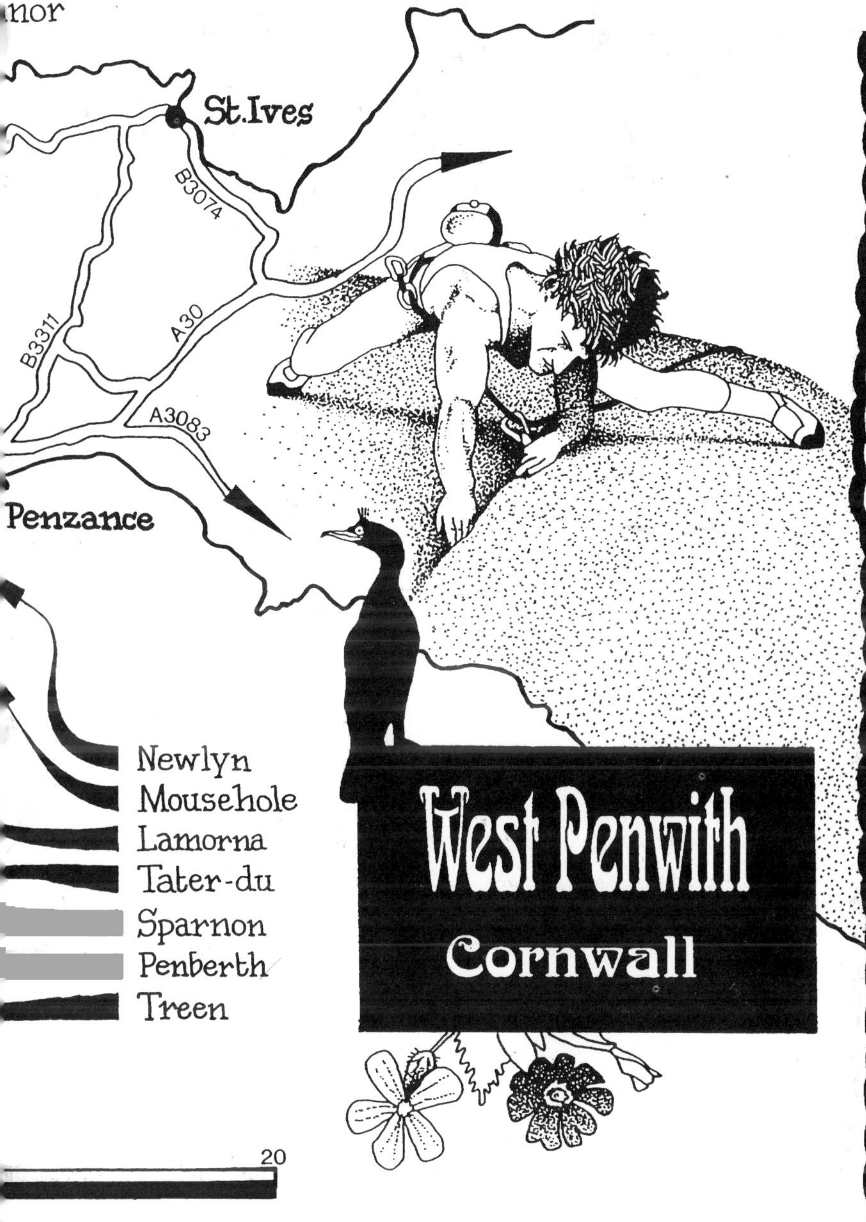

St.Ives

B3074

B3311

A30

A3083

Penzance

Newlyn
Mousehole
Lamorna
Tater-du
Sparnon
Penberth
Treen

20

West Penwith
Cornwall

Cornish Rock

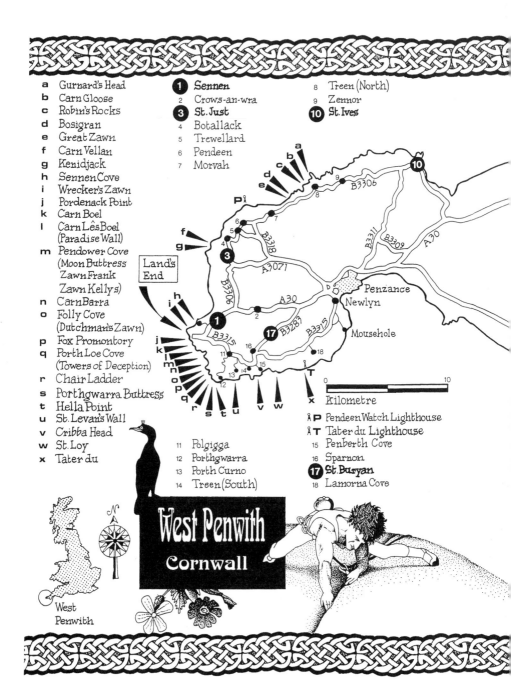

a	Gurnard's Head	**1**	Sennen	8	Treen (North)
b	Carn Gloose	2	Crows-an-wra	9	Zennor
c	Robin's Rocks	**3**	St. Just	**10**	St. Ives
d	Bosigran	4	Botallack		
e	Great Zawn	5	Trewellard		
f	Carn Vellan	6	Pendeen		
g	Kenidjack	7	Morvah		
h	Sennen Cove				
i	Wrecker's Zawn				
j	Pordenack Point				
k	Carn Boel				
l	Carn Lês Boel (Paradise Wall)				
m	Pendower Cove (Moon Buttress Zawn Frank Zawn Kellys)				
n	Carn Barra				
o	Folly Cove (Dutchman's Zawn)				
p	Fox Promontory				
q	Porth Loe Cove (Towers of Deception)				
r	Chair Ladder				
s	Porthgwarra Buttress				
t	Hella Point				
u	St. Levan's Wall				
v	Cribba Head				
w	St. Loy				
x	Tater du				

Land's End

Penzance

Newlyn

Mousehole

0 — 10 Kilometre

⚲ **P** Pendeen Watch Lighthouse
⚲ **T** Tater du Lighthouse

11	Polgigga	15	Penberth Cove
12	Porthgwarra	16	Sparnon
13	Porth Curno	**17**	St. Buryan
14	Treen (South)	18	Lamorna Cove

West Penwith
Cornwall

West Penwith

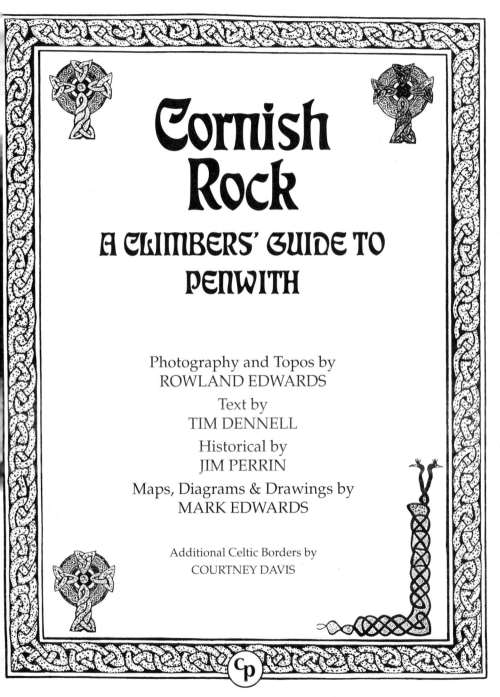

Cornish Rock

A CLIMBERS' GUIDE TO PENWITH

Photography and Topos by
ROWLAND EDWARDS

Text by
TIM DENNELL

Historical by
JIM PERRIN

Maps, Diagrams & Drawings by
MARK EDWARDS

Additional Celtic Borders by
COURTNEY DAVIS

CICERONE PRESS
MILNTHORPE, CUMBRIA, U.K.

© Rowland Edwards 1996
ISBN 1 85284 2083
First printed in 1997
A catalogue record for this book is available from the British Library

"We shall not cease from exploration
And the end of all our exploring
Will be to arrive where we started
And know the place for the first time."

'Little Gidding'
from *The Four Quartets* by T.S. Eliot

Text printed by St Edmundsbury Press, Bury St Edmunds, Suffolk
Colour printed by Steve Newbury Print & Design, Chorley, Lancashire
Cover printed by Carnmor Print & Design, London Road, Preston,
Lancashire.
Binding by Hunter & Foulis Ltd, Edinburgh

Front Cover: Atlantic Ocean Wall E5 6b, Land's End. Climber: Mark Edwards
Back Cover: Eat 'Em and Smile E6 7a, Dutchman's Zawn. Climber: Mark Edwards

THE AUTHORS

Rowland Edwards, originally from Bolton in Lancashire, first began climbing in the 1950s and is a British and Alpine guide. He has based his rock climbing school in West Penwith since 1978 and since 1982, also operates the school in Spain. Formerly a senior instructor at Plas Y Brenin in Wales for 12 years; he has climbed extensively throughout the world producing over a thousand significant new routes, predominantly in North Wales, Cornwall and Jordan. He now spends most of the year running the climbing school and developing new areas in the mountains of the Costa Blanca, Spain. He also wrote the first guide to North Wales limestone.

Tim Dennell is a native of the south-west and a climbing enthusiast who has climbed extensively throughout the area and now lives in London. He has collaborated on three interim climbing guides to areas in south Devon and is a former south-west area reporter for *Climber* magazine. For two years he sat on the Environmental Liaison Committee for the Penwith and Lizard area. He has worked in administration, the book trade, as a teacher and as an outdoor education instructor. He is also a counsellor.

Jim Perrin is a well-known climber, author, essayist and observer of the climbing scene. As well as writing for most of the British outdoor titles and contributing a monthly column for the magazine *Climber,* he is a regular contributor to the national daily press. He has written several books, the second of which, *Menlove,* was the first outright winner of the Boardman Tasker Prize for Mountain Literature. Two collections of his essays have been published, *On And Off The Rocks* and *Yes, To Dance* as well as a forthcoming biography of Don Whillans.

Mark Edwards is Rowland's eldest son and has been climbing since the age of 16 producing a large number of high standard routes both in Cornwall, Spain and Jordan. An instructor at his father's school, he climbs in both the traditional and sports styles to the highest standards. He has put up some of the most serious and technically demanding routes in West Penwith, many still without second ascents. He also trained as a graphic design artist at a local art school.

ACKNOWLEDGEMENTS

All guidebooks produced as collective endeavours involve a synthesis of ideas but, by and large, the following demarcation lines have been adhered to. Photography, topos and route-checking by Rowland Edwards. All text unless otherwise specified by Tim Dennell. Maps, diagrams, drawings and route-checking by Mark Edwards. The Historical by Jim Perrin.

We would like to thank the following for sparing the time and energy to read and comment on the manuscript, or sections thereof, or for providing advice, information, comments or photographs. However, responsibility for the views expressed and any errors or omissions remain, of course, entirely our own.

Faber and Faber Ltd for their kind permission to quote from *The Four Quartets*, 'Little Gidding' by T.S. Eliot. Cassell PLC for their kind permission to reproduce five Celtic design map borders by Courtney Davis and used on those for the title page, Porthgwarra area, St. Levan, Cribba Head and Bosigran. All rights to these patterns and designs are reserved to the authors and they may not be reproduced in any form whatsoever for commercial gain without prior permission in writing from the publishers, Cassell plc. (Other borders produced by M. Edwards and T. Dennell.) Lauren (I've been called worse) Cole for her computing expertise and endless patience. Bernadette Lintell and Ida Sabelis for their translations. Of the National Trust: Peter Mansfield, Regional Agent; John Brooks, Countryside Manager and Katherine Hern, Advisor on Nature Conservation. Nicola George, Assistant Conservation Officer for English Nature. Kath Pyke, Access and Conservation Officer for the BMC. David Flumm, Warden of the Royal Society for the Protection of Birds. All members of the West Cornwall Environmental Liaison Committee chaired by Mike Banks. Don Buckfield, Land's End Sector Officer HM Coastguard. Lieutenant T.C. Getsy of 771 Squadron, RNAS Culdrose. Mr Arthur Duplock of the Plymouth Branch of the Red Cross. HM Coastguard Station, Falmouth. Peter Kaye and crews from RNAS Culdrose for the aerial photography. Robin Dennell, Gay Jones and Prudence de Villiers for their proofreading and constructive suggestions. To those who endure, support and encourage our endeavours; Esther, Carmel and Jayne. The climbers: Jim Adamson, Mike Barnes, Paul Birchell, Dave Blackwell, Ian Blake, Dyane Cooper, Noel Crane, Martin Crocker, Brian Dent, Carl Edwards, Jayne Fisher, Andy Grieve, Nick Hancock, Peter Kaye, Pete Longley, Shane Ohly, Ken Palmer, Paul Rigg, Scott Rourke, Frieke Schepman, Pete Saunders, Rob Smart, Rob Southall, Tony Thompson, Paul Twomey and Steve Waldren and all those others who generously gave their time, comments or route information. Last, but by no means least, Walt Unsworth and Brian and Aileen Evans of Cicerone for their encouragement and wisdom.

Authors' note: it is the nature of contemporary guidebooks that an attitude is struck over the issue of bolting; this guide inevitably is no exception, whilst hopefully not blurring its main function.

CONTENTS

INTRODUCTION 9
  Cornish Rock - The Climbing 9
  How to use this book 9
The Basics 12
    How to get there 12
    Getting around 12
    Staying there 13
    Food and drink 14
    Pubs 14
    Phone and postal services 15
    Fuel 15
    Where to play 15
    Useful information 16
    Some Cornish words 16
    Bienvenue à Penwith en Cornwall 18
    Wikommen in Cornwall 19
    Welkom in Cornwall 20

The Green Pages 21
    Conservation and access 21
    Groups and clubs 22
    SSSIs 22
    Access and restrictions 22
    Nests 23
    The environmental challenge 23
    Plant life and climbers 24
    Birds and climbers 25
    Wildlife and climbers 26

Accidents, Safety, Rescue & First Aid . 28
    Waves 28
    Protection 29
    In situ protection 29
    Getting lost 30
    It's all common sense 30
  ● Getting help 31
    Helicopter rescue 32
  ● Basic first aid 32
    Snake bite 33
    Carrying a casualty 33
    Hospitals 33

The Rock and Climbing 34
    Granite, greenstone, slate 34
The Sea and Climbing 36

Tides, sea conditions 36
The Weather and Climbing 39
Grades 40
    The British grading system 40
    Aid grades 41
    Grading problems and symbols 41
    Stars 42
    The finest technical pitches? 42
    Tables of international grades 43
Ethics 45
    BMC area policy 46
    Some suggestions 47
    Gardening 48
Historical by Jim Perrin 49
Symbols, Abbreviations and Terms 54

THE CLIFFS
 1) Gurnard's Head 57
 2) Carn Gloose 61
 3) Robin's Rocks ٥3
 4) Bosigran 65
 5) Bosigran Ridge & Bosigran Great .....
      Zawn 86
 6) Carn Vellan 96
 7) Kenidjack 102
 8) Sennen Cove & Irish Lady Cove . 108
 9) Land's End 131
10) Pordenack Point 159
11) Carn Boel
      The Immaculate Crack Area ... 170
12) Carn Lês Boel 173
13) Pendower Cove 183
14) Frank's Zawn & Zawn Kellys 188
15) Carn Barra 193
16) Dutchman's Zawn 204
17) Folly Cove 208
18) Fox Promontory 211
19) Porth Loe Cove 215
      The Towers of Deception 217
20) Chair Ladder 218
21) Porthgwarra Buttress & Hella
      Point 242
22) St. Levan's Wall 247
23) Cribba Head 250

24) St. Loy 254
25) Tater Du 256

MAPS AND DIAGRAMS

1) West Penwith, Cornwall 2
   The area and cliffs
2) Gurnard's Head
   Gurnard's Head, Carn Gloose
   & Robin's Rocks 56
3) Bosigran 65
4) Carn Vellan 96
5) Kenidjack 102
6) Land's End Area
   Sennen Cove to Carn Boel 107
7) Sennen Cove 108
8) Land's End 130
9) Prodenack Point 159
10) Carn Boel 169

11) Porthgwarra Area
    Carn Lês Boel to Hella Point .. 172
12) Carn Lês Boel 173
13) Pendower Cove 182
14) Frank's Zawn, diagram 189
15) Zawn Kellys 190
16) Carn Barra 193
17) Folly Cove & Dutchman's Zawn 204
18) Chair Ladder
    Porth Loe Cove, Chair Ladder
    Porthgwarra Buttress & Hella
    Point 218
19) St. Levan 246
20) St. Burryan Area
    Cribba Head to Tater du 249
21) Cribba Head 250
22) Tater du 256
23) West Penwith, Cornwall. Roads, ...
    towns and villages - ....
    .. Inside back cover (also page 13)

Advice to Readers

Readers are advised that whilst every effort has been taken to ensure the accuracy of this guidebook, changes can occur which may affect the contents. It is advisable to check locally on transport, parking, accommodation, pubs and shops etc. but rights of way can change as can the cliffs themselves. The publisher would welcome notes of any such changes, comments about grades and First Known Ascents etc. It is always advisable to monitor the climbing press regarding the access and conservation situation in the area.

INTRODUCTION

CORNISH ROCK - THE CLIMBING

I, who shall remain Nameless, was back in Penwith chasing a Dream, or was I just suffering from Déjà Vu by repeating Ding? Banged my head on a Doorpost after having drunk too much from a Little Brown Jug and heard an Anvil Chorus sing.

All this time I climbed with a Saxon covered in woad, an Illustrated Man called Andrew; Crazy from the Heat we sat in High Spirits on the Grand Plage and watched a Variety Show. After the Last Dancer had given us a Private Performance I had a Baptism of Fire, almost Virgin on a Crisis, after a Golden Brown Free Spirit called Alison gave me the Evil Eye when on A Swift Flight of Fancy I tried to feel her Rib.

I retired to an Armchair with an Irish Whiskey in a state of total Kafoozalem. Andrew had an Initiation into playing Black Jack with Lost Souls Kate, Delilah, Gillian and Crazy Man Michael, so at a Right Angle to them I Zig Zagged to the Doorway. Gillian got Dead Lucky and pulled an Ace of Spades and the Crazy Man wept Tears of a Clown as he lost all Hope and forfeited a String of Pearls and Cool Diamonds. He had nothing left but a bad case of the High Street Blues but it was really Much Ado About Nothing.

Down these Mean Streets a man must go and I had a pocketful of Burning Gold. I tried to saddle Pegasus, whom I'd left in a Hayloft, but My Mule Don't Like You Laffin and a passing dog with No Name and a mouth like a Shark took a Monster Munch out of my leg but left behind a Terrier's Tooth. I may have the Patience of a Paragon but I swung on my Axis and with some Finesse, and the cunning of Daedalus, put a Muzzle on the Behemoth in a Titanic Cress-Cendo of Footless Madness. My strength of Samson had something to do with all the Protein and Opium I'd had and I climbed a Hot Line out of Desolation Row, like a Saddle Tramp with Dangerous Visions, up the Staircase and took an Astral Stroll across the High Frontier to a Gig In The Sky.

That night I Pendulumed across a Chimney onto the Big Top and sought Absolution in the arms of Pauline, a Painted Lady and we listened to the Echoes of Voices from the Steeple until Reveille. The next day, a Day-tripper on the Edge of Time at World's End, my Dream turned out to be no Ghost, but a Liberator and, I realised I really had found Xanadu and not a Fool's Lode.

HOW TO USE THIS BOOK

It is hoped that this guide to the West Penwith district of Cornwall is as functional, informative, and accessible as it can be This is a photo-topo visitors' guide and contains selected cliffs and climbs; it is not a definitive guide, though it more

Gig In The Sky, E2 6a, Pordenack Point. Climber: Rowland Edwards. Photo: Esther Edwards

than adequately covers each cliff shown and holds enough routes to satisfy even the most rock hungry of climbers.

The introductory chapters provide information invaluable to visitors to the area and can be used both to plan a trip and help add to the enjoyment of a visit. It is worth dipping into at some point, before rather than after in the case of the accident and rescue section. The cliffs are arranged in a north to south order, as you would pass them on a drive along the coast road from St. Ives to Newlyn. Each cliff is introduced with maps and brief information on its location, parking, approach, character, aspect, tides, type of climbs and environmental concerns etc. which is then followed by the relevant topos and text. The topos and diagrams are at the heart of this guide and should be used in conjunction with the text to identify any desired route, descent or abseil point. Once you have located one major line or feature then the rest should fall into place. On a few climbs where a logical or even graded combination of pitches exist we depict these at the expense of historical purity.

The routes have been depicted, where possible, in relation to your direction of approach. Where this is not possible, or there are a number of approaches available, then they are depicted from left to right. The routes are all numbered in sequence as you would pass their starts. Each route has a number which remains constant even if it appears on more than one topo. If there is a jump in the numbers on a topo, this means that the missing routes are on another topo. If, after a route name, the letter T is found inside brackets followed by a number e.g. (T2) then this is informing you which other topo for that cliff it also appears on. Any information as to its character and first ascent details are only given once, for the topo on which its features and line are most pronounced. In order to minimise confusion as to where routes go, should they cross, they are numbered at start and finish and if necessary elsewhere on the line to help you follow its path. In some cases the same section of cliff is shown more than once, but with different routes or from a different angle, so as to clearly show where each route goes without causing confusion.

As well as pitch lengths, grades and stars, that give a subjective opinion as to quality, we use symbols e.g. 🔗🏊 🌶 ☺ etc. to let you know roughly what to expect; but where thought necessary this is supplemented by some text as to the climb's character, type of protection or, in a few instances, description to help you find your way. The occasional route, not found on a topo, is covered solely by description. These are indicated by a letter rather than a number. We also provide first ascent details. Each route number is also preceded by the initials of the cliff it is on, just to help you find your place in the book more easily.

The glossary of abbreviations and symbols is presented at the beginning of the cliffs section and is repeated on page 265 for ease of reference. It sounds complicated, but in practice is very easy to use.

THE BASICS

West Penwith is the area that forms the most south-westerly peninsula in England. (The Lizard is the most southerly point, Land's End the most south-westerly.) It is the area lying beyond Penzance and St. Ives and is reminiscent of Western Ireland. Its landscape is of two distinct types.

In the north-west, between St. Ives and St. Just, the cliff tops are covered by rugged moorland, the cliffs themselves drop precipitously into the sea and arriving at the start of a climb can be an adventure in itself. It has the feel of a true wilderness area.

South-east of St. Just the land has become more tamed; rolling pasture unfolds, the cliff tops are less harsh, covered in maritime heath; a blaze of purple and yellow in summer. The headlands and cliffs, often no less precipitous, often jut out into the sea and are marked by prominent black, gold and green castellated buttresses.

Much of the coast is owned by the National Trust, who do not just own the land but also manage it. For example, government grants are distributed to farmers to keep the "old" field systems (the field boundaries at Bosigran date back to prehistoric times), graze livestock on heath-land and not use pesticides; much of the work they do is unseen by the visitor but of vital importance in preserving this unique area.

HOW TO GET THERE
1) By Car
Land's End is approximately 205 miles (330kms) from Bristol, 378 miles (608kms) from Sheffield, 320 miles (515kms) from London and 368 miles (592kms) from Folkstone or Dover. From Bristol the M5 provides motorway to Exeter where, at junction 31, you can either join the dual carriageway of the A30 to Penzance via Okehampton, Bodmin and Redruth (probably quickest) or continue down the A38 via the Tamar bridge to join the A30 at Bodmin.

2) By Train, Coach or Air
There is a regular rail service from Edinburgh, London or Bristol to Penzance. A branch line runs from St. Earth to St. Ives. There is a daily coach service from London Victoria via Heathrow, and also one from Bristol to Penzance. Genuine rock stars may be interested in the Land's End Aerodrome which has links with Exeter, Newquay and the Isles of Scilly; there are flights from London to both Exeter and Newquay. There are ferry services from Brittany, Ireland and Spain to Plymouth.

GETTING AROUND
The A30 continues from Penzance to Sennen and Land's End. Major roads also lead to St. Just or Pendeen. A narrow coast road (B3306/B3315) winds its way from St. Ives southwards round to Newlyn via Zennor, Pendeen, St. Just, Sennen

and St Buryan. As well as providing access to cliffs, this road, and the villages along it, will provide virtually everything you will need, e.g. accommodation, food, drink etc. Car theft and break-ins are not a major problem in this area and long may it stay this way. The area is ideal for a cycle tour, but bikes are not welcomed on the coastal path.

There is a local bus service from Penzance to Sennen and Land's End, from Penzance to St. Just via Pendeen and from Land's End to St. Ives via St. Just; other villages are also serviced. Some bus stops have timetables and further information can be obtained from Western National at the Penzance Bus Station, tel: (01736) 69469.

In Penzance the rail, coach and bus stations are conveniently situated alongside each other along with a tourist information office. It is useful, but not essential, to have the Ordnance Survey map 'Land's End, The Lizard and the Isles of Scilly'. 1:50,000 Landranger series, sheet 203. Do note that some place names occur more than once. e.g. Treen. Cliffs are given a grid reference at the start of each chapter.

Our maps use scales marked in kilometres; 1km is the equivalent of 1,094yds or .62 of a mile, 10kms is equal to 6.2 miles and so on.

STAYING HERE

At Bosigran there is a Climbers' Club Hut, the Count House, which is open to members of the CC, their affiliates and guests. The Climbers' Club or British Mountaineering Council can provide details of how to go about booking places.

There is a youth hostel at Kellynack, near St. Just; the address is Letcha Vean,

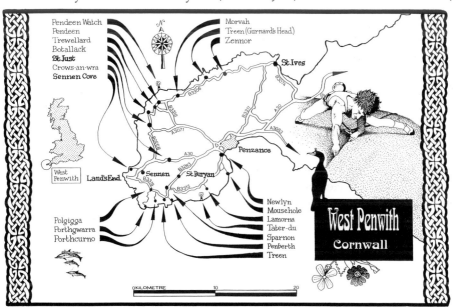

St. Just. Tel: (01736) 788437. There is also a youth hostel just outside Penzance at Castle Horneck, Alverton, Penzance. Tel: (01736) 626661. Whitesand's Lodge in Sennen offers bunk-house accommodation.

Many farms in the area offer bed and breakfast, as do hotels and guest houses, and the prices tend to be standardised throughout the area.

There are camping and caravanning sites at Trewellard, Botallack, Kellynack, around Sennen, St. Buryan and at Treen (south). The one at Kellynack is very sheltered, the one at Botallack has an off-licence, whilst the "Seaview" at Sennen has excellent facilities but is within staggering distance of two pubs, one with a disco, and can be noisy at night in summer, so take your pick. Camping on the cliff tops is actively discouraged.

FOOD & DRINK

Most pubs also serve meals; it pays to shop around. But don't expect to get food late at night in a pub, particularly when it's busy. Most villages have a café serving the ubiquitous cream tea and the occasional restaurant is found. For a major treat visit St. Ives or Penzance - and a visit to a Cornish meadery is a must. There are fish 'n' chip shops in Pendeen (closes approx 7.30pm), St. Just (closes approx. 9pm), Sennen and Sennen Cove (closes approx. 8pm). Times can vary according to the number of tourists.

If you're catering for yourself, St. Just has a co-op mini-market (open 9am - 8pm weekdays, 10am - 4pm Sundays), a baker, a butcher, a fruit & veg shop etc. Pendeen, Trewellard, Botallack, Sennen and Sennen Cove all have shops selling food, milk and the like. The local shops also double as newsagents, off-licences. etc. Don't leave shopping until too late in the day, though shops may be open later in the height of the tourist season. If all else fails (out of season the area hibernates) the Wimpy Bar in Penzance is open every day. For breakfasts, the cafés on the sea front in Sennen Cove are well recommended.

PUBS

At Zennor, the Tinner's Arms has a distinctive red light on its wall which has long guided travellers in to enjoy an open fire, real ale from the cask and the company of the odd feline or two. The Gurnard's Head Hotel is popular with climbers staying at Bosigran and it's well worth checking out its menu.

In Pendeen the Radjel is a foxy little pub and the nearby North Inn also offers a warm welcome. The pubs in Trewellard and Botallack are worth visiting to escape from rooms full of climbers reading guidebooks.

St. Just is a positive metropolis; The Star is many people's favourite and consequently often packed; it also has a family room. The Commercial Hotel hosts discos during the holiday season and is popular with the armed services visiting for training purposes (on the cliffs that is, not in the pub). The King's Arms, Wellington Hotel (which welcomes children) and Miner's Arms all offer a formidable welcome.

In Sennen Cove the Old Success isn't as popular with climbers as it once was, but it is with tourists. The First and Last Inn on the road above the cove is popular with tourists, climbers, surfers and locals alike; both serve excellent meals. Further on the Wrecker's Inn has weekend discos during the summer months; be in by 11pm or else there will be no admission. This closes at 12.30am and is popular with the young 'holiday' crowd. At Treen (south) the Logan Rock Inn is very popular with those camping nearby.

Ales to look out for include Hicks from St. Austell Breweries, Flowers, and Sharp's Doom Bar. Then there are the ciders. Most pubs have cigarette and condom machines.

PHONE & POSTAL SERVICES ✆ ✉

There are phone boxes at Morvah, Trewellard, Botallack, St. Just, Sennen, Sennen Cove, Land's End, Porthgwarra and St. Buryan. The Count House has a telephone, as do most pubs. For Emergency Services dial 999 and ask for the Coastguard (mountain rescue), Ambulance, Police or Fire Service as appropriate. The Coastguard co-ordinates cliff rescues; the call is free as is the rescue. There are post offices at St. Just, Sennen and St. Buryan. They close for lunch (12 noon-1pm). Post boxes are at Zennor, Treen (north & south coasts), Morvah, Pendeen, Trewellard, Botallack, Kellynack and Sennen Cove. Some shops sell books of stamps and they all sell the compulsory postcard.

FUEL

Don't leave buying it too late, as even in summer the average closing time is 6pm. Petrol stations can be found at Trewellard, St. Just, Sennen and Buryas Bridge. There are 24-hour stations in Penzance and at Loggan's Moor on the A30 near Hale.

WHERE TO PLAY

One of the best beaches in the area, and which is popular with surfers, is at Sennen Cove (for surf shops visit St. Ives). Other good ones for a family day out are at Porthcurno, Porthgwarra, Porth Chapel and St. Levan; all of which are very clean and the water clear. The celebrated open air Minack Theatre near Porthcurno is open during the summer months; book and arrive early, and take your own cushions and a blanket for evening performances. The Geevor mine and museum at Levant near Pendeen is a monument to the area's once thriving tin industry.

At Chysauster near Nancledra an Iron Age village has been recreated on the foundations of the original. The whole peninsula is littered with Iron and Bronze Age remains (and legend) including standing stones, stone circles and burial chambers. An easy walk begins at Lanyon near Morvah and takes in the holed stone, Men-an-tol, the Nine Sisters stone circle, the Ding-Dong tin mine and the Lanyon Quoit.

St. Ives is a tourist resort stuffed full of art galleries, gift shops and cafés. It also has two beaches and a Tate Gallery which is worth a visit if only for the building's architecture. Penzance has many restaurants, bars, clubs and the like, and the nearby St. Michael's Mount is worth walking over to at low tide, or by boat at other times - a good wet day outing. Penzance and St. Ives both have cinemas. For updated local information, the *What's On* magazine is fairly comprehensive.

The nearest indoor climbing walls are in Helston and Plymouth.

USEFUL INFORMATION

- The nearest **Hospital** is the West Cornwall Hospital, St. Clare Street, Penzance. Tel: (01736) 62382.
- St. Ives, Penzance and St. Just have **chemists** and **doctors'** surgeries. Bank holiday cover is provided as it is for **dentists**. They also have **vets**.
- A Lloyds and Barclays **bank** are both situated in St. Just; neither, however, have a cash dispenser! The nearest **cash points** are in Penzance or St. Ives.
- A part-time **police station** is in St. Just, the main police station is in Penzance. Tel: (01736) 62395.
- To contact the **Penzance Tourist Information Office** Tel: (01736) 796297.
- If you need to wash clothes, **launderettes** can be found in Sennen Cove, Penzance and St. Ives.
- The nearest shops selling **process paid film** are in Penzance or St. Ives.
- A **climbing shop** is in Truro (Penrose Sports, town quay); 30 miles (45kms) from Land's End.
- **BBC Radio Cornwall** can be found on 103.9 MHz. VHF/FM.
- A 45 metre rope is 147.6ft long. A 50 metre one, 164ft long.
- The **Climbers' Club** publishes two definitive guides to the area covering both the north and south coasts.

SOME CORNISH WORDS

ALS/BOEL/VOEL	Cliff
BOS/BOD	Dwelling. Romantics say that Bosigran means the dwelling of Ygrain (Igrane), mother of the legendary King Arthur. Pedants say that it's a dwelling either by the home of a crane or at the head of a dry valley.
CARN	Cairn or rock pile
CARREK	Rock
CHY	House
CRIB	Ridge or crest
DHU/DU	Black

ENYS	Island
KELLYS	Lost, hidden or grove
MAEN/MEN	Stone
MEUR/VEO	Big or great
MOR	Sea
NANS/NANT/LANT	Valley
PENN/PEN	Head, end or top
PENWYTH	Extremity (of the land)
PEDN/PEDEN	Headland
POLL/POL	Pool
PORTH	Harbour or cove
ROS	Heath or moor
TOL	Holed
TRE	Hamlet or homestead
TREATH	Beach
WHEAL	Mine
ZAWN/SAWN	Cleft

Sennen Cove - Pedn Mên Du - is the headland of black stone; Chair Ladder - Tol Pedn Penwith - is the holed headland of Penwith; Zawn Kellys is the hidden cleft and so on.

The ancient burial chamber of Lanyon Quoit. (1700 - 1500 BC)

BIENVENUE À PENWITH EN CORNWALL

Bienvenue à Penwith en Cornwall, région où vous trouverez les meilleures falaises granit pour itinéraires d'escalade en Grande Bretagne. La plus grande partie de ce guide est écrit en Anglais, mais le topos vous apportera toutes les informations nécessaires sur les difficultés pour suivre un itinéraire. Les pitons ou repères sont très rares dans cette région et vous devez placer les vôtres par vous-même sur la plupart de ces itinéraires. Les itinéraires non munis de pitons sont indiqués par un **R** suivant le degré de difficulté.

Un ◉ indique que vous devez l'envisager avec prudence et précaution jusqu'à ce que le degré de difficulté soit indiqué ou confirmé, et un ☠ vous indique qu'en cas de chute, vous pouvez être blessé très sérieusement ou gravement. Un ⚕ symbole indique que la roche à cet endroit est extrêmement friable et que l'itinéraire doit être évité, bien que sur d'autres itinéraires il peut également y avoir des chutes de roche sans que vous ayez rencontré ce symbole. Quelques itinéraires ont un ☺. Ceux-ci sont très fiables et sans danger et peuvent être envisagés avec confiance. Mais il vous incombe à nouveau de placer vos pitons. Beaucoup d'autres itinéraires sont également sans danger.

Une ★ ou ★★★★ étoiles en regard d'un itinéraire signifie que celui-ci est d'une excellente qualité, allant graduellement d'une échelle de un à quatre. Mais rappelez-vous toujours que tous les itinéraires indiqués dans ce guide sont de bonne qualité.

Il y a beaucoup de campings disponibles dans cette région et la plupart des fermes et pensions de famille louent également des chambres pour la nuit. La plus grande majorité des magasins se trouvent à Saint Juste et Sennen. Ces deux villages sont munis de station service. Il est important que vous sachiez que c'est une région dite "à marée". Beaucoup de magasins vendent des calendriers de marées et les horaires de marées sont aussi indiqués dans le journal local.

En cas d'accident grave, composez le 999 et demandez les Gardes Côtes (Coastguard). Donnez votre nom, les détails de l'accident et le numéro de téléphone d'où vous appelez aux Gardes Côtes. En Grande Bretange, le 999 ainsi que les secours sont gratuits.

Cette région est très belle et très riche en plantes rares ainsi que mouettes et goélands. Il est très important que ceux-ci ne soient pas détruits, endomagés de quelque façon que ce soit, ou tués. Déplacez-vous avec attention afin d'éviter les nids d'oiseaux.

Passer un très bon séjour en appréciant la région et les itinéraires d'escalade.

*　　*　　*

WILKOMMEN IN CORNWALL

Wir heißen sie herzlich wilkommen in Penwith, Cornwall - Heimat der schönsten Kletterrouten in Granitfelsen der großbritanischen Küste. Der Großteil dieses Führers ist auf englisch, aber die Topos werden Ihnen, zusammen mit den Schwierigkeitsangaben (UIAA/F/US/UK), alle Informationen bieten die sie benötigen um die einzelnen Routen zu klettern.

Haken sind seltsam in diesem Gebiet. Sie werden meistens die eigenen Sicherungsmaßnahmen treffen müssen: "Friends" und Nuts sind von jeher eine große Hilfe... Diejenigen Routen die (ganz oder zum Teil) nicht mit Haken gesichert sind, sind mittels einem "R" neben der Schwierigkeitsstufe gekennzeichnet.

Eine 💣 besagt, daß die Route sehr vorsichtig angegangen werden muß weil sie noch nicht offiziell bestätigt worden ist. Und ein ☠ heißt daß ein Sturz schwere Verletzungen, wenn nicht schlimmeres, zur Folge haben könnte. Ein ✠ Symbol bei einer Route heißt daß sie überdurchschnittlich von Steinschlag gefährdet ist und eigentlich nicht geklettert werden sollte. Allerdings können auch andere Routen etwas Steinschlag aufweisen. Einige Routen haben ein ☺ Symbol. Das sind die sicheren, benutzerfreundlichen Routen. Allerdings sind Sie immer selbst für die erwünschte Sicherung verantwortlich. Und es gibt fast überall noch sehr viele (Neben) Routen die sicher gemacht werden können. Ein Stern ★ bzw. Sterne ★★★★ bei manchen Routen beziehen sich auf die Attraktivität der Routen, von einem Stern aufwärts bis zu vier (sehr attraktiv) - obwohl alle in diesem Führer beschriebenen Routen ihren Reiz haben, versteht sich.

Es gibt viele Möglichkeiten zum Zelten in diesem Gebiet; daneben bieten die meiste Bauernhöfe und "Guest Houses" Zimmer an. Einkaufsmöglichkeiten gibt es in St. Just und Sennen; in beiden Dörfern gibt es auch Tankstellen.

Sehr wichtig ist es in diesem Gebiet Rücksicht zu nehmen auf die Gezeiten: ein großer Unterschied zwischen Ebbe und Flut, die sehr schnell auftreten und manchem Kletterer schon den Ruckzug abgeschnitten haben. Viele Geschäfte verkaufen deswegen Gezeiten-Tabellen, die übrigens auch meist in den lokalen Zeitungen abgedruckt werden. Im Falle von ernsthafen Unfällen ist die Nortrufnummer 999; man fragt dann den "Coastguard" (Küstwache). Jedes Kapittel für die unterschiedlichen Kliffen fängt an mit der jeweiligen Coastal Guard Bezeichnung; melde dem "Coastguard" diese Bezeichnung (Name), Besonderheiten des Unfalls und die Telefonnumer des Geräts von wo aus sie anrufen. In Großbritanien sind Anruf, Rettung und Krankenhausbetreuung gratis.

Cornwall ist ein sehr naturreiches Gebiet; es gibt viele seltene Pflanzen und Seevögel. Sehr wichtig ist, daß dies weiterhin so bleibt und daß sie nicht beschädigt oder vernichtet werden. Deswegen: seit vorsichtig beim gehen und vermeide Brutstätten. Viel Spaß im Urlaub und beim Klettern!

*　　*　　*

WELKOM IN CORNWALL

Welkom in Penwith, Cornwall, de beste plaats voor het beklimmen van granietrotsen aan zee in Groot Brittanië. Het grootste deel van deze gids is in het engels; maar de Topos (kaarten) zullen je, in combinatie met de moeilijkheidsaanduiding (volgens UK/F/US/UIAA-skala), alles bieden wat je nodig hebt om de routes op eigen mogelijkheden in te schatten.

Haken en ringen zul je vrijwel niet tegenkomen in dit gebied. Je zult meestal zelf voor beveiliging moeten zorgen (daar heb je je "Friends" en nuts voor...). Routes die in het geheel of op onderdelen zelf gezekerd moeten worden, zijn aangegeven met een "**R**" naast de moeilijkheidsfactor. Een 💣 geeft aan, dat de betreffende route met de grootst mogelijke voorzichtigheid moet worden benaderd, omdat deze nog niet volledig geregistreerd is en een ☠ betekent dat op die plaats een verhoogd risico bestaat op akelige blessures bij een val, zo niet erger.

Een ⚲ symbooltje geeft aan, dat er veel losse stenen op de route liggen en er dus eigenlijk niet geklommen zou moeten worden. Maar ook op sommige andere routes kunnen losse stenen voorkomen. Een paar routes zijn voorzien van een ☺. Deze routes zijn "gebruikersvriendelijk" en relatief veilig. Wel ben je altijd zelf verantwoordelijk voor het zekeren; ook veel andere routes kunnen nog veilig gemaakt worden.

Een ster ★ of sterren ★★★★ bij routes betekenen, dat deze al naar gelang het aantal sterren buitengewoon aantrekkelijk zijn. Dat wil natuurlijk niet zeggen dat de anderen onaantrekkelijk zouden wezen.

Er zijn veel mogelijkheden om te camperen in het gebied. De meeste boerderijen en "guest houses" bieden de mogelijkheid om kamers te huren. Winkels zijn er voornamelijk in St. Just en Sennen, alwaar ook benzinestations zijn. Het is belangrijk je bewust te zijn van de getijden in deze streek (snelle wisseling tussen eb en vloed en met een groot hoogteverschil; menigeen zag daardoor zijn terugweg afgesneden). Veel winkels verkopen dan ook getijde-tabellen en bovendien kun je die in de meeste lokale kranten vinden.

Bij ongevallen kun je het noodnummer 999 bellen en naar de "Coastguard" (Kustwacht) vragen. Aan het begin van elk rots-hoofdstuk staat de identiteitsaanduiding van die specifieke plek; geef die naam, bijzonderheden over het ongeluk en het telefoonnummer van waar je belt door aan de Coastguard. In Groot Brittanië zijn het telefoneren, de reddingsoperatie en eventuele ziekenhuiskosten gratis.

De streek is rijk aan natuurschoon en er komen veel zeldzame planten en zeevogels voor. Het is belangrijk om ervoor te zorgen dat deze niet beschadigd of vernietigd worden. Let daarop bij het lopen en vermijdt broedplaatsen van vogels. We wensen je veel plezier tijdens je verblijf en met het klimmen.

* * *

THE GREEN PAGES

CONSERVATION AND ACCESS

Penwith is an astonishingly beautiful and unique area that has changed slowly over the years. Even along its roads there is a profusion of wild flowers, a rare sight nowadays. The local council has a policy of encouraging the farmers not to cut the hedgerows until late summer so that visitors can enjoy them to the full and allow natural re-seeding to occur.

Just under half the cliffs along this coast are owned by the National Trust who have to attempt the tricky balancing act of conserving them whilst maintaining land and recreational use. The Trust also manages areas of cliffs on behalf of other landowners. Some cliffs are owned by farmers and other individuals. Land's End is owned by a company operating a tourist complex; the owners have demonstrated admirable ability in restoring previously damaged areas, carefully landscaping the grounds and preserving the immediate surroundings. Few visitors stray more than a few yards from the complex grounds, but they do roam the headlands.

The south-west coast path circumnavigates the entire coastline and the area attracts tourists, walkers and bird watchers as well as climbers. Maintaining access to the cliffs is dependent upon maintaining a sustainable level of recreational use in the places we go and climb.

The conservation and access situation is changing quite quickly at the time of writing. Do keep in touch with the situation through the climbing press and BMC newsletters. If at all in doubt then contact the BMC. Also read any notices or leaflets in the area.

PLEASE

- READ THE ENVIRONMENTAL CONCERNS SECTION AT THE START OF EACH CLIFF CHAPTER .
- AVOID NESTING BIRDS.
- PRE-PLACE AN ABSEIL ROPE, WHERE REQUESTED, TO AVOID DAMAGING CLIFF TOPS.
- ON APPROACHES BE AWARE OF SENSITIVE AND EASILY ERODED AREAS, AVOID SHORTCUTS & CONTROL DOGS.
- PICK UP ALL LITTER - including cans, wrappers, cigarette ends etc.
- ONLY NEW ROUTE ON CLEAN ROCK, DON'T GARDEN OR BRUSH LICHEN.
- PLEASE INFORM ENGLISH NATURE OF ANY PLANNED DEVELOPMENT OF AREAS AND SEEK THEIR ADVICE REGARDING ENVIRONMENTAL CONCERNS.
- DON'T TRY AND DRIVE THROUGH A HERD OF CATTLE BEING DRIVEN ALONG A ROAD.
- PARK CONSIDERATELY.

GROUPS AND CLUBS

Anyone bringing a large group into the area should think of obtaining advice as to the current situation. Do not take groups abseiling or top-roping into areas where they can do a lot of environmental damage in one visit, but use described approaches and keep them together, on rock platforms if possible. Take into account the popularity of the cliff, access to toilet facilities and the nature of the approach. Please do not let members abseil in big boots and don't monopolise routes.

✿ SSSIs ✿

A majority of the Penwith coastline has now been designated Sites of Special Scientific Interest. A SSSI is a legal designation applied to land of special nature conservation interest for its flora, fauna, geological or physiograpical features and is of national (in some cases international) importance. English Nature is responsible for the notification of SSSIs which are protected by the provision of the Wildlife and Countryside Act 1981 as amended in 1985. The environmental concerns section in each cliff introduction tells you whether the cliff is a ` SSSI ` or not. Remember this will probably apply to the approach as well.

A ✿ indicates that a particular route is environmentally sensitive and that care should be exercised. Refer to the appropriate environmental concerns section for guidance. Unless stated otherwise the suggestions we make for each cliff are very much our own; good practice now could make all the difference in the future. We leave the choice up to you.

ACCESS AND RESTRICTIONS

Access restrictions are currently rare.

1) ✗ **Porthmoina Island - Bosigran:** The BMC and National Trust have agreed that this is to be left as undisturbed as possible, as a wilderness area. Please do not visit it or set up a tyrolean from it. There are one or two alternative climbs nearby.

2) ✓ At **Land's End** climbers are allowed to enter FREE OF CHARGE. Tell them at the gate you're climbers. Some supporting evidence such as ropes may be required. This agreement is STRICTLY on the basis that you're there to climb - you may use the cafés, but not visit the other attractions or exhibits.

3) ✗ At **Tater Du** the owner has asked climbers to observe nesting restrictions between March 1st and July 1st and people living in nearby houses are very sensitive about people taking short cuts across their land.

4) ✗ For **St. Loy** the farmer who owns the **Trevererven Farm and campsite** has asked climbers not to park on his road, campsite or by his farm. St. Loy can be approached from Treen (south) and the Logan Rock by a stiff 40-minute walk along the coast path. Worth the effort.

5) ✓ **Kenidjack**. A few years ago a group of travellers camped in the tiny quarry

above the cliff. Ultimately their tepees were bulldozed and burnt and large boulders placed in the lanes to prevent them from returning; these are subject to mysterious forces and periodically move position. The travellers do return, occasionally, and you may have to park where you can and walk to the crag. The travellers have never caused any trouble to climbers, nor have there been car thefts, so please treat them with tolerance.

6) ✗ At **Carn Barra** there is an agreement between the BMC, English Nature and National Trust that climbers should avoid the lichenous upper buttresses. These have not attracted climbers in the past.

⚞ NESTS ⚟

People don't own them, birds do! On some cliffs, or even for a particular route and known nesting site, we are suggesting visual inspection first and even voluntary restraint by avoiding the route or nests during the nesting season. From April through to August expect to find nests, eggs or chicks on ledges. All wild birds and their eggs are protected by law under the Wildlife and Conservation Act of 1981. Seabird chicks can be quite big, but they will be more scared than you are, and their parents might respond by trying to frighten you away. Some species are more aggressive than others. Fulmars in particular have a very unpleasant defence mechanism - they spew 'oil' at you - and may try to bite your ropes, helmets, etc. **If at all possible go around them, onto another route, lower off, or decide at the start, if you can see a nest or chick, to leave it to another day.** When all else fails the chick will jump off and even if it lives it is unlikely to survive predators and storms. Regularly used known nesting sites (and many seabirds do not actually build nests but just lay eggs on ledges) are indicated by a ⚞. Please refer to the text for that cliff. There are at present no BMC agreed bird nesting restrictions in Cornwall though they do advise minimal disturbance and avoiding routes with nesting birds; the suggestions in this book are purely our own, we leave the choice to you.

THE ENVIRONMENTAL CHALLENGE

The biggest challenge to climbers today lies in maintaining access to the cliffs, hills and mountains whilst preserving the natural environment: maintaining access is in itself not enough. The way we treat the natural environment as a whole is of equal importance. Damaging cliff tops on approach, disturbing nesting birds, turning the cliff base into a toilet, leaving litter and gardening routes are all practices damaging to our sport, and more importantly, to the planet on which we all rely and which we hold in trust for future generations. Disregard for the natural environment is also the quickest way to lose access.

We need to become more pro-active and to consider measures that can be put into place to prevent problems arising and which preserve the environment. The 'new' areas prevention is always better than a later 'cure' as harm to the environment is often irreversible.

An aesthetic reason is involved as well; we shouldn't just preserve cliffs because we are asked to, because something is rare or because damage needs repairing. We should do it because we ourselves like being in a beautiful place, because one reason we climb is that it takes us into such places, and we wish to pass it on undamaged to our children and grandchildren.

Every year the BMC and local climbers meet with landowners and conservation bodies to produce good working arrangements to protect wildlife, the environment and access. Look around you when you climb. Are there many paths when only one would do? Is erosion wearing away a descent gully? Are there any flowers, trees or bushes missing from when you last visited? Have the boulders been turned into a toilet? How much litter is there? Do the routes look old and worn?

We have a unique opportunity to conserve a wonderful area that has not suffered the ravages other areas have, and we should not let the opportunity slip through our fingers: be environmentally aware, act considerately.

* * *

The BMC works to resolve access and conservation problems in England and Wales through patient negotiation by volunteers and staff as well as practical contributions from the BMC Access Fund. Each year the BMC represents your views to landowners and conservation bodies to produce good working arrangements that protect wildlife, the environment and climbing. If you have any inquiries about the climbing arrangements, etc. please contact the BMC. If planning new routes please contact English Nature regarding any possible environmental concerns for that cliff.

The British Mountaineering Council
177-179 Burton Road
West Didsbury
Manchester M20 2BB
Tel: 0161 445 4747

English Nature
Trelissick
Feock
Truro
Cornwall TR3 6QL
Tel: 01872 265261

The National Trust
Countryside Manager
Treveal Farm
Zennor, St. Ives
Cornwall TR26 3BW
Tel: 01736 796993

PLANT LIFE AND CLIMBERS

Penwith has a rich spread of plant life, much of it of international and national importance, including species that only survive on cliffs subject to great exposure, but which have a moist, mild and frost free climate. Because of its southerly position it also supports species that are more commonly found in Mediterranean countries, a mix unique in Britain. Cliff top plant communities here are also very special because they have remained unaffected by human influence for thousands of years; which is very rare in Britain except in a few cliff top and mountain areas.

Unfortunately for us, these plants are in the very locations that we use for climbing, on the cliffs and cliff tops. They live on the cliffs in cracks and on ledges, on the rock in the form of lichens, on the cliff edges where rock meets soil, a little way back as maritime grassland on the tops themselves and in the heathland and scrub that covers the land behind the cliffs.

A short area of cliff can support several distinct plant habitats. The gullies climbers use to descend the cliffs are often dark, wet and sheltered and support many rare plants that are very fragile and easily damaged. On the south coast in particular, the soil is very sandy and easily eroded; and many plants have short roots and are easily uprooted or damaged. Once paths start being worn rainwater takes over and the path acts as a river bed, channelling water down it. In a very short space of time considerable amounts of earth and vegetation can disappear as the path widens and people are less careful where they step. The very tops of the climbs can be covered by a shallow layer of soil. This is easily removed by climbers' feet, particularly on popular cliffs such as Carn Barra, and produces a major conservation headache. Penwith has 25 species of plant that are extremely rare, some which now only exist in a few square kilometre sized areas, and which are vulnerable to extinction. These are now protected species under law.

Many important lichens also live on the rocks. The most obvious are the grey / green 'hairy' *Ramalina* species that covers many buttresses above the sea, and the golden *Xanthoria* (which is also very slippery when wet). It is lichens that give Penwith rock its distinctive green, gold and black colouring. There is a voluntary agreement discouraging new routing on the buttresses covered by *Ramalina*, on the upper cliffs of Carn Barra. But parts of other cliffs such as Chair Ladder, Pordenack Point and the unclimbed upper reaches of Bosigran are also covered with this lichen and we ask you to think of avoiding climbing through heavily lichenous areas. Even if the first ascender did not clean or remove the lichen, given time repeat ascents might clean it from the rock. The choice is yours.

Some people take the attitude that "if it's not rare, then we don't care". This is to be regretted for two reasons. Firstly, most plants that are now rare once were very common only a few decades ago and if we do not look after our more common species now they could easily go the same way. Secondly, no other users of the land would be tolerated if they tore up the plants, swept wide expanses of rock clean of lichen, trampled over habitats away from the paths or frightened birds off their nests. There is no good reason for climbers to be an exception.

Refer also to the gardening section.

BIRDS AND CLIMBERS

The cliffs are a major nesting site for many species of seabird such as herring gulls, black-backed gulls, fulmars, shags, cormorants, kittiwakes, guillemots and razorbills. These last two are under careful watch as their numbers have greatly declined. The nesting season is roughly from April into August though the odd late arrival may be found in September. There are surprisingly few places where birds can nest that are inaccessible to foxes, mink or weasels etc. The numbers of seabirds is not as great as those in Wales and Scotland but are just as important in maintaining the geographic range of their breeding sites.

Climbers are not a major threat to colonies at present, if only because it is so unpleasant climbing through one, but can threaten individual nests on cliffs. All wild birds are protected by law. The seasonal distribution is changing quite rapidly in Penwith at present; for example, kittiwakes are being replaced by fulmars (now Britain's most common seabird) at Chair Ladder, but this certainly is not due to climbers; declining fish stocks or pollution are the greatest threats along with the spread of wild mink in south Penwith.

Please do all you can to avoid climbing near a nest and interrupting incubation of eggs (guillemots rest their eggs on their feet during incubation and sudden disturbance can catapult the egg to destruction) or frightening a chick into jumping off; if it lives it will only survive a few days at the most. In the environmental concerns sections we have made suggestions as to areas and routes where it's worth looking out for nesting birds or to avoid during the height of the nesting season and we have highlighted individual routes with a 🐦 symbol.

Over 150 rare migrants visit the area and at a number of sites peregrine falcons breed. This bird is rare and it is a major offence to disturb the bird on or near its nest and climbers could be prosecuted if they knew where a nest was and chose to climb near it anyway. If you suspect you are near a nest, move away from it as quickly as possible and never touch a nest or eggs. Peregrines are unlikely to continue nesting anywhere near where climbers may disturb them. Ravens, jackdaws, stonechats and warblers also nest on cliffs so please also avoid disturbing them or their nests.

WILDLIFE AND CLIMBERS

The countryside is teeming with wildlife. Foxes are common and patrol cliffs at night looking for gulls. Badgers are not unusual and go foraging down the roads at night, so drive carefully. The fields and heathlands contain rabbits, mice and other small mammals providing abundant food for buzzards and hawks. At Bosigran wild goats have been introduced to graze the heathland.

There are a number of grey seal colonies along the coast and it is likely one will pop up to solemnly observe your antics, particularly on the south coast between Land's End and Chair Ladder. In recent years a pod of bottlenose dolphins have been regular visitors to the area, stopping over for a number of days and occasionally swimming in to Sennen beach to play alongside surfers. Basking sharks and porpoises also swim in to feed in the bays.

Adders have a brown zig-zag down their backs and can be found in the heathland and basking on rocks in the hot sun, particularly at Bosigran. They will try and move out of your way if disturbed and only bite if trodden on. Do not try to kill them. (Their bite is rarely fatal. Refer to the first aid section.) Grass snakes (which are silver/green and harmless) and small lizards can also be seen.

Many different insects such as dragonflies live in the vegetation and wetlands and a variety of slugs and snails can be seen after rain, as can many species of butterfly during a summer (the bracken is vital to their survival) and at night owls and bats are active.

A guide to plants and wildlife can add to the enjoyment of a visit.

Shag

ACCIDENTS, SAFETY, RESCUE & FIRST AID

- At Sennen Cove a young climber was swept off the main platform by a 'freak' wave; once in the water there was no chance of saving him. At least four other climbers have also been swept to their deaths along the coast.

- Two climbers have died falling from the crux of Anvil Chorus, yet it is a very protectable pitch.

- Two more died when the leader fell at Bosigran and the belay pegs failed. In the Variety Show area of Great Zawn a climber attempted to climb hand over hand back up his abseil rope; after 40ft he ran out of strength and fell as he wasn't carrying prussik cord.

- In the Great Zawn itself a second fell off under an overhang and was left dangling in space. He didn't know how to prussik; the leader didn't know how to tie off a belay plate, remove himself safely from the belay system or set up a pulley system. They were there for twelve hours before being found.

- At Sennen Cove an 'extreme' leader was badly injured when a hold snapped on Banana Flake (V. Diff.) He had placed protection, but he was too far above it for it to stop him hitting the ground.

Climbing is a very unforgiving activity and there are lessons to be learnt from all the above.

WAVES

'Freak' or large waves are fairly common and strike all along the coast, but 99% of the time there is no one in their path or around to see them. The size of the wave isn't the most vital factor; the angle at which they approach the cliffs and how the rock funnels them can be as important.

Keep your gear on a bandoleer, then if you are swept in you can ditch it quickly and not be pulled under by its weight. Descending to sea level when there is a

Sea thrift

English stonecrop

Sea aster

Sea milkwort

Cliff bluebell

Spring squill

1

high sea running is putting yourself into a high risk situation and should be avoided. If caught out then rope up and treat the traverse or boulder hop as a pitch with one of you attached to a belay, then if you're washed into the sea there is a chance of being pulled back out.

Always find out the times of high and low tides before you set out. Tide tables are available (and cheap) from most shops, and local papers also carry them.

Not using a ground belay at the start of a pitch at sea level places both belayer and leader at risk; remember, it should be able to hold you against upward, outward and downward pulls as a wave will push, lift and pull.

PROTECTION

If you are carrying a lead rack and climbing roped up, it is worth placing runners at regular intervals, even when on easy ground. Think ahead; don't hit the crux, find you've placed no protection up to that point, that there's none when you need it most, or find that a hold snaps or that it's a loose finish. There is no such thing as an easy solo; rain, salt water, grit, darkness or loose holds can turn an easy route into a horror show. Even when placing protection, be generous; on many routes you are climbing away from ledges; with rope stretch you can easily fall more than twice the distance between you and the last runner, and if that fails..... Protection is only as good as the person placing it. Learning to place good protection is a hard earned skill; being able to judge how good it is an art. If at all in doubt then double it up.

On traverses protection should be placed to safeguard the second and not just the leader. At Carn Barra, several leaders were injured falling off Grand Plage. Their protection was quite good, but their seconds had walked back from the wall. The angle of the rope lifted out the runners as the leader fell.

IN SITU PROTECTION

On sea cliffs all ironmongery corrodes and deteriorates rapidly and can become useless even in a few months. Often it is not the eye of a peg or bolt that suffers most, but the part inside a crack or hole. Some may also have been "cut to size" to fit the crack, many are remains of protection used on a first ascent. Always back up all pegs. Stainless steel pegs would seem to be the solution, but are brittle and sometimes have fractured after only a few falls so always treat them with caution. Bolts are controversial.

Fixed slings, tape or lengths of rope are dramatically weakened by ultraviolet rays from sunlight; again it doesn't take long. Replace it or use a back up. Your life is worth more than the price of a sling. The same advice about backing up protection applies also to jammed nuts, hexes or camming devices abandoned in cracks. You don't know how many falls they've taken or exactly how corroded they are.

GETTING LOST

When visiting a new cliff it's always worth climbing a few easy routes just so you know where the escape routes are, what the rock is like and so on. Going off route can happen; if necessary carry this guidebook in a wallet on your harness or, if you want to cut down on weight, carry a photocopy of the relevant page. If you think you're off route or may be on something too hard for you, then there is no shame in backing off and returning to climb your route another day.

Always allow more time than you expect to climb a big route; quite a few people have been benighted because they hadn't made a realistic assessment of the time they needed. Allow extra time, if you're visiting a new cliff, to find it, find the descent and find the route.

If there is any doubt about the outcome carry a head torch, wear an extra layer of clothing (even if you sweat early on) and let someone know the cliff and route you are on and the time you expect to be back. And do tell them you've got back safely, don't just slope off to the pub.

IT'S ALL COMMON SENSE

Helmets are a matter of personal choice. If you don't ever wear one, ask yourself "How bad do things have to get before I would?" Head injuries can be, and are, caused by climbers dropping equipment onto other climbers, dislodging rocks and the like. Pulling abseil ropes through can pull rock down with it. Tourists lob stones over cliff edges - particularly at Sennen Cove and Land's End - and a helmet is reassuring should a fulmar decide to 'have a go!' On some, if not all the cliffs in the area, do consider wearing one; they do save lives.

Climbers have died in abseiling accidents. Penwith granite is extremely rough, and slate and greenstone often have sharp edges so try and protect ropes over edges when abseiling. Never abseil, or belay, on only one anchor point - something only ever needs to go wrong once and you may not live to regret it. Also always check your harness buckle and screwgate before going over the edge.

If you can't see where your abseil ends, tie a knot in the end of the rope and untie the knot when the last person is down so it doesn't jam when you pull it back up. Knowing how to use an auto brake to protect an abseil is also useful. Pulling your abseil rope down after you cuts off your escape, and you'd be surprised how many people have abseiled down and discovered that they'd left their climbing ropes on the top.

Keep ropes away from the sea (a rope bag can be very useful); ropes can be washed into a crack or under a boulder and a lot of ropes have been lost or cut that way. Salt water can harm ropes; when they dry out tiny crystals are left inside, so as you fall the fibres stretch and tauten and can be cut by these crystals. If your ropes go into the sea, wash them in tap water soon after; your metal equipment too as even salt in the air can affect Friends, karabiners, etc.

Do carry prussik loops and practise prussiking before you go for a climb, as hanging under an overhang on Astral Stroll is not a good place to start learning;

5mm or 6mm kermantle nylon cord is ideal, cut into two lengths of three metres and one and a half metres. Knowing how to tie off a belay plate, escape from a belay system and set up a 2:1 pulley system just using common climbing equipment are all useful skills. A lot of rescues could have been avoided if the climbers involved had known them; having read it in a book is one thing, doing it for real is another thing completely, so practise somewhere safe first. Some experience of first aid is also useful.

Most accidents happen when people get cold, tired, rushed, scared, over-excited or forgetful. Inexperience, getting into bad habits or an unwillingness to learn 'new tricks' can also play a part. Monitoring your own emotional and mental states is a vital climbing skill and if you and your climbing partner become tired, rushed, irritable or whatever then start checking each other's anchors, ropework and so on.

If caught in a thunderstorm, get off the cliff as lightning can be very scary. Avoid towers, and large boulders (even sheltering under a boulder could be dangerous) and suspend your metal gear from a rope below you if you're stuck on a ledge. Instances of climbers being struck by lightning are, however, very rare.

● **GETTING HELP** ✆

Telephone 999 and ask for the Coastguard. In Britain the call is free, as is the rescue and any hospital treatment.

Each cliff has a coast guard identity that can be different from the names used by climbers. This is given at the start of each cliff introduction: note it before you visit a cliff. We also indicate where the nearest phone ✆ may be found. (Where possible these are phone boxes rather than in private premises that may be closed. Where this is unavoidably the case we also give the location of the next nearest phone. Calls should only be made in cases of genuine emergency.) Give the cliff's coast guard identity, and the grid reference, if possible, to the Coastguard. They will also ask for the number of the phone you are calling from, a brief assessment of the accident and any possible identifying landmarks. They will also need an idea of the type of injuries and number of people involved. Any major landmarks you can describe to help them locate the approach and casualty will be a great help. If you can, meet them and guide them to the exact location. If there are spectators then ask them to act as 'marker posts' along the approach path.

Instead of a conventional ambulance you may be sent an air ambulance which will land as close as is practical; this carries two paramedics and a stretcher. If they decide that it is too difficult to carry a stretcher they will summon a Royal Navy rescue helicopter to organise an air lift from the site of the accident, but can also call upon the lifeboat services.

HELICOPTER RESCUE

All rescues are co-ordinated by the crew and in most situations a winchman (who is also a first aider) will be lowered to the ground to act as a ground controller. The Sea King helicopter will approach three times: to lower the winchman, to lower a stretcher and then to lift the casualty and winchman.

You could help by:

1) Clearing objects such as rucksacks, ropes, coats, branches or litter from the landing or hover zone. The down draught from the rotors could blow them around and injure someone or they could get sucked into an engine. Remove them, tie them down or lie on them.

2) Attempt to clear spectators from an area at least 50 metres from the hover or landing zone. Put out all cigarettes and dogs should be removed and kept on a lead.

3) Do not move as the helicopter approaches. If with the casualty, crouch over them with your back to it to shield them from flying grit, sea spray etc. Cup your hands over their eyes (or a wound) if necessary.

4) Do not touch a winch line until it has touched the ground; they can carry a static charge.

5) Obey all instructions from the crew, paramedics and coastguards.

6) If a helicopter lands stay well clear, kneel down and do not approach it. The crew will come to you.

● BASIC FIRST AID

Always look to your own safety first. Your priorities are to check to see if the casualty is conscious and still breathing. Then if s/he is bleeding and whether there are any broken bones. Breathing and circulation take priority over anything else, after that comes bleeding and then broken bones. Don't panic at the sight of blood; a little goes a long way and a body can afford to lose one pint without becoming close to danger, but lose three and the body has too little to function.

- All unconscious casualties must be placed in the recovery position to keep the airway open; first check to see if anything is blocking the mouth.

- Do not move a conscious casualty should spinal injuries or head injuries be suspected, unless leaving them where they are places them in greater danger or they need resuscitation.

- If the casualty is not breathing you then need to check if the airway is obstructed by his/her vomit, tongue or sweets, etc. then check to see if the circulation has stopped.

- To check pulse, feel for the artery at the side of the Adam's apple and windpipe.

- If breathing has stopped, but there is a pulse, begin resuscitation while someone goes for help. If on your own then administer artificial ventilation for one minute and then go and call for help, return and continue.

- If breathing has stopped and no pulse can be detected it is vital that paramedics get to the scene quickly. If you can, send someone to telephone for help while you start artificial ventilation and chest compressions; if on your own then go for help first, then return and begin resuscitation. Once you start administering ventilations and compressions you should continue until the paramedics arrive.
- Bleeding can be stopped by applying direct pressure; never use a tourniquet. If the bleeding is from a limb, raise it higher than the rest of the body and let gravity work for you. If the bleeding is profuse and does not stop after applying pressure with bandages, apply pressure to the artery a little way above the wound. Scalp wounds can bleed heavily; pads placed over the wound should control bleeding.
- Keep the casualty warm; if practicable and safe to do so place insulating material between them and the ground. Never give a seriously injured casualty anything to eat or drink.
- Hypothermia can develop surprisingly quickly, particularly in wet, windy conditions and it can kill. Your priority is to prevent a casualty from losing more body heat and to keep them warm by sheltering them from the wind, insulating them with more layers and administering warm drinks and high energy food. A bivy bag is a useful item.

SNAKE BITE

Cases of snake bite are very rare in the UK and rarely fatal. An adder is either grey or brown and has a distinctive brown zig-zag down its back. Check if there are puncture wounds in the skin, in which case the casualty should be immediately carried to a car and taken to hospital. The very old and very young are most at risk. Do not cut open the wound or attempt to suck out venom.

CARRYING A CASUALTY

As a general rule always carry a casualty feet first. When carrying a casualty suffering from a stroke or cerebral compression (caused by skull fracture for example) down a slope or steps, their head must never be lower than their feet. There are two exceptions to this general rule: when carrying a casualty with either serious limb injuries or hypothermia down a slope or steps.

HOSPITALS

The nearest hospital is the West Cornwall Hospital, St. Clare Street, Penzance. Tel: (01736) 623 82. Some casualties and those lifted by Sea King helicopter will be taken to the Royal Cornwall Hospital at Treliske near Truro. Tel: (01872) 742 42 or to Derriford in Plymouth. Tel: (01752) 777 111.

THE ROCK AND CLIMBING

Geologists will cringe, but the rock you climb on is one of three different types.

GRANITE

An igneous rock (it was once molten magma) and what Penwith is famed for. Granite has superb frictional properties and can be very rough. On harder crack climbs it is worth thinking of taping up. It occurs all along the coast but in different guises. On the north coast at Bosigran it is in great sheets and blocks, split by cracks and roofs. In places it has a skin of black tourmaline that has less friction, but where weathered provides good protruding jugs. Bands of quartz and feldspar also appear. The rock is generally sound, though care should be taken with large blocks balanced on ledges. The rock has a curious ability to 'sweat', giving it a greasy feel on occasions, most noticeable on hot days and is the result of a salt rich atmosphere.

At Sennen Cove the granite is wonderfully rough and juggy; its friction is excellent and holds are positive. It has a dark side of course such as Black Zawn where the rock can be very treacherous when wet. The 'black' commonly seen on rock near sea level is actually a lichen (*Verrucaria*) which bonds to the rock and swells up and becomes slippery when wet.

The black protruding bumps occasionally seen in granite are the remains of slate that was trapped and cooked in the lava and are obvious on the great flake of Windows of Perfection/Dextrose. On many climbs along the coast sharp feldspar crystals provide key holds. But between Sennen and Chair Ladder the rock becomes kaolinised in places (that's loose to you). The feldspar crystals in the rock rot away and no longer bind tightly with the remaining quartz and mica crystals. Exceptions to this stand proud: most of Land's End and Pordenack Point, Carn Boel, Carn lês Boel, Carn Barra, Fox Promontory and the like. It becomes generally solid again at Chair Ladder. Kaolinised rock comes in different forms. It can have a gritty outer layer that leads to a feeling of insecurity on some climbs; but when cleaned off by repeat ascents, the rock underneath is solid and provides outstanding climbs.

At worst a mixture of rock and earth appears in a thick band in the upper part of the cliff, though the rock below it is perfectly sound granite. This upper band is very fragile and vulnerable to a climber's passage and this provoked a debate about the desirability of lower offs at the top of the good pitch, purely on environmental grounds. These could solve the problem but are controversial. We also suggest pre-placed abseil ropes, though even these could cause some damage. At very worst, this band of earth and rock extends to sea level and gives a climbing experience not unlike climbing through a tray of compressed cat litter, though as the lower section is sea-washed most loose grit has been removed.

GREENSTONE

Another form of igneous rock that has been metamorphosed (or changed) usually by being placed under great pressure into something 'new'. It tends to have less cracks and sometimes less protection than granite but incut holds and horizontal breaks provide holds.

Near the tops of cliffs the quality of rock deteriorates, holds become prone to snapping and some can resemble bricks piled on top of each other. Most of this has now disappeared from popular routes, but be careful. The majority of greenstone is in north Penwith. Gurnard's Head is the most famous cliff; it peters out as you go towards Sennen and makes a final, unexpected, appearance at Tater Du, though in a slightly different form to that of its north coast cousins, being pillow lava.

SLATE

A sedimentary rock (formed by layers of silt and sands being compressed into rock). Carn Vellan and Kenidjack are two prominent examples. Holds can be more varied than on greenstone, but small flakes and jugs tend to be brittle and snap, so protect and survive. Take care with your protection; runners can rip and cracks shatter when loaded with your weight. At the top of some cliffs, e.g. the upper tiers of Carn Vellan, the rock deteriorates and care is needed with loose blocks on these pitches. Like its Llanberis cousin, Cornish slate (and greenstone) can be very slippery when wet.

THE SEA AND CLIMBING

TIDES

Buy a tide table for the area you are climbing in. Local newspapers also carry them. Tides are caused by the gravitational pulls of the moon and sun; each day the earth and moon are in different positions, in relation to the sun and each other, and consequently their gravitational effects are different. However the moon and earth have fairly regular orbits and pass through the same positions at regular intervals.

Tides have a rhythm as well. The moon orbits the earth once in a lunar month. Near full moon or new moon the gravitational pull of the sun and moon are in alignment (either with or against each other) pulling the oceans towards the opposite sides of the planet (the earth's spin also helps). This causes SPRING tides, which happen twice a month. You'll like spring tides because more rocks are uncovered at the base of tidal cliffs and this allows you to get into places that are inaccessible otherwise, providing the sea is calm of course. But spring tides also come up higher than at other times, and mean there is also a greater chance of cutting you off or chasing you up a cliff.

When the moon and sun are not in alignment with each other their pull is not so great. When at right angles to each other NEAP tides occur. The distance between high and low water is the least of all the tides and they also happen twice a month. There are also seasonal variations as the spring tidal ranges in March and September are greater than those in June or December. The tides can rise and fall by as much as 23 *vertical* feet in Penwith, so check carefully before setting out.

The times of high and low tides will be slightly different every day, roughly six hours apart, which is why you need a tide table. Spring tides are shown in a table by a symbol of a full or eclipsed moon by the day at which they are at their peak. The exact time of a tide will vary from place to place on the coast, and the tide table will tell you how to take this into account if you need total accuracy. Access to a cliff will be at its best two hours either side of a low tide. As a rough guide, low tides tomorrow will be between 20 to 90 minutes later than today's, as will the times of high tides. It is also worth discovering the rule of twelfths as tides do not rise or fall at a uniform rate. They start at a slow rate, speed up and then slow down again.

SEA CONDITIONS

Waves are formed far out at sea by winds. Exercise common sense, err on the side of caution when making decisions, and read the accident and rescue section.

The sea can produce big waves even on a fairly windless day, a lot depending upon the direction and angle from which they approach a cliff. At Sennen Cove, when spray buckets over the top of Demo Route it is the direction of wave

Mastodon, E3 5c, Gurnard's Head. Climbers: Rowland and Mark Edwards. Photo: Esther Edwards

approach that is as important as the size of the wave. Some cliffs funnel waves in, up sloping underwater platforms to collide with vertical walls, which can send water high up a cliff, e.g. Sennen Cove , Gurnard's Head and Carn Gloose.

You will also find when boulder hopping that the sea can be fairly calm, then five large waves come along, then it goes calm again. Look before you leap, watch what is happening at the base of a cliff before making a decision - a quick glance might not tell you the whole story. Also it helps to know if the tide is rising or falling before setting out.

The wind blows water droplets against cliffs, which can make it greasy even when the sea isn't rough. Be observant and flexible in your plans.

If listening to a shipping forecast, Penwith is in LUNDY and adjacent to PLYMOUTH. Local media also give a surf forecast indicating the expected sizes of waves. We tell you in each cliff introduction if it is tidal or not.

Carn Galver Mine, Bosigran

THE WEATHER AND CLIMBING

Penwith is famous for its mild maritime climate, which can mean climbing in shorts and tee shirts in early February whilst Scotland enjoys excellent snow and ice. Penwith is ideally suited to all year round rock climbing and, by picking the right cliffs, can be surprisingly warm, providing you're out of any wind. Good all year round climbing areas are the World's End and Day Tripper areas of Land's End, Carn Barra, Paradise Wall at Carn Lês Boel, Pordenack Point and Sennen Cove. When the sun's out people have sunbathed at Bosigran in February and only rain really stops play here.

But wherever land meets sea there is a clash of temperatures that produce their own effects, often only along the coastal strip. Penwith is famous for its thick mists, particularly at night, and these can be warm and wet or cold and dry ones. These can often sit on cliff tops, leaving the cliffs themselves free, so its often worth going for a look.

Being westerly Penwith is also the first land mass any cloud or weather front meets after its journey across the Atlantic; one cloud can dump its rain on you as it passes, whilst every other cliff is sunny! You can "see" rain out at sea so try and judge where it's heading. The weather can be changeable so it can be worth sitting out rainstorms. Many cliffs are very fast drying; granite ones in particular, though cracks will take longer. Any cliff with a lot of vegetation on top will be slow to dry because the soil traps water and causes seepage, Carn Gloose is one of these. Strong winds cause problems. Climbers have had to grip tightly during gusts at Bosigran. It also makes spoken communication impossible, so have a system of rope signals worked out. Land's End acts as a wind break and cliffs may be more sheltered past this. From rain as well.

Sunburn can be intense as you'll also catch rays reflected up from the sea and dehydration has been a problem for a few. For a weather forecast phone Weathercall on (01891) 505 304. They charge approx. 36p a minute at cheap rate times (1996). The Plymouth Weather Centre can be contacted on (01752) 251 860. BBC Radio Cornwall can be found on 103.9 MHz.

GRADES

THE BRITISH GRADING SYSTEM

The British grading system is used in this guide, with a few exceptions for historical accuracy. Once you understand it, it does make sense for the 'traditional' routes, those where you have to place your own protection. (Though a novice group was once discovered attempting to top rope an E1 in the belief that the E stood for easy!)

Firstly there is a descriptive grade, which takes into account all the factors that make up a route's overall difficulty, except how hard the individual moves are. These can include how much or how little protection there is, how strenuous it is, the quality of the rock, whether it is sustained or just has a short, sharp crux. It also reflects its situation, difficulties of retreating etc. The routes are graded for dry conditions.

The grades are in the following order, developing from the easiest to the hardest: Easy, Moderate, Difficult, Very Difficult, Severe, Hard Severe, Very Severe, Hard Very Severe and Extremely Severe (also described by the letters E or XS). After this comes a technical grade that indicates how hard the hardest move on the route is thought to be. This is done by allocating a number 1-7 to the degree of difficulty of the move and refined by being sub-divided by one of three letters: a, b, or c. For example 4a, 4b, 4c and so on up to 7b. The system is open ended. Grades 1, 2 and 3 are often thought to be superfluous, as they are given for routes at the lowest point of the scale, so only the descriptive grade is given, e.g. Moderate and Difficult. There is some overlap at times but the grade is trying to tell you something. A VS 5a for example should be well protected and have a short crux sequence. A HVS 4c is likely to be committing and poorly protected. Extreme grades also attempt to let you know what's in store. An E1 5c should be pretty safe, and have only one hard move. By the time you get to an E4 5c you're being told it's committing, sustained and strenuous, possibly with very poor protection or loose rock.

The system works well up to a point. By the early 1980s British climbers had developed traditional style climbing so that extremely strenuous, technical and dangerous climbing was at a very high level. However, some French climbers were doing more strenuous and technical ones on 'blank' limestone walls by using bolts, red pointing and so on. This has been adopted by some British climbers, particularly at the leading edge, in order to push standards further still. British grades have difficulty in accurately describing such climbs because the emphasis is on cumulative technical difficulty and the climbers are playing by different rules, thus French or sports grades are used to describe such routes. These have the letter F in front of them, e.g. F7c. Some have been climbed in this area, but are now de-geared; we depict them solely for historical accuracy.

An International grades comparison table is provided for quick reference by overseas visitors.

AID GRADES

Aid routes are graded on a rising scale from zero to four, where one aid move on an in situ runner equals A0 and the most serious, technical routes where the aid is placed by the leader A4.

GRADING PROBLEMS & SYMBOLS

There will always be arguments over grades as factors such as height can play a part, as can preference for a particular type of climb. The grades in this area have had a tough reputation. In part, this is because the majority of climbers who repeat the routes live outside the area and depart taking their thoughts with them. We have revised some grades in this guide.

Some routes can change through rock fall; famously a 120ft classic route vanished in a storm a few years ago, and the sea can hurl boulders at a cliff in a storm, so be observant.

Many routes have had few ascents, others have yet to receive a second ascent. In these cases the grade is that of the first ascender and a ☄ indicates where it is felt to be important that the route be approached warily. As well as indicating that the grade is unconfirmed, this symbol can also indicate that any in situ protection should be treated with caution, or be missing. Just to confuse you when you thought you had the hang of grades, routes given the same grade may not be of exactly equal difficulty as one may be bolder or more strenuous than another for example; we try to provide additional guidance. Next to some grades a plus or minus sign (+ or -) indicates if it is thought to be a hard, or a soft touch within its descriptive or technical grade. On multi-pitch routes where there may be confusion as to which technical grade the descriptive grade refers to, we highlight the appropriate one by both putting it in bold lettering and underlining it, e.g. HVS **4c**, 5a (this indicates that the 4c pitch is very bold).

On a few selected routes we use a ☺ symbol to indicate that it can be protected well and would be a good *gradebreaker* for those pushing their grades - but remember you are responsible for placing the gear and having a decent lead rack.

On some others we use a ☻ to indicate that it is exceptionally bold. This only takes into account **lack of protection**, e.g. as on Hell Hath No Fear. We indicate in the text if very specialist equipment is required. We assume most leaders will own Friends or other camming equipment and have a number of small and large rocks, etc.

If the grade is followed by a **R** this indicates that the route may be run-out in places but otherwise there is good protection; it can also mean that you have to climb some way above the ground before you get your first runner. Remember, this is a subjective opinion and merely supplements the grade and your own judgement.

On sports routes at Carn Vellan we use a ✛ to show that the bolts have been cut and a ☹ to show how unhappy this makes sport-climbers and pluralists .

Finally, if a ⚜ appears it indicates that a route is very loose and should be approached with extreme care; on the south coast in particular, slightly gritty rock can be something of a shock to those used to Peak gritstone or Welsh limestone, so remember this symbol is reserved for routes of outstanding instability and that the nature of a climb can change.

Between them, the above should provide all the information you'll need.

Rock climbing is a high risk sport and the user of this book should assume full responsibility for his/her own safety. One of the challenges of climbing is to go into a high risk situation in as safe a manner as possible. One way to maximise that possibility is to seek proper training by a qualified instructor. The BMC can provide details of such providers in each part of the country. The inclusion of a cliff in this guide does not indicate an automatic right of access.

★★★★ STARS ★★★★

Stars by the side of a route name indicate the quality of a route. All the routes in this guide are good so the stars merely help indicate those of outstanding quality.

The system goes from one to four stars on a rising scale taking into account the quality and variety of all pitches, position, and the nature of the challenge. They are to be found next to the route descriptions.

Fifteen routes have been awarded four stars. These have been selected as the finest representatives of their grade from Moderate, Difficult, V. Difficult, Severe, H. Severe, V. Severe, HVS and E1 through to E8 in the area. A few stand head and shoulders above the rest whilst others have fierce competition. Interestingly, though not a criterion in the selection, many are also landmarks in the area's development. In selecting these, discussion (including environmental concerns) also produced twelve individual pitches that offer the finest moves at their technical grade; again there was fierce competition. Three of these also came high in other criteria and thus gained the four star accolade.

THE FINEST TECHNICAL PITCHES?

3b.	Corner Climb	5b.	Pitch one, Bishop's Rib
3c.	Pitch three, Terrier's Tooth	5c.	Pitch two, Mastodon
4a.	The slab pitch, Pegasus	6a.	Immaculate Arête
4b.	Demo Route	6b.	Tears of a Clown
4c.	Pitch two, Little Brown Jug	6c.	Amazonia
5a.	Pitch two, Suicide Wall	7a.	Pre-Marital Tension

All this is, of course, purely subjective but we hope will provide enjoyable climbing and many fun debates.

GRADES AT A GLANCE

LOW TO INTERMEDIATE GRADES			
GB	**FRENCH**	**ALPINE (UIAA)**	**USA (YDS)**
MODERATE - 1	I	I	5.2
DIFFICULT 2a	2	II	5.3
VERY DIFFICULT 2b/3c	3	III	5.4
HARD VERY DIFFICULT - 3c	3+/4-	IV-	5.5
SEVERE 4a	4-	IV	5.6
SEVERE 4b	4	IV	5.6/5.7
SEVERE 4c	4+	V	5.7
HARD SEVERE 4a	4	V	5.7
HARD SEVERE 4b	4+/5	V	5.7
HARD SEVERE 4c	4+/5	VI-	5.7
VERY SEVERE 4b	5a	V+	5.8
VERY SEVERE 4c	5a	V+/VI-	5.8
VERY SEVERE 5a	5a/5a+	VI-	5.8/9
HARD VERY SEVERE 4c	5a+	VI-	5.8/9
HARD VERY SEVERE 5a	5b	VI	5.8/9
HARD VERY SEVERE 5b	5c+/6a	VI+	5.9
E1 5a	5c+/6a	VI+	5.9/5.10a
E1 5b	6a	VI+/VII	5.10a

An exact comparison of different grading systems is difficult to achieve because they're subjective and you're not comparing like with like, but these charts are as precise as we can make them. There may be exceptions however (and in other parts of the country, on other types of rock and climbs, especially bolted limestone) so use your own judgement as well.

ADVANCED GRADES			
GB	**FRENCH**	**ALPINE (UIAA)**	**USA (YDS)**
E1 5b	6a	VI+/VII	5.10a
E2 5b	6a+	VII-	5.10b/c
E3 5b	6b/6b+	VII+	5.10c
E1 5c	6a+	VII-	5.10
E2 5c	6a+/6b	VII	5.10b/c
E3 5c	6b+	VII+	5.11a
E4 5c	6c/7a	VIII-	5.11c/d
E3 6a	6b+/6c	VII+	5.11a
E4 6a	6c+	VIII-	5.11b/c
E5 6a	7a/7a+	VIII+	5.12a
E6 6a	7b+/7c+	IX	5.12a
E4 6b	6c/7a	VIII-	5.11c/d
E5 6b	7a+/7b	VIII+	5.12a
E6 6b	7b+/7c	IX-	5.12c/d
E7 6b	7c+/8a	X	5.13d
E5 6c	7b/7c	VIII+	5.12b/c
E6 6c	7c/8a	IX	5.12d/5.13a
E7 6c	8a/8a+	X-	5.13b/d
E8 6c	8b/8b+	X/X+	5.13c/d-5.14b
E7 7a	8a+/8b	X/X+	5.13d-5.14b
E8 7a	8b+/8c	XI-	5.14a-5.14b

€THI€S

In theory this should be easy. The traditional British ethic, as hallowed as the sound of leather on willow, the opening bars of *Jerusalem* or warm beer on a warm night, is essentially as follows. "A leader climbs from the bottom of the cliff to the top, without falling (or using knees), placing protection as they go, which is then removed by the second as they climb."

This was born of necessity, as the first climbers had no protective equipment, except a rope. They did fall, occasionally, of course which led to the development of equipment and the proliferation of ethical arguments. Even now the purest ethical statement is an on-sight solo. The traditional ethic works well on the majority of climbs, even those in the extreme grade. This is how they were first climbed, and why they shouldn't be turned into retro-bolted 'ladders'. But every generation cheats; few today would consider climbing Demo Route in nailed leather boots with a hemp rope around their waist, yet this was how it was first climbed. Each generation has used new equipment, tactics and approaches and had a natural desire to push standards higher. Each generation has introduced something new, be it rubbers, pebbles, pitons, aid, pre-inspection, chalk, pre-practice, dogging, training, camming devices, 'sticky' boots, bolts or whatever. Time has discarded that which was poor, kept that which was useful, and each new generation rectified the previous one's ethical lapses whilst introducing ones of its own. Only time will tell if standards have now risen so far that this process will slow or grind to a halt. Different ethical approaches have also developed for different types of challenge.

Ethics have been argued passionately in Penwith in recent years, largely due to the reintroduction of bolts into the area. It is only right and proper that each new development should be closely scrutinised and arguments tested and developed. The bolt debate in the area has been in fact four separate debates that have evolved alongside each other over the years. To make a definitive statement on ethics is difficult as they have developed over the decades and doubtless will evolve further. But it may be worth considering the following. Despite much speculation it is not clear how standards will continue to rise in future years. Without doubt, honest competition always provides the greatest spur to achievement. The traditional ethic is still very much alive in Penwith, as the majority of routes in this guide show. On granite Tears Of A Clown, Pre Marital Tension, Storms Over Africa, Question Mark, Titanic and Rats In A Rage all demonstrate different styles of approach; and evolution. Top rope practice prior to a bold ascent (whilst detracting from the On Sight ethic) may be an indication of how standards will be forced. It will be interesting to see how far this approach can be taken. Whether it could be applied to a route such as Red Rose is debatable. There is quite deep division in the south-west, but not the immediate area, over the suitability of Carn Vellan as a sport climbing venue and the use of bolts on it (e.g. Monster Munch). The issue has been settled (if not resolved) for the time being, but it would only be personal example that would finally decide the matter. Our contention is that the roof section here is suitable for bolt protected climbing and that the two styles of climbing can co-exist in Penwith. In the meantime the potential for futuristic additions (e.g. The Lid, free) remains and it will be interesting to see how these are approached by future generations.

The use of bolt lower-offs to protect the environment (e.g. Isis) is controversial and it is the author's opinion that they should not be ruled out, even if only as a means of last resort both to maintain access and conserve more fragile areas. In the meantime we are suggesting pre-placed abseil ropes on some routes (with the exception of Pendower Cove) in an attempt to preserve environmentally sensitive upper sections, though even this may cause some damage.

With conservation issues rising up the agenda it may also be the case that climbing ethics can no longer take precedence over environmental ones, but go hand in hand, i.e. do we always have to finish on the very top of a cliff, come what may?

The issue of deteriorating pegs on sea cliffs and that repeated peg placements degrade the climb (e.g. Suicide Wall) remains with us. Bolts have been placed on quite a few routes in the area, after a first ascent using pegs, in an effort to maintain it in the state known to the first ascender (e.g. Atlantic Ocean Wall). This has met with vocal opposition but no clear cut answer has emerged apart from a completely in situ protection on sight free ascent. An ethic of 'ethical de-gearing' seems to be finally emerging in the area, in order to remove redundant pegs from routes; many are products of the 1960s and 1970s. This involves an ascent of the route and removal of any pegs not used. It is likely that the tradition of placing pegs will continue in Cornwall and it should be left to competition to dispense with them. If this ethic were also applied to bolts it would allow routes to evolve and personal example to be the final arbiter in ethical disagreements. But this also requires patience. Each placement, and the reason for it, should also be considered on its own merits. We suggest that with protection pegs, any de-gearing should also be by someone operating at around the standard of the climb, particularly in the case of long established routes below the leading edge standard of today (e.g. Beowulf, Ghost etc.).

NB. On a personal note the author also finds that where deeply held convictions are in conflict compromise should be considered in order to resolve the situation.

BMC AREA POLICY

There is strong local opinion, and current area BMC policy, against the use of bolts on sea cliffs or natural outcrops in Cornwall. It is also policy to remove bolts placed and it is current practice to render any placed useless, or to remove them. (1995)

It would be pointless producing a rule book laying down how one should or should not climb, akin to the FA rule book. But ethics are also about how we treat the cliffs, the land and each other.

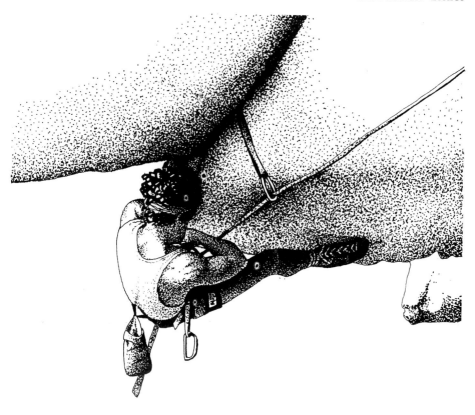

Super Jam E5 6b. Sennen Cove

SOME SUGGESTIONS

- There are very thin lines between gardening, cleaning, removing loose rock, comfortising, chipping and defacing the rock, so do as little as you can, even if it means leaving the route. See also gardening.
- Where peg protection is not eliminated by subsequent ascenders, or they are thought to be useful, then thought should be given to periodically re-equipping the route and how best this can be achieved.
- Any new routes should be notified to English Nature for advice as to environmental sensitivity, and new routes may have to be considered by the environmental liaison committee before being publicised.
- Every effort should be made to remove jammed, abandoned protection, e.g. rocks, etc.

PLEASE

- Ask permission before using an abseil rope already in place.
- Don't abseil down a route someone is climbing up.
- Remove an abseil rope as soon as possible to prevent obstructing a route.
- Respect other cliff users.
- Don't destroy vegetation.
- Don't litter, light fires or use the crag as a toilet.
- Have fun; climbing is about enjoyment. Whatever differences exist in the climbing world, what unites us is the fun, pleasure and satisfaction we gain from the routes we climb.

GARDENING

- Any gardening should be strictly avoided. What to you is common grass and bramble could contain plants of great rarity. Once removed even common species can take decades to regrow and have little chance if repeat ascenders climb the route.
- Avoid stepping on, pulling on or disturbing plants and the earth they are in when climbing - for you it is a transitory experience, for them their entire one.
- Gardening can also cause access problems.

HISTORICAL
AN OUTLINE HISTORY

There is a claim made every so often that the sport of sea-cliff climbing was invented in Cornwall. It is one we should view with circumspection, ears attuned to the habitual arrogance of our own tribe. How much can we justly pretend to know of the activities of smugglers, tin-miners, simples-gatherers, egg-collectors or even venturesome children in a region before our interest asserted year-round proprietorial rights over it? The activity of climbing has a prehistory, the only clues to which lie in miners' or herbalists' lore and local traditions - indigenous relics brushed aside by the colonialists and imperialists who founded our formal sport. It seems to me extremely unlikely that a local population would have been unacquainted throughout previous centuries with the cliff descents, the nesting rakes, the fishing ledges, the exposed mineral lodes; and yet as climbers we assume our sport's incursions on this terrain to have been the first. And to validate that belief we buttress our own story with dates.

In 1858 a 27-year-old Cambridge clergyman, Leslie Stephen, made an ascent, "gangling and prehensile", of a chimney on Gurnard's Head - the which, given that Stephen was a member of the Alpine Club, was naturally assumed to be its first, and (though we do not know its whereabouts) is therefore, to confer respectability, generally placed at the head of the chronicle of Cornish climbing. Stephen's account of his climb, characteristically droll, inspired no spirit of emulation amongst his fellow alpinists. Nor, forty years later, did Walter Parry Haskett Smith's literary incentives attract the ascending ranks. "To the true-souled climber," he wrote, in his entertaining and remarkable gazetteer, *Climbing in the British Isles* , "who can enjoy a tough bit of rock, even if it is only fifty, aye, or twenty feet high, the coast of Cornwall with its worn granite cliffs and bays has much to offer." The true-souled climbers, sniffy at the idea of expending noble effort on 20 feet of rock, disdained the offer and kept to the 1,000-foot Welsh precipice of Lliwedd. Amongst their number, however, there was by fortuitous accident of history a man with Cornish connections whose part in the exploration of Lliwedd was significant, and of Cornwall seminal.

He was Arthur Westlake Andrews, an Oxford Blue in athletics (his event was the high jump), a gold medallist in the European mile, a singles semi-finalist at Wimbledon, and a scholar of independent means. His uncle, the great jurist and liberal M.P. John Westlake, owned a house at Zennor where Andrews, his brother and sister, spent most of their childhood holidays. From the opposite end of the twentieth century it's tempting, given the quality and difficulty of Andrews' explorations elsewhere (he "rubber-roamed, goat-like, up ribs - solitary and sturdy wanderings in rubber and audacity, high among the Lliwedd cracks and juts", wrote Geoffrey Winthrop Young), to wonder why he did so little in Cornwall, and so late. His recorded explorations here didn't start until 1902, when he was 34, and they ended in 1923 with his crossing of the *Green Cormorant Ledge* - a remarkable achievement for its time, and all the more so given that Andrews was by then in his mid-fifties. But to take the tally of recorded climbs as the sum total of the man's achievement is to dismiss him too easily. He created an interest, set a mood which endured throughout 50 years of activity in the area. His only significant *ascents* might be those of the *Bosigran* and *Rosemergy* ridges - suitably alpine features which he climbed with his sister Elsie in 1902 and 1906 - but his contribution was far more wide-reaching.

In brief, he invented the concept of the sea-level traverse (his grand design, humorously expressed and still unrealised, was a traverse between high and low water mark of the entire coast of Britain) and made some remarkably serious sallies in this now-unfashionable direction around the peninsula of Penwith; through the attraction of his personality he enticed most of the leading climbers of the first decades of the century down to Cornwall, where most of them - Winthrop Young, Farmer, Mallory, Odell, Haskett Smith himself - left some slight legacy; he extolled the virtues of the light rubber shoe as climbing footwear well before it became popular elsewhere; after buying it in 1922, he held house-parties from his home at Tregerthen in which the centrality of *play* was paramount; he held forth for decades on the many dimensions of the environments in which climbing takes place, and thus established a tradition of awareness and concern which continues to this day; he popularised, with articles, poems and descriptions from the Climbers' Club Journal of 1905 to the first Cornish climbing guide of 1950; finally, and most tangible in its influence, he persuaded his brother in 1938 to lease to the Climbers' Club as a base - the first such outside the mountain areas of Britain - the Count House at Bosigran.

He didn't just attract those of his own turn-of-the-century generation down to Penwith. This was the man who had lectured the worthies of the Alpine Club on the autonomous value of rock-climbing. So in due course and because of him the two great climbers of the 1930's arrived in Cornwall. Colin Kirkus came in 1938, climbed a few easy new routes at Bosigran, Chair Ladder and Porthgwarra, of which the *Black Slab* at Bosigran alone is of any great quality. In terms of climbing at the extreme standard of the day, since the accident at Easter 1934 on Ben Nevis in which Maurice Linnell had been killed Kirkus was a spent force. A flicker of the former spirit remained, though, and took him on a solo reconnaissance of the main face at Bosigran. He climbed to within 30 feet of the top of what is now *Nameless* before retreating from the indefinite and disconcerting final corner. After him, in the war years, drained with the effort of conscientious objection, came Menlove Edwards: "...such a very large amount of fine climbing faces", he wrote in the Count House log-book. Under Andrews' tutelage he made various sea-level traverses, a route on the east face of Porthmoina Island, the first direct ascent of Bosigran's *Western Ridge*. For the most part he bathed, crazily, in the waves, against the rocks - deep play, and fatally witness to it were Royal Marine Commandos (three of whom died in copying him) from the Commando Cliff Assault Wing, which was to move the history of Cornish climbing on to its next phase.

The CCAW came to be sited in St Ives through the influence of Noel Odell, who had himself been introduced to the Cornish cliffs by Andrews before the Great War. At first its activities comprised nail-shod desecration of the easy and obvious features, but with the cessation of hostilities in 1945, the challenge of climbing began to elicit more sophisticated attention. Joe Barry - father to the more famous John and a short and unbelievably tough Ulsterman was the driving force of the early generations of the group, amongst whom or associated with whom were Eric Stones, Tommy Genge, Jim Cortlandt-Simpson, Jimmy Flint and Mike Banks. Much of their initial activity went unrecorded, only the highlights standing out. But those highlights - *Demo Route* and *Genge's Groove* at Sennen, *South Face Direct* on Chair Ladder and Bosigran's version of *Zig-Zag* - were ripening the area to climbing maturity. Its growing repertoire attracted others, who added to it. Martin Ridges of the Manchester University Mountaineering Club discovered *Diocese* on Chair Ladder; the sandstone climber Dennis Kemp on a wild day in 1953 solved the problem corner of *Nameless* at the top of Bosigran's main face which had forced Kirkus to retreat fifteen years earlier; Menlove Edwards punned Chair Ladder's *Nearly* into existence after a failed attempt by Nea Morin. The holiday atmosphere of Cornish climbing, originating in A.W.Andrew's sea-play and compounded by the CCAW's ancillary activities of drinking, devil-may-care driving and attendance of every local dance from Redruth to St. Just, exerted a powerful influence. By the mid-1950's, Cornish climbing was popular, and poised to make the leap which would bring it in line with the top British standards of the day. The remarkable feature of the advance, when it came, was the number of climbers it involved.

The first signs were in a renewal of activity amongst the commando climbers. Shaking themselves free from a fug of alcohol and dance-hall which had descended on them after the departure of Joe Barry, they started once again to produce good new routes: Zeke Deacon's elegant and exposed pitch *The Mitre* in 1954, and Mike Banks' forceful *Zig-Zag* at Sennen the following year pointed the way. It was taken up by a group of gritstone-trained climbers who arrived at Bosigran in the summer of 1955. Peter Biven, his brother Barrie and their elder mentor Trevor Peck were already responsible for some of the great test-pieces in Derbyshire. They and the CCAW team of Deacon and Rawdon Goodier in the space of a year wove a web of lines across the faces of Bosigran, defining in the process some of the classic routes on Cornish granite: *Doorpost, Suicide Wall, Little Brown Jug, Anvil Chorus, Thin Wall Special, Paragon, Ghost, Phantom* and *Great Zawn Chimney* - the last three with considerable aid - came from the Biven-Peck combination. Deacon and Goodier, meanwhile, added *String of Pearls* - surely the best of all girdle traverses - *Raven Wall* and *Autumn Flakes* , as well as the estimable *Bishop's Rib* at Chair Ladder. Occasionally, the overweening voice of modern criticism attacks these routes for their innovatory and liberal use of pitons for protection and aid. It should be heard with caution, and tempered with the awareness that before the use of wire runners, nuts, tapes, harnesses, Friends, chalk, perlon rope, specialist rock-boots, abseil cleaning, inspection and rehearsal of moves, to climb lines on sight, dealing as you went with vegetation, choked cracks, sugary granite, and oppressed by ignorance of what was to come was an entirely different, and significantly more serious proposition, regardless of aid used, than to climb the same routes in the style of today. When they were first done in 1957 by, respectively, Deacon and Banks and the Bivens, *Green Cormorant Face* and the *West Face* - the first routes of quality in the Great Zawn - could not have been climbed without recourse over brief sections to artificial aids. We who follow cleanly years later are hard pressed to imagine the conditions the first ascensionists faced. Perhaps we're equally hard-pressed to grasp the scale of Joe Brown's achievement the same year in leading *Bow Wall* - a climb of sumptuous quality, perhaps the finest to that date in Cornwall, and of a steepness which had previously only been encountered on outcrops. It set the *imprimatur* of the Master upon this coast.

After *Bow Wall*, anything at Bosigran was bound for a time to appear as anti-climax. The main developments now came elsewhere, in particular with a series of routes by Zeke Deacon and various new commando partners - notably Viv Stevenson and "Mac" Macdermott - at Land's End and along the south coast: *Death Rattle Gulch* and *The Parasite* at Land's End, *Excelsior* and *Detergent Wall* at Chair Ladder, stand out as clearly now in terms of star-rating as they did in their day for seriousness. All this promise, however, led to little more than a decade of consolidation. The best routes produced in the decade 1959-1969 - *Beowulf* (on which Peter Biven used three bolts, but which was climbed free almost immediately by Phil Gordon - nephew of Winthrop Young and a technical master of the 1959 generation who was too graciously unmotivated ever to fulfil his extraordinary early promise), *Paradise, Behemoth, Omen, Desolation Row, Boldfinger* - with the possible exception of the last, which is both technically hard and serious, and *Behemoth*, which was one of the first of the hard greenstone classics, did not mark any significant advance. The latter climbs did signal the emergence of a talented group of Exeter climbers - Frank Cannings, Pat Littlejohn, Keith Darbyshire foremost among them - who emerged from the long shadow Peter Biven's ability and character cast over that town to assert their own talent and outlook. But in Cornwall, as elsewhere, the 1960's were a period of relative stagnation, awaiting galvanism.

There were flickerings of progress before the mid-1970's. Littlejohn's enormous appetite for rock and cool ability was apparent in routes like *The Adversary* in Zawn Duel, climbed in 1972; Derbyshire-based climbers Tom Proctor and Edwin Drummond free-climbed the old aid routes of *Ghost* and *Phantom* on successive days in 1973. But in 1974 came the true harbinger of the new, with visiting American climber Henry Barber's lead of the Great Zawn's monolithically serious and excellent *Deja Vu*. Thereafter, the great aid-reliant routes to its right - *Dream, Liberator, The West Face* - were freed from iron bondage by Ron Fawcett, Pete Livesey and Jill Lawrence - predators from the north who trained for climbing, pursued it on the steepest limestone, brought a technological armoury of micro-nuts, chalk and, a little later, Friends to the task. The stage was set for Cornwall to witness the next phase of development. The pointers to it crowded in as the 1970's drew to a close. Littlejohn raised his game with his ascent of the magnificent *Burning Gold* on Carn Les Boel - an event finessed by Ron Fawcett with his bold and technical *New Medium* at Bosigran. These, however, were mere preliminaries.

The man initially responsible for a pioneering effort which has continued right through to the present day made his first new climb in Cornwall - Candy Man in the Great Zawn - in 1973. Rowland Edwards is a powerful, passionately keen Welshman, brought up in Bolton, who had crucially influenced Welsh climbing for much of the 1960's and 1970's. In 1978 he moved to Sennen to start a climbing school. From that time to the present day he and his son Mark have dominated Cornish climbing: *Mastodon, Rock Dancer, Astral Stroll, Immaculate Arete, American Dream, Ziggurat, Atlantic Ocean Wall* all belong to the early phase of their activity and each is of high quality, the last named being one of the prime rock-climbs in Britain. Gradually, in the early 1980's, Mark's ability caught up with and surpassed that of his father and he too began to create a series of routes which ranked with the hardest in the country. With some of them - *Red Rose* at Sennen in particular, and his awesome sports climbs under the great roof of Carn Vellan, he invited controversy through the nature of his protection, and precipitated a debate which resulted in the BMC's policy that bolts should not be placed on Cornish sea-cliffs. The arguments raged viciously backwards and forwards, disinformation abounded, recriminations and mendacities were hurled about, and magazine editors stocked their correspondence columns with glee. The simple truth that Edwards father and son are exceptionally gifted climbers whose contribution to Cornish cliff exploration is unparalleled has sadly all too often been overlooked. It's my hope that this guide, written by an honest broker, Tim Dennell, in collaboration with the Edwards's, will set the record straight, allow the scale of their achievement to be appreciated. As climbers, we come to Cornwall to hear the wave sound and the gull's cry, not the grinding of axes. We come to enjoy some of the loveliest environments, best rock and most pleasing routes Britain has to offer. Here, for your own judgement and delectation, and it's to be hoped beyond the reach of stale and artificially prolonged controversy, in modern style and at reasonable cost the riches are spread out before you. May the disinterested reach their own conclusions!

Jim Perrin

SYMBOLS, ABBREVIATIONS & TERMS

❀ SSSI ❀ = Site of Special Scientific Interest.

❀ = Environmentally Sensitive - refer to appropriate text for that route or cliff.

🦅 = Known nesting site. check visually prior to an ascent or avoid during spring and summer.

☠ = Very Bold. Route noted for lack of protection possibilities.

💣 = Approach warily as the grade may be unconfirmed or the route may have in situ protection missing.

R = Route may be run out in places or the first protection may be some way above the ground.

☺ = Well protected, makes a good 'gradebreaker'.

⚲ = Rock particularly loose on this route.

✚ ☹ = Bolts cut or removed from this sports route.

(T) = Also shown on other topo(s). The number is also given.

A + (plus) or - (minus) sign next to the grade indicates whether a route is thought to be a hard or soft touch within its grade. If a technical grade is highlighted by being both in bold and underlined then it is this grade that the descriptive grade primarily applies to, e.g. HVS **4c**, 5a (1st pitch bold) E2 5a,

5b etc.

FA ~ First Ascent with aid or in situ protection if followed by

FFA ~ First Free Ascent.

FKA ~ First Known Ascent.

FKFA ~ First Known Free Ascent.

alt/var ~ Alternate/Various leads.

TR ~ Top Rope.

A ~ Abseil Point.

B ~ Belay.

D ~ Descent or Downclimb.

P ~ Pitch.

PR ~ Peg Runner - the presence or quality of which cannot be guaranteed.

PB ~ Peg Belay - the presence or quality of which cannot be guaranteed.

BR ~ Bolt Runner - the presence or quality of which cannot be guaranteed.

BB ~ Bolt Belay - the presence or quality of which cannot be guaranteed.

SS ~ Stainless Steel.

XS ~ Extremely Severe.

Friends ~ Friends, Quadcams, Camalots and other comparable camming devices.

TCUs ~ Triple Camming Units including Friends 0.5 and .00.

Rocks ~ Rocks, Wallnuts, Gems, Stones etc. on both wire and tape.

Micros ~ Smallest rocks, Wallnuts etc. and RPs, HBs etc.

Silence of a Lamb, E5 6b, Gurnard's Head. Climbers : Rowland Edwards and Ian Blake

Gurnard's Head

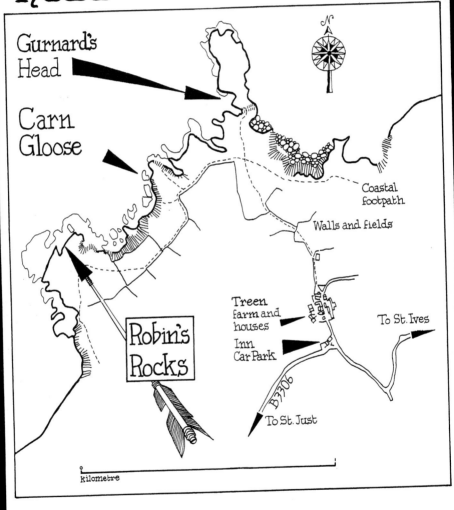

Gurnard's Head

Carn Gloose

Robin's Rocks

Coastal footpath

Walls and fields

Treen farm and houses

Inn Car Park

To St. Ives

To St. Just

B3306

kilometre

THE CLIFFS

Gurnard's Head

COASTGUARD IDENTITY: Gurnard's Head.

NEAREST PHONE: ✆ Treen - north (pub) or in Zennor.

OS REFERENCE: 432 385

TIDAL? Yes. The platforms at the base of Mastodon, Shark and Tropospheric Scatter can be reached by an abseil at low tide when the sea is calm. Right Angle is non-tidal but requires calm seas for an ascent involving the downclimb.

ASPECT: Westerly and north-westerly, it catches the sun in the afternoon and evening.

CHARACTER: A committing cliff made of steep, almost vertical, walls of compact rock. (A gurnard is a species of fish.)

ROCK: Greenstone.

TYPE OF CLIMBS: Committing, quality climbs, some multi-pitch.

PROBLEMS: Waves can send spray high up the cliff, lower parts of the cliff can be slow drying.

ENVIRONMENTAL CONCERNS: ❀ SSSI ❀ Erosion at the start and finish of Right Angle. There is concern from the National Trust about potential damage to valuable vegetation on the start of the first pitch of this route, so please exercise great care. It is a species of sea aster that lives in crevices, rare in the UK and only found in three places in Penwith. This cliff is one of them. There are valuable plants and also a prehistoric fort on the headland itself. On the cliff top plants can be damaged by trampling. Fulmar, herring gull and shags breed in the area. The cliffs and zawns between Gurnard's Head and Carn Gloose are a very sensitive area for nesting birds. If there are nesting birds on the Right Angle wall consideration is required.

PARKING: By the Gurnard's Head pub or discreetly down the road past the pub in the Treen hamlet.

APPROACH: Refer to both the West Penwith - Cornwall and Gurnard's Head maps. From the Gurnard's Head pub or Treen hamlet walk down the short road to a small white coastguard house. Bear left at this and walk down a narrow pedestrian cut-through to fields, the start of the path and a good view of the headland. Follow the path and down seven stone steps into another field until a low stone stile is reached. Continue through fern and bracken to a junction with the coast path which forms an obvious crossroads. Carry straight on towards the headland. The dramatic cliffs are tucked away on its left side where the headland meets the mainland.

DESCENTS: For the start of Right Angle, descend the slope at the top of the right-hand wall (facing out) until it is possible to downclimb a short chimney to the start of the route. It can also be reached by a short traverse from a little lower which we recommend. The Behemoth cave can be reached from the sea level belay of Right Angle; a little ingenuity may be needed when the rock is wet. This can also be reached by an abseil down Right Angle, anti-social on a busy day. The rock platforms at the starts of Mastodon, Shark and Tropospheric Scatter can be reached by abseils down Shark or Probe.

Topo 1
Gurnard's Head, Right Angle Wall

The Right Angle Wall
Topo 1

GH 1)
Right Angle (T2) 🏵 ★★★
Hard Severe 4a, 4a, 4a 235ft **R**
P1) 40ft P2) 75ft P3) 120ft
Consideration is required should birds be nesting on the Right Angle Wall. **It is very important you don't disturb vegetation on the first pitch. We suggest the alternative start, traversing in a little lower.** Superb, joyous climbing in great position on good rock. Friends are useful. A competent second is essential as P2 involves some committing downclimbing though a back rope can be arranged at the expense of a piece of gear.
(FA I. Peters, J. Bember 1966)

GH 1a)
Right Angle Variation 20ft Hard Severe 4a
A worthwhile variation, particularly when high seas are running, is to P2 & Severe 4a. Instead of downclimbing, continue traversing along a break to a stance level with the roof of the cave, below the final slab and corner.

GH 4)
Pure Juice (T2) 295ft E1 4a, 4a, **5b**, 4c

GH 8)
Mastodon (T2) 180ft E3 5b, **5c, 5c** ★★★

Behemoth Wall
Topo 2

GH 1)
Right Angle (T1) 235ft Hard Severe 4a, 4a, 4a **R** 🏵 ★★★

GH 2)
Nemesis 170ft Hard Very Severe 4a, **5a**
P1) 50ft P2) 120ft
(FA R. Edwards, S. Salmon 1978)

**Topo 2
Gurnard's Head
Behemoth Wall**

GH 3)
The Kracken 130ft Hard Very Severe **5a**, 4c
P1) 70ft P2) 60ft
(FA J. Hart, J. Loxham alt 1977)

GH 4)
Pure Juice (T1) 295ft E1 4a, 4a, **5b**, 4c

P1) 40ft P2) 75ft P3) 115ft P4) 65ft
A harder variation on the theme of The
Kracken.
(FA R. Edwards, S. Salmon 1978)

GH 5)
Behemoth 160ft E2 5b, 5b, 3c ★★★

59

P1) 60ft P2) 70ft P3) 30ft
Diverse, committing and absorbing. Start from the ledges inside the cave. The corners of the first pitch can be free climbed in dry conditions, but aid is sometimes resorted to when wet, still not a soft option. Spare karabiners and rocks, etc. are useful for the hanging belay.
(FA P. Littlejohn, S. Jones alt 1969)

GH 6)
Magog 160ft E5 6b 💣 ★
P1) 60ft P2) 70ft P3) 30ft
Begin from inside the cave, climbing a short arête and chimney to the left of the Behemoth start, breaking out through the roof at a junction with Mastodon.
(FA N. Crane, C. Waddy alt 1994)

GH 7)
Leviathan 130ft E4 6a, 6a, 3c **R** 💣 ★
P1) 60ft P2) 70ft P3) 30ft
The start of a harder companion to Behemoth, this climbs the good looking arête on the right-hand side (facing in) of the cave. Climb to the Behemoth stance and begin to traverse right as for that route, before climbing up the wall to rejoin Behemoth just before the final stance.
(FA S. Ohly, M. Raine 1994)

GH 8)
Mastodon (T1) 180ft E3 5b, 5c, 5c ★★★
P1) 65ft P2) 75ft P3) 40ft
Exemplary, exquisite climbing that should be savoured by everyone with the ability. Spare small rocks and quickdraws useful for the hanging stance. The first pitch is serious when wet.
(FA R. Edwards, S. Salmon 1978)

GH 9)
Black Magic 110ft E2 5b+ ★★
Overshadowed by its neighbours and consequently underrated.
(FA R. Edwards, S. Salmon 1978)

GH 10)
Shark 90ft E1 5b ★★
A fine pitch, climbing the corner and finishing up the wall on the right. Good protection throughout.
(FA P. Littlejohn, S. Jones 1969)

GH 11)
The Silence Of A Lamb 110ft E5 6b 💣 ★★
A striking line up the arête right of Shark starting via a rising traverse from the base of Shark, past a PR & BR (removed).
(FA R. Edwards, I. Blake 1991)

GH 12)
Tropospheric Scatter 95ft E4 5c+ ★★★
Sustained climbing following cracks up the wall. A long reach is an advantage.
(FA R. Edwards, S. Salmon 1978)

GH 13)
Art Of The Slate 90ft E5 6a ☠ ★
The crux is low down but it is bold throughout. It still awaits an on sight ascent.
(FA M. Edwards, S. Anson 1989. FFA M. Edwards solo 1989)

The next three routes are not depicted on a topo.

GH a)   **Probe** 50ft Severe
Climbs the corner on the right-hand (facing in) end of the cliff. Start by climbing slabs leftwards to enter the corner.
(FA Unknown, possibly 1960s)

GH b)
Babylon And Back E3 6a, 💣 ★
A girdle of the cliff which starts from two-thirds height up Probe. It crosses the wall to the arête of Silence Of A Lamb and enters Shark. From here it crosses to the traverse of Behemoth, reverses this to join P2 of Mastodon. It then leaves this above the cave to cross Pure Juice and finishes up a shallow groove between that route and The Kracken.
(FA M. Raine, S. Ohly alt 1994)

GH c)
Parabola 140ft E2 5b
A left to right girdle. Start as for Right Angle and join Pure Juice to the belay, descend to a nose and climb around this to a crack. Climb the crack and move right to a pedestal. Belay. Climb another crack then traverse right around the arête to an easier finish.
(FA R. Edwards, R. Perriment 1980)

Monster Munch F8b+, Carn Vellan. Climber: Mark Edwards

Carn Gloose

COASTGUARD IDENTITY: Carn Gloose - Near Gurnard's Head.

NEAREST PHONE: ✆ Treen - north (pub) or in Zennor.

OS REFERENCE: 429 384

TIDAL? Does not affect Astral Stroll, High Frontier or Dangerous Visions except in rough seas.

ASPECT: South-westerly. Astral Stroll catches the sun from mid-morning onwards. North-westerly. Dangerous Visions catches the afternoon sun.

CHARACTER: An overhanging, dark cliff, often approached with a sense of foreboding. When dry and the sea is calm, however, it allows itself to smile a little; don't let the cliff psych you out.

ROCK: Slate.

TYPE OF CLIMBS: Committing adventures into the unknown.

PROBLEMS: Difficulties in locating starts of routes and route-finding. Rough seas can affect the routes and the cliff is slow drying and seeps after rain. The few remaining pegs are corroded.

ENVIRONMENTAL CONCERNS: ❀ SSSI ❀ Ideally we would suggest that a visit should consist of changing, descending, climbing the route followed by departure with no exploratory scrambling on the upper part of the cliff. The slopes at the top of the cliff are valuable and vulnerable. There is a little erosion on them at present. The area is also a nesting site. Take care to exit the cliff as cleanly as possible. Please do not trample on or pick any flowers or small plants such as cliff bluebell. Any new routing activity is best left until midsummer onwards.

PARKING: By the Gurnard's Head pub or discreetly down the road in the Treen hamlet.

APPROACH: Refer to both the West Penwith - Cornwall and Gurnard's Head maps (page 56). From the Gurnard's Head pub or Treen hamlet walk down the short road to a small white coastguard house. Bear left at this and walk down a narrow pedestrian cut-through to the fields and the start of the path (signed). Follow this and down seven stone steps into another field until a low stone stile is reached. Continue through fern and bracken to a junction with the coast path which forms an obvious crossroads. Turn left and after passing a low stone wall and ascending a slight rise Carn Gloose comes into view. It is 350m further on and is the large rocky headland with an obvious notch in its spine.

DESCENTS: For Astral Stroll scramble down the right side (facing out) of the headland until it steepens. A short abseil or downclimb leads to a platform. Traversing left (facing out) around an arête leads to the first view of the main cliff and is the start (P1) of Astral Stroll. For Dangerous Visions, walk past the headland and a wall, then scramble down slopes on its left-hand (facing out) side to reach a ridge leading to rock and the cliff base.

CG 1)
High Frontier (T2) 160ft Hard Very Severe 4b, **5a**, 3c
P1) 30ft P2) 80ft P3) 30ft
(FA R. Edwards, M. Edwards 1980)

CG 2)
Babylon Five 120ft Very Severe 4b, 4b, 4c ❂
P1) 30ft P2) 40ft P3) 50ft
(FKA T. Dennell, S. Pac, alt J. Adamson 1991)

CG 3)
Astral Stroll 180ft E1 4b, **5b, 5b,**5a ★★★★
P1) 30ft P2) 40ft P3) 50ft P4) 60ft
Low in its technical grade but in exciting, committing, ethereal position. Large Friends, are useful. With good ropework both the main pitches can be run together. Incompetence and indecision have led to some epics. Retreat is, ah, interesting and has resulted in the odd swim.
(FA R. Edwards, C. Bryan 1980)

Cool Diamonds E5 6b, Paradise Wall. Climber: Dick Swindon

Carn Gloose

CG 4)
Space Race 220ft E2 4b, 5b, 5b, <u>5c</u>
P1) 30ft P2) 40ft P3) 50ft P4) 60ft
(FA R. Edwards, P. O'Sullivan, P. Lloyd 1980)

Dangerous Visions Area

These routes are not depicted on a topo

Descending the slopes on the left-hand (facing out) end of the cliffs gains a sloping rock platform. From right to left (facing in) the first route is reached.

CG a)
Hornpipe Corner 100ft Very Severe 4c
This climbs the prominent corner crack. The upper section has some suspect rock.
(FA M. McDermott, R. Payne 1967)

CG b)
The Loose Goose 110ft Hard Very Severe 5a
This climbs the wall, starting about 12ft left of Hornpipe Corner, passing an overhang and finishing on suspect rock.
(FA S. Lewis, A.N. Other 1982)

After this the cliff becomes increasingly undercut. The massive overhangs are currently breached by only one route, but potential exists for further hard lines.

CG c)
Dangerous Visions 205ft E6 6a, 5b+
★★★
P1) 120ft P2) 85ft
In the first section of the overhanging area, two grooves can be seen suspended above the platform. This route takes the second one from the right, which is gained by lassoing a spike following by a prussik. Climb the groove to a roof, pass this, then trend up and left to belay above a small roof. P2 trends up and rightwards and finishes direct via a short corner/groove.

The first free ascent came after a number of attempts, placing protection on the lead. More pegs were placed subsequently to encourage further ascents, though it has now been led without them.
(FA R. Edwards, M. Edwards 1980. FFA P. Littlejohn 1996)

Robin's Rocks

COASTGUARD IDENTITY: Robin's Rocks.

NEAREST PHONE: ℭ Count House or Morvah; Treen north (pub) or at Zennor.

OS REFERENCE: 426 381

TIDAL? Yes, so visit when the tide is on its way out. Sensible Shoes can be started by downclimbing a corner during high tide. Avoid the area if the sea is rough.

ASPECT: North-westerly. Best visited in the afternoon, if the tide is low, to catch the sun.

CHARACTER: An amiable cliff that packs a punch. Well worth the walk to visit, especially on a sunny day.

ROCK: Greenstone.

TYPE OF CLIMBS: Challenging single pitches.

PROBLEMS: Tides. A 20-minute walk in, but not too strenuous.

ENVIRONMENTAL CONCERNS: ❀ SSSI ❀ Stick to the paths, leave no litter, tread lightly and avoid any nests in spring. Act considerately.

PARKING: By the Gurnard's Head pub or discreetly down the road in Treen hamlet.

APPROACH: Refer to both the West Penwith - Cornwall and Gurnard's Head maps (p56). From the Gurnard's Head pub or Treen hamlet walk down the short road to a small white coastguard house. Bear left at this and walk down a narrow pedestrian cut-through to the fields and a path (as for Gurnard's Head). Follow the path down seven stone steps into another field until a low stone stile is crossed. Continue through fern and bracken to a junction with the coast path which forms an obvious crossroads. Turn left and walk southwards past the ridged headland of Carn Gloose (the ridge has an obvious notch in its spine) and crossing a stone wall to reach a wooden stile. Fifty metres further on the coast path 'dog legs' sharply. From this bend a small path leads down to old spoil heaps and past a manmade ravine towards large blocks on the cliff top. Sensible Shoes can be started at high tide by striding over an impressive narrow canyon onto the top of its buttress.

DESCENTS: The main platform is reached by walking left (facing out from the main cliff) and down to the platform. Or by abseil.

RR 1)
Sensible Shoes 120ft Very Severe 4c **R**
★★★
A great little route and shown here with the direct start. Care required if this is wet. The original start and a very worthwhile one (**1a**) downclimbs the corner to join the traverse. A back rope can be arranged to protect the second if double ropes are used.
(FA P. O'Sullivan, C. Woodhead 1978. Direct Start M. Edwards, C. Johns 1988)

The overhangs have yet to be breached.

RR 2)
Black Cleft 70ft Very Severe 4c
The line that skirts the first overhang by moving around the corner onto the canyon wall and finishes up this.
(FA R. Edwards, J. Miguel-Fraile 1991)
The canyon has been climbed at Severe standard, **Porthmeour Chimney**.
(FA W. Andrews 1908)

The Main Cliff

RR 3)
Black Sapper 110ft E4/5 6a ★★
An excellent route that deserves more traffic.
(FA P. Littlejohn, C. King 1978. Variation M. Edwards 1989)

RR 4)
Off The Mark 120ft E7 6c ☠ 💣 ★★★
With titillating run-outs and absurdly steep, strenous climbing, this stimulates the senses. A variation is to start as for Black Sapper before climbing to join this route at the same grade.
(FA M. Edwards, R. Edwards 1989)

RR 5)
The Silver Arrow 110ft E5 6b 💣 ★
This climbs the wall past 5 SS pegs. A belay can be found at half height if required.
(FA M. Edwards, R. Edwards 1991)

RR 6)
Tuco The Terrible 110ft E2 5b ★★★
A gracious, challenging climb. The first greenstone extreme. A belay can be taken at half height if required.
(FA W. Carver, M. Hands 1969)

RR 7)
Black Napkin 100ft E2 5c **R** ★
(FA P. Saunders, G. Butler 1988)

RR 8)
Monsoon 60ft E3 6b 💣 ★★
(FA M. Edwards, R. Edwards 1992)

RR 9)
Robin Hood 60ft E1 5b
(FA M. Edwards, C. Johns 1991)

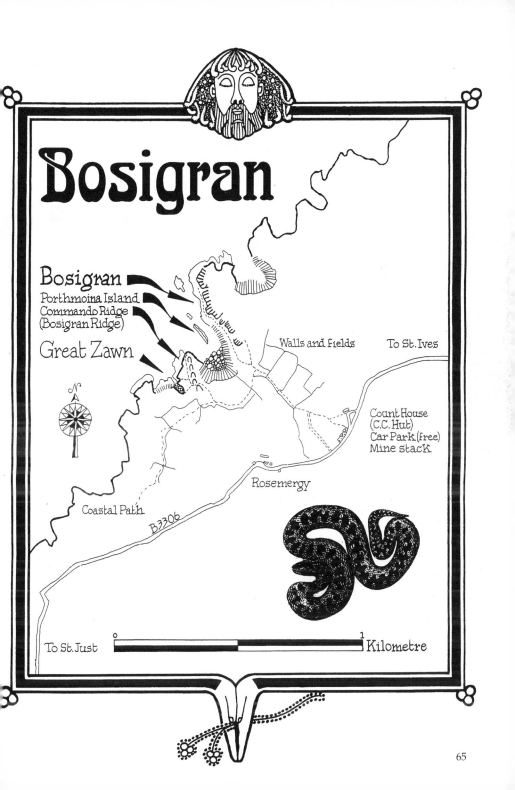

Bosigran

Bosigran
Porthmoina Island
Commando Ridge
(Bosigran Ridge)

Great Zawn

Walls and Fields

To St. Ives

Count House
(C.C. Hut)
Car Park (free)
Mine stack

Rosemergy

N

Coastal Path

B3306

To St. Just

0 ───── 1 Kilometre

65

Bosigran

COASTGUARD IDENTITY: Bosigran's Main Face.

NEAREST PHONE: ✆ The Count House or in Morvah.

OS REFERENCE: 416 370

TIDAL? Not tidal or affected by the sea except for Seaward Cliff. Care required around the Ochre Slab area if the sea is rough.

ASPECT: South-westerly/westerly, it starts to catch any sun from around 10am onwards.

CHARACTER: The jewel in Penwith's crown. Now perhaps the jewel has lost a little lustre from being handled too many times. With major routes at all grades, this cliff still epitomises Penwith for many climbers.

ROCK: Solid granite, smooth in places.

TYPE OF CLIMBS: Both single and multi-pitch routes featuring cracks, corners, slabs and roofs. Something for everyone.

PROBLEMS: Walls under overhangs can take a while to dry. It can become crowded, particularly at weekends.

ENVIRONMENTAL CONCERNS: ❀ SSSI ❀ The prominent rock island beneath the main face is Porthmoina island. The BMC and National Trust have agreed that this is to be left in as undisturbed a state as possible, as a wilderness area. Please do not visit it or set up a tyrolean from it. There is some path erosion and concern about possible disturbance of plants in the

gullies, in particular dwarf oaks in Simon Gully and cliff bluebells in the surrounding Maritime Heathland. There has also been a decline in nesting gulls, peg damage to cracks and removal of lichen. There are Iron Age remains on the top of the headland. We ask you to please avoid nests and young gulls and attempt not to tread on or disturb plants in the gullies. We also ask you not to push new routes through major areas of lichen. Ravens and jackdaws also nest here. Please take litter home. The area is being monitored by the NT.

PARKING: Roadside car park next to two prominent ruined mine buildings (of the Carn Galver mine). An old pump house and chimney stack.

APPROACH: Follow paths from the car park, through bracken and gorse initially and then through fields and over stiles towards the sea. Just past old ruins walk downwards following a track and then bear right and walk and scramble over boulders around to the wide ledge and path at the base of the cliff, which is around 100ft above sea level.

DESCENTS: Two major gullies at either end of the main cliff, marked on topos. Care required as both involve some downclimbing and so as not to disturb valuable plants in Simon Gully.

Bosigran - Topo 1 (p66)

B 2)
Alison Rib (T2) Difficult ☺ ★★★★

B a)
Big Top (T p68) Very Difficult ☺ ★

B 20)
Doorpost (T3) Hard Severe 4b ☺ ★★★★

B 26)
Suicide Wall (T5) E1 5c (or 5a) ★★★

B 47)
Kafoozalem (T7) E4 6a ★★★

B 56)
Black Slab (T9) Difficult ☺ ★

Alison Rib Area - Topo 2 (p68)

B 1)
Fafnir 200ft Difficult
Finish as for Alison Rib or pick a line up the slabs to the top.
(FA P. Biven, C. Fishwick alt 1961)

B 2)
Alison Rib (T1) 220ft Difficult ☺ ★★★★
P1) 150ft - then a short walk to P2) 40ft
Pure pleasure. This both satisfies the timorous novice and revitalises the jaded. The rib can only be climbed to the thread belays,

Alison Rib, Difficult, Bosigran.
Climber: Sigrid Merc

67

Topo 2
Alison Rib Area

TO SIMON GULLY

B 5)
Oread 165ft Very Difficult
+ **R**
Thoughtful protection.
(FA P. Jaynes, E. Byne 1955)

B 6)
Oread Bypass 160ft
Very Difficult + **R**
Care required placing
protection.
*(FA E. Byne, C. Ashbury
1955)*

B 7)
Picnic 60ft Very Severe 4b
★
Not for teddy bears. An
enjoyable, short pitch.
*(FA B. Biven, P. Biven, T.
Peck, C. Fishwick 1958)*

The next two routes are not
depicted on an area topo.
Refer to Topo One. Fifty
feet left of Alison Rib, at
the base of the descent
gully, is a large detached
buttress.

B a)
Big Top (T1) 80ft
Very Difficult ☺ ★

comfortably, in one pitch with a 50m rope. Do
climb the rib, not the right-hand slab. Good
belays can be found if you wish to split the
pitch. Large Friend useful for the final crack.
(FA D. Romanis 1923)

B 3)
Kate 150ft Very Difficult
P1) 70ft P2) 92ft
A short, but flirtatious, main section.
(FA C. Fishwick, R. Mavin 1963)

B 4)
In Between 150ft Very Difficult ☺ ★
Overly modest, it's a choice climb. A belay can
be found on ledges at around 60ft if desired.
(FA P. Biven, R. Woodman, C. Fishwick 1963)

Embryonic Vector. Climb cracks snaking up
large blocks, passing a small overhang, to the
prominent overhang neb, move right and
climb the crack and slab to an easier finish onto
the top of the buttress.
(FA C. Fishwick, T. Peck 1958)

Left of Big Top a slender wall is split by a
prominent dog leg crack.

B b)
Trapeze 80ft
Hard Very Severe 5a+ ★
Deceptively hard; if you wondered where the
crux was then traverse right to finish, most are
content to finish direct.
(FA T. Peck, P. Biven 1964)

Andrew, Hard Very Difficult, Bosigran. Climber: Thor Veen

The Main Cliff - Doorpost Area
View 1 Topo 3 (p70)

B 8)
Andrew 200ft Hard Very Difficult 3c, 3c+, 3b, 3c+ ★★
P1) 50ft P2) 50ft P3) 40ft P4) 60ft
A compelling route that maintains interest throughout. Hidden on the topo is the final pitch (see photo). As you move right (facing in) around a corner, you'll reach a small stance under a large, leaning groove. This is awkward to start (Welsh 4a or Cornish 3c?) before you can bridge out, and up, to reach the upper slabs. Care is required with protection as the angle of the rope can lift gear out.
(FA P. Biven, T. Peck, J. Andrew 1958)

Topo 3
The Main Cliff
Doorpost Area
View One

**Topo 4
The Main Cliff
Doorpost Area
View Two**

B 10)
Anvil Chorus (T4) ★★★
200ft Hard Very Severe 4b, 4b, **5a**, 4c
P1) 60ft P2) 50ft P3) 55ft P4) 25ft
The second pitch of this route is shown here
for those who want a tougher alternative (4b)
to the second pitch of Andrew. Large Friend
useful. All of Anvil Chorus is shown on Topo
Four.

B 11)
Venusberg 190ft Very Severe 4a, 4a, 4c+, 4c
R ★
P1) 35ft P2) 55ft P3) 65ft P4) 35ft
Keeps coming at you; an 'in your face' climb
on the final two pitches. Not soft touch even
with modern protection. Friends useful.
(FA P. Biven, C. Fishwick 1961)

B 14)
Thick Wall Special 180ft E4 5c, 4c ☠ ★
P1) 70ft P2) 110ft
To finish, climb the hanging arête above until
the final ledge shared with Little Brown Jug
(B16) is reached.
(FA P. Livesey and party 1976)

B 15)
Feast Of Fear 120ft E6 6b ☠ ★★
P1) 25ft P2) 60ft P3) 35ft
Teetering on the brink of extinction.
(FA M. Edwards, R. Greaves 1985)

B 16)
Little Brown Jug ★★★
200ft Very Severe 4b, 4c/5a, 2a **R**
P1) 120ft P2) 70ft P3) 10ft
From a whisper to a song. There are both 4c
and 5a ways of doing the crux moves on P2. A
lot depends on your ability to read the rock.
Small Friends, rocks and larger gear for the
brisk final crack are useful.
(FA P. Biven, B. Biven 1955)

B 16a)
Direct start to Little Brown Jug 70ft Hard
Very Severe 5a **R**
Take the small triangular roof on the left and
climb direct to join the shallow corner crack.

Anvil Chorus, Hard Very Severe. Bosigran.
Climber: Ans Knoope

B 18)
Thin Wall Special 200ft E2 **5b**, 4a, 5a+ **R**
★★
P1) 80ft P2) 40ft P3) 80ft
Contrasting pitches with stimulating
protection and a good finish.
(FA P. Biven, T. Peck 1956. FFA Unknown)

B 20)
Doorpost (T1) ☺ ★★★★
200ft Hard Severe 4a, 4b, 4a
P1) 70ft P2) 45ft P3) 85ft
THE classic of the area at its grade, offering
continually varied and interesting climbing;
the technical difficulties ease on P3 allowing
vertigo to become your companion. If after

reading this you still haven't climbed Doorpost, then make it your next route. The final two pitches can be run together with good ropework. Good protection throughout, particularly with Friends of all sizes and varied sized rocks. The first pitch is slow drying. Slings are useful for the final thread belay.
(FA B. Biven, T. Peck, P. Biven 1955)

B 21)
Bow Wall (T5) 220ft E2 3b, 4c+, 5b, 5b, 4a
★★★★

B 22)
The Marksman (T4) 180ft E7 5b, 6c+ 5a
💣★★
P1) 60ft P2) 60ft P3) 60ft
Exhilarating, wild and exacting in dramatic position. Two SS pegs should be in place, the placements aren't 'bomber'. Tackle the roof with boundless enthusiasm.
(FA M. Edwards unseconded 1994)

The Main Cliff - Doorpost Area
Topo 4 View 2 (page 71)

B 9)
Ledge Climb 180ft Difficult ★
P1) 50ft P2) 70ft P3) 80ft
Hidden on the topo around a corner is a gauche chimney which leads to the start of the ledge. The summit of Bosigran is 335ft above sea level, so the moves across the ledge are an exposure explosion for the uninitiated.
(FA P1 G. Mallory and party 1922. Final Pitch, A. Andrews, J. Farmer 1905)

B 10)
Anvil Chorus (T3) ★★★
200ft Hard Very Severe 4b, 4b, **5a**, 4c ★★
P1) 60ft P2) 50ft P3) 55ft P4) 25ft
Don't be laid-back on the layback; protect and survive on the big corner pitch (pitch 3). A flexi-Friend 1-2 placed in the first 10ft of the corner crack would help prevent the angle of the rope lifting out runners in the event of a fall.
(FA P. Biven, T. Peck, B. Biven 1956)

B 12)
Doorway 190ft Severe 4a, 3a, 4a ☺ ★★
P1) 70ft P2) 35ft P3) 85ft
The final pitch is slow drying, but well worth doing after a somewhat disjointed start.
(FA J. Cortland-Simpson, W. Hutchinson 1949)

B 13)
Visions of Johanna 180ft E2 5b, 3a, 4c R ★
P1) 70ft P2) 30ft P3) 80ft
The first 20ft is the crux and is bold. There are hidden holds. A variation is **She** which climbs directly to the roof and pulls over this to join the groove at E2 5c.
(FA P1 M. Springett, F. Cannings, P. Biven 1968. P3 J. Taylor 1968. She M. Edwards 1983)

B 17)
Toad Wall Special 200ft E3 5c+, 6a ★★
P1) 120ft P2) 80ft
A determined approach required, reach helps.
(FA P1 S. Lewis 1982. P2 S. Lewis, C. Mellor 1983)

B 19)
Shaft 200ft E3 5b, **6b**, 5a
P1) 80ft P2) 40ft P3) 80ft
The first pitch can be used as a direct start to Doorpost. A thin crack to the left goes at HVS 5b.
(FA R. Edwards, M. Edwards 1983)

B 22)   **The Marksman (T3)** 180ft E7 6c+
💣 ★★

The Main Cliff - Suicide Wall Area
Topo 5 (p74)

B 21)
Bow Wall (T3) 220ft E2 3b, 4c+, 5b, 5b, 4a
★★★★
P1) 25ft P2) 60ft P3) 50ft P4) 40ft P5) 40ft
This route has all the hallmarks of excellence: history, variety, quality and exposure. Pure exhilaration and a milestone in any E2 leader's climbing life. Be selfish, lead all of it. A large Friend and competent second desirable. The start, P1, is a scramble onto a small pillar by the coal face, often soloed.
(FA P1, P2 & P3 J. Brown unseconded 1957. FA/ FFA P4 & P5 B. Biven, T. Peck 1958)

B 23)
Vulcan 200ft E5 5a, 6b, 5a
★★
P1) 50ft P2) 60ft P3) 90ft
A searing crux pitch. Large
Friends and a half size
Friend reassuring.
*(FA M. Jones unseconded
1968. FFA K. Carrington, A.
Lowe 1981)*

B 24)
New Medium 180ft E4
4c, 6a+ **R** 💣 ★
P1) 45ft P2) 135ft
Airy and exposed. The
pegs in the roof are in poor
condition and may need
replacing.
*(FA R. Fawcett, M. Rhodes,
S. Foster 1978)*

B 25)
The Ghost 180ft E3 4c, 5c,
4a **R** ★★★
P1) 60ft P2) 80ft P3) 40ft
A walk on the wild side.
Start at the base of the coal
face. The second pitch is
slow drying, micro wires
may be of some use on the
slab. Good protection at
the start of the traverse,
keep reaching right (PR) and go for the easy
ground and better protection.
*(FA P. Biven, T. Peck 1958. FFA E. Drummond,
T. Proctor 1973)*

B 26)
Suicide Wall (T1) 140ft E1 4b, 5a, **5c** (or 5a),
5a **R** ★★★
P1) 40ft P2) 40ft P3) 30ft P4) 30ft
A former test piece of the area, still no
pushover. Start by ascending the diagonal
break across the coal face. The traverse can be
achieved either up the diagonal rake or by
climbing to the wide break and crossing this.
Large Friends useful. Whichever way, the crux
is right at the end. Thoughtful belays.
Combined tactics at the start of P3 reduces the
overall grade to HVS 5a. The crux is now very
polished.
(FA P. Biven, T. Peck, B. Biven 1955)

*Ghost, E3 5c, Bosigran.
Climber: Mark Edwards*

B 27)
The Phantom 195ft E3 4c, 5c, 6a **R** ★
P1) 90ft P2) 55ft P3) 50ft
A bold move away from good protection on
an airy crux. Large pieces of protection useful;
finish up the rightward slanting groove.
*(FA P. Biven, T. Peck. FFA E. Drummond, T.
Proctor 1973)*

B 28)
The Absolution 180ft E6 5c, **6b**+, 5c **R** ★★
P1) 80ft P2) 100ft P3) 40ft
The Littlejohn touch. Committing, serious and
technical. Compelling. Smallest TCUs
comforting
*(FA P. Littlejohn, F. Ramsey 1987. P3 M. Edwards,
R. Edwards 1987)*

B 29)
Beowulf (T6) 190ft E2 5a, **5c**, 5b R ★★
P1) 80ft P2) 60ft P3) 50ft
A fine crux pitch. Peg runner on P2. Large
Friend and varied rocks useful. The first ascent
used bolts for protection and direct aid. Shock!
Horror! Gordon led the route free on an early
repeat ascent and the bolts used for protection
thereafter until finally removed in 1974. A
measured response that allowed the natural
development of the route.
(FA P. Biven, T. Peck 1966. FFA P. Gordon 1960s)

B 30)
Nameless 190ft Very Severe 3c, 4b, 4c
★★
P1) 90ft P2) 40ft P3) 30ft
An imposing line, inimitably exposed with an
air of seriousness; not one for those who are
not comfortable at this grade, particularly if
it's wet. Avoid in spring as the gulls on the
top pitch have a nasty reputation!
(FA D. Kemp, N. Morin 1953)

B 32)
Paragon (T6) 200ft Hard Very Severe **5a**, 4c,
5a, **5a** R ★★
P1) 60ft P2) 70ft P3) 30ft P4) 40ft
Superior, attractive climbing.
(FA P. Biven, T. Peck 1956)

Nameless, Very Severe 4c, Bosigran.
Climber: Jort Veen

The Main Cliff - Autumn Flakes Area
Topo 6 (p77)

B 29)
Beowulf (T5) 190ft E2 5a, **5c**, 5b R ★★

B 31)
Paradise 195ft E1 4b, 4c, 5c
P1) 60ft P2) 80ft P3) 55ft
*(FA P1 & P2 P. Biven, T. Peck 1967. P3 P. Rigg
and party 1973. FFA P. Littlejohn, H. Clarke 1978)*

B 32)
Paragon (T5) 200ft Hard Very Severe **5a**, 4c,
5a, **5a** R ★★

B 33)
Broadstairs 180ft E2 5a, **5b**, 4c
P1) 40ft P2) 80ft P3) 50ft
*(FA J. Deacon, S. Jarvis 1959. FFA P. Littlejohn
and party 1971)*

B 34)
Autumn Flakes 175ft Hard Severe 4a, 4a, 4b
★★
P1) 20ft P2) 65ft P3) 90ft
A good combination of pitches for a competent
VS leader are the first two pitches of Autumn
Flakes together with the last two pitches of
Nameless (B30).
(FA R. Goodier, P. Henry 1955)

B 35)
Zig Zag (T7) 150ft Very Severe 3c, 4c, 4c ★★
P1) 30ft P2) 40ft P3) 80ft
A testing crux pitch.
(FA J. Cortlandt-Simpson, W. Hutchinson 1948)

B 36)
Dominator (T8) 120ft E3 6a ★
Steep climbing on hidden holds.
(FA R. Edwards, M. Edwards 1983)

B 37)
Patience (T8) 125ft E3 6a ★
Start up wall left of the flake. The crux is
technical, strenuous and committing; don't
dither.
*(FA T. Peck, B. Biven 1957. FFA P. Littlejohn,
C. Ward-Tetley 1970)*

Topo 6
The Main Cliff
Autumn Flakes
Area

LARGE
FLAKE

CAVE
FLAKE

B 38)
Saddle Tramp (T7) 130ft E4 6b **R** ★
Start up the hidden crack left of the flake.
(FA J. Moran unseconded 1978)

The Raven Wall Area
View One Topo 7 (p78)

B 35)
Zig Zag (T6) 150ft Very Severe 3c, 4c, 4c ★★

**Topo 7
The Raven Wall Area
View One**

B 38)
Saddle Tramp (T6) 130ft E4 6b **R** ★

B 39)
Grendle 130ft E2 5c ★
Moving left onto the wall is easier, but bolder,

than taking the groove direct.
(FA M. McDermott, I. Peters 1966. FFA P. Littlejohn, F. Cannings 1971)

B 42)
Kafoozalem (T1) 120ft E4 6a ★★★
Unrelenting, uncompromising, unforgettable. The 'tat', just right of the start of the crack, is part of Evil Eye.
(FA F. Cannings, P. Badcock 1964. FFA J. Moran, D. Banks 1977)

B 45)
The Armchair 120ft Hard Very Severe 5a, 5a
🪨 ★
P1) 50ft P2) 70ft
Often led in one run-out. Finish up the hidden corner. Slow drying and also do check to see if gulls are nesting in spring.
(FA J. Smoker 1958)

B 46)
Lurch 100ft E3 + 6a
Finish up the hidden corner.
(FA P. Livesey solo 1976)

B 47)
The Leer 165ft E3 5b, 6a **R**
P1) 80ft P2) 80ft
A left to right rising traverse of the cliff. Two breaks run across the wall in the upper part. These belong to Diamond Tiara. The Leer takes a lower line.
(FA P. Littlejohn, C. King 1978)

B 49)
Artificer 80ft Hard Very Severe 5b **R**
(FA P. Littlejohn, S. Jones 1969)

B 49a)
Artifact E4 6b ☠
A direct start to Artificer and very bold.
(FA N. Dixon unseconded 1984)

The Raven Wall Area
View Two Topo 8 (p80)

B 36)
Dominator (T6) 120ft E3 6a ★

B 37)
Patience (T6) 125ft E3 6a ★

B 40)
Raven Wall 120ft E3 5c+ **R** ★★★
Fair protection, but you have to work for it

**Topo 8
The Raven Wall Area
View Two**

from enigmatic rests between intricate moves. Climb slabs, as depicted, to the corner and then climb this moving right, to a crack, then back left at half height and finish direct up the groove. Some reach helps, but isn't essential. *(FA J. Deacon, R. Goodier 1955. FFA P. Littlejohn 1977)*

BIG
FLAKE

B 41)
Evil Eye 120ft E5 6b ☠ ★★★
Micros useful. An intense and serious climb, the technical crux is at the top of the slim groove followed by the bold headwall. Evil Eye, it's looking at you!
(FA P. Littlejohn, C. King 1978)

B 43)
Diamond Face 120ft TR 7a+
Yet to be led, a tenuous line up the golden wall with a ferocious crux. A line to the left may require a 'new generation' of sticky boots.
(FTR M. Edwards 1990)

B 44)
Beaker Route 140ft Hard Very Severe 5a, 4c, 4a 🐎 ★
P1) 45ft P2) 65ft P3) 40ft
(FA H. Nichol, R. Brooke 1955)

B 48)
Daedalus 150ft Hard Very Severe 5a, 5a, 5a
P1) 50ft P2) 60ft P3) 40ft
(FA P1 & P2 P. Littlejohn, P. Biven 1969. P3 P. Littlejohn, S. Jones 1969)

B 50)
Sinistra 100ft Very Severe 4c, 4a ★
P1) 60ft P2) 40ft
Often passed by, but worth a second look. Finish up the hidden corner.
(FA D. Holdroyd, A Blackshaw, A. Day 1955)

To the left is the broad descent of Seaward Gully. Descend down the right-hand (facing out) side of this.

Girdles of the Main Sections of the Cliff

Though not depicted on the topos two substantial girdles of Bosigran are as follows.

B c)
String of Pearls ★
600ft Hard Very Severe **5b**, **5b**, 4b, 4c, 4c, 4c, 3a, 4c
This starts as for Beaker Route and follows a logical, if meandering, line of weakness at

Topo 9
The Ochre Slab Area

around half height until it finishes up the final pitch of Little Brown Jug. The adventurous may wish to pick out a likely line on the photographs.
(FA R. Goodier, J. Deacon alt 1955)

B d)
Diamond Tiara
600ft Hard Very Severe 4c, **5b**, 4a, 4a, **5a**, 5a, 4c, **5a**
This is a higher level girdle. It starts up Sinistra and crosses Raven Wall and Zig Zag on its way to the ledge above the hard section of Suicide Wall. It moves up the final crack of this then breaks right to go under the roof of Doorway. You then climb down and follow an obvious break around before climbing to join, and finish up, Little Brown Jug.
(FA P. Biven, J. Deacon, T. Peck 1956)

Note: ascents of these girdles are rare nowadays. Unless you wish to meet lots of other climbers and hear from them the richness and inventiveness of the English language, any attempt is best left to a very quiet day.

The Ochre Slab Area
Topo 9 (p82)

B 51)
Dong 150ft Severe 4a, 4a, 4b ★
P1) 30ft P2) 60ft P3) 60ft
Escapable but fun, if you like that sort of thing.
(FA M. Banks, B. Grey, J. Deacon 1957)

B 52)
Ding 160ft Very Severe 4c, 4b ★★★
P1) 85ft P2) 75ft
Enchanting. Delectable rock and testing moves produce a stylish jaunt. An unsung little gem.
(FA J. Deacon, B. Grey, M. Banks 1957)

B 53)
Dung 160ft Hard Severe 4b
(FA D. Hope, D. Atkin 1972)

B 54)
Gollywog's Cakewalk 130ft Hard Severe 4b, 3c
P1) 70ft P2) 60ft
(FA D. Bassett, G. Barber 1962)

B 55)
Red Slab 100ft Severe 3c, 4a ★
P1) 70ft P2) 30ft
(FA K. Lawder, J. Andrew 1954)

B 56)
Black Slab (T1) 110ft Difficult ☺ ★
The slab is gained by a step from a spike, sling useful. At the huge overhang at the top of the slab (belay, Friend useful) traverse left (facing in) to a ledge and climb a short, wide groove to the top. Now, where's the belay?
(FA C. Kirkus, P. Fallows 1938)

B 56a)
Black Slab Direct 110ft Difficult
(FKA R. Edwards 1961)

B 57)
Ochre Slab Route 1 130ft Very Severe 4c, 4c R ★★
P1) 90ft P2) 40ft
Two contrasting pitches. The final pitches takes the large roof above the slab via the 'chimney' cut into it; often failed on, but there are good holds around the lip.
(FA T. Peck, B. Biven 1956)

Ding, Very Severe 4c, Bosigran.
Climber: Ian Blake

Topo 10
The Seaward Cliff Area

B 58)
Marking Time 50ft E6 6b 💣 ★★
Climb directly through the roof. Large Friend
and smaller camming equipment useful.
(FA M. Edwards unseconded 1994)

B 59)
Ochre Slab Direct 130ft E1 <u>5a</u>, <u>5b</u> ☠ ★
P1) 90ft P2) 40ft
Two quite challenging pitches.
(FA P1 T. Peck 1964. P2 R. Edwards 1984)

B 60)
Ochre Slab Route 2 130ft Severe 4a, 4a **R**
★★
P1) 90ft P2) 40ft
(FA Unknown 1950s)

The Seaward Cliff
Topo 10 (p84)

This area is tidal and easily affected by any swells.
These routes can only be viewed from the base of the cliff and are depicted **right to left** on the topo. **Hope** (67) is the escape route should it be required, the other routes are all bold leads and some were notorious 'sandbags' at their original grades. All the following routes are tidal and require calm conditions.

B 61)
Strike 150ft E2 5b+, 3c ☠
P1) 80ft P2) 70ft
Originally graded at HVS 5a. Good climbers they were back in the 1960s. A serious route.
(FA F. Cannings, J. Davis 1966)

B 62)
Silas Marner 160ft E2 **5b**, 5a **R** ★
P1) 80ft P2) 80ft
Gain the black seam and climb up to the notched overhang. Move left making a long step onto a slab and follow this to a large ledge.
(FA P. O'Sullivan, B. Adams 1990)

B 63)
Boldfinger 150ft E3 5c ☠ ★★
Excellent climbing, but sparse protection. Small rocks essential as is a 2/2½ Friend. There are placements above the hard moves on the first roof, the next roof is also bold and fingery.
(FA F. Cannings, J. Davis 1966)

B 64)
Geronimo 150ft E1/2 5b, 3c **R** ★★★
P1) 90ft P2) 60ft
Reasonable protection and wild moves over the roof.
(FA F. Cannings, P. Biven 1968)

B 64a)
A Variation 90ft E2 5b **R**
Follow the parent route to the roof, traverse right then move up and right.
(FA P. O'Sullivan, P. Bingham 1990)

B 65)
The Pessimist 150ft E2 5b+ **R** ★★
P1) 90ft P2) 60ft
A nice climb and surprisingly independent. Starts as for Hopeless Slab until the scoop, move right and up into a sloping crack in an overlap. Climb this and immediately step left into a thin crack on the slab. Follow this, past a hard move at its end to a small ledge. Climb the groove above to finish.
(FA P. O'Sullivan, B. Adams 1990)

B 66)
Hopeless Slab 150ft Hard Very Severe **4c**, **4c**, 3c ☠ ★
P1) 40ft P2) 30ft P3) 60ft
1) Step up and follow good holds to a shallow scoop on the left (shared with The Pessimist). Small rocks useful. Traverse left to the edge of the slab and belay. An escape into Hope is possible from here.

2) Move up and then right onto the slab and head for a small black slab above. Go up this and then layback up to a large ledge and belays.

3) Climb the slabs to reach the top.
(FA P. Biven and party 1955)

B 67)
Hope 150ft Very Difficult
P1) 55ft P2) 95ft
This climbs the easiest line up the left-hand (facing in) side of the slab.
(FA Unknown, possibly 1950s)

Bosigran (Commando) Ridge
&
Bosigran Great Zawn

COASTGUARD IDENTITY: Great Zawn near Bosigran.

NEAREST PHONE: *C* The Count House or Morvah.

OS REFERENCE: 415 368

TIDAL? The first pitch of Commando Ridge is tidal, but at high tide it is possible to scramble down to the start of the second pitch. Great Zawn, no, but it is affected by rough seas.

ASPECT: Bosigran Ridge is north-westerly. Great Zawn is westerly; but to catch the sun go for Xanadu in the morning and routes on the West Face in the afternoon. The depths of the zawn remain sombre.

CHARACTER: Bosigran Ridge: an alpine arête rising from the sea. Great Zawn: the emperor of Penwith giving superbly atmospheric, serious and committing zawn climbing.

ROCK: Solid granite, very smooth in places inside the zawn.

TYPE OF CLIMBS: Bosigran Ridge: a popular lengthy route of great interest and some commitment. Great Zawn: brilliant multi-pitch routes in the extreme grades, cracks, slabs and roofs a speciality. One good HVS climb makes a visit by an intermediate grade leader a must.

PROBLEMS: Slippery rock when wet. Nesting birds sometimes on Xanadu, old peg remains and a long abseil entry into the Great Zawn for the West and East faces.

ENVIRONMENTAL CONCERNS: ❀ SSSI ❀ Fragile maritime heath and heather on approach. Stick to existing tracks. Nesting cormorants sometimes on Xanadu. Avoid this route in the spring if they're present. You should be able to see from the abseil point. Green Cormorant Face is also a nesting area so check visually first if possible. Ravens and jackdaws also nest in the area.

PARKING: As for Bosigran in the roadside car park, by the old Carn Galver mine buildings.

APPROACH AND DESCENTS: Refer to the map titled Bosigran (p65). Follow paths from the car park, over stiles towards the sea. (As for Bosigran p67) just before old ruins bear left and follow a path across a stream via a tiny bridge. Where the path branches at a little waymarker take the right-hand fork (ignore the NT coast path) to a prominent ridge (Bosigran Ridge) with a good view across to Bosigran itself.

Bosigran Ridge: Continue until the Commando plaque on the ridge itself. Cross the ridge at the first notch above the plaque (20ft downclimb or abseil), descend the left flank to its foot and skirt round its base (tidal) onto a small tilted, tidal platform. This is the start of the first pitch and can be wave-washed in rough seas. If it is out of reach then the start of the second pitch can be gained by carefully scrambling down the slopes on the right side (facing out) of the ridge, from the plaque; great care required if wet. The ridge is best viewed from the main cliff of Bosigran.

Great Zawn: For the Seaward Face and Variety Show follow the path along the left side (facing out) of Porthmona Cove up to where it meets Bosigran Ridge and the prominent memorial plaque. Cross the ridge, at the notch above the plaque, and drop down its left side (facing out). About halfway down bear left and scramble down and away from the ridge leftwards (facing out) towards ledges. These give a good view of the mouth of the zawn and a short abseil gains a large platform. Variety Show starts from this, but is affected by rough seas. It is also possible to jump from the platform (jibber) over to a small ledge where Déjà Vu and Dream can be started from, but this is for thrill seekers only. (A start from boulders inside the zawn is more

**Topo 2
Bosigran Ridge
The Upper
Pitches**

**Topo 1
Bosigran Ridge
The Lower
Pitches**

4b PITCH

APPROACH
DOWN
SIDE OF
RIDGE

APPROACH
AND WAY
OFF

B

GREAT ZAWN
(HIDDEN)

PINNACLES

B

B

DOWN
BEHIND
PINNACLE

B

GREAT ZAWN
(HIDDEN)

DOWN
BEHIND
PINNACLE

B

GROOVE

B

B

B

LOW WATER
APPROACH

popular, but serious when wet.) It is also possible to arrange two consecutive abseils down Green Cormorant Face to its start. Refer to the text.

For the West and East Faces: cross the ridge as for the above; descend only a little way and follow a faint path round leftwards (facing out) to reach another notch from where a short downclimb reaches a grassy terrace at the top of the right side (facing out) of the zawn. This gives a good view of the headwall and the East Face. On the left, where the terrace is narrowest, an obvious spike of rock provides an abseil point (back it up with rocks in the cracks above) and a long abseil leads to a steep, grassy slope above the zawn floor. This slope can be treacherous when wet and it is possible to continue abseiling, down a doubled climbing rope attached to the end of the abseil rope, to the boulders, pulling it through when down. Desolation Row starts from this steep slope; a belay can be found in the blocks and/or by attaching the second to the abseil rope, if it's long enough.

BOSIGRAN (COMMANDO) RIDGE

Topos 1 & 2 (p87)

BR 1)
Bosigran Ridge 660ft Very Difficult 3c (or Severe 4b) ★★★
The spark that lit the flame. Stimulating climbing simulating an alpine experience. Usually climbed in eight pitches. Arrows indicate the direction of part of the route that is hidden on the topo. Some competence at the grade is required by both leader and second. Many finish at the Commando memorial plaque, but it is possible to continue at Severe 4b standard. The first pitch is the crux, after which there are many variations. The route is escapable at several points. Check visually, from the old ruins, to see if the start is wave-washed before attempting to descend to the base.
(FA A. Andrews, E. Andrews 1902. P1 J. Farmer, A. Andrews 1905)

BOSIGRAN GREAT ZAWN

The Seaward Face
Topo 1 (p89)

GtZn a)
Exit Route 70ft Hard Severe 4a+
Not shown on the topo, but also the abseil line, this takes the corner just to the left of Smiley Culture.
(FA Unknown)

GtZn 1)
Smiley Culture 70ft E3 5b **R**
(FA P. Rogers, H. Simons 1986)

GtZn 2)
The Variety Show 150ft Hard Very Severe 5a, 4b ★★
P1) 90ft P2) 60ft
It's showtime! A lovely first pitch, not to be missed. Competence required.
(FA T. Peck, B. Biven, C. Fishwick 1958. FFA P. Littlejohn, F. Cannings 1970)

Great Zawn Approach

BOSIGRAN RIDGE

ABSEIL POINT (HIDDEN)

WEST FACE

SEAWARD FACE

A

LEDGE AND JUMP

GtZn 3)
Three Score Years And Ten, Amen 90ft
E5/6 6a ☠ ★★★
PR used on FA at one-third height. A heartfelt route name after a mix up in calls resulted in the rapid descent of the leader down the route, instead of him being lowered to the ground. The injuries were surprisingly light given the distance fallen; may it be at least that many years, amen.
(FA M. Crocker unseconded 1992)

GtZn 4)
Great Zawn Chimney 160ft E2 5b ☠ ⚓
Very bold with loose rock.
(FA T. Peck, P. Biven 1956. FFA P. Littlejohn, S. Jones 1969)

GtZn 5
Zarathustra 150ft E2 5b, 3c
P1) 90ft P2) 60ft
(FA P. Littlejohn, F. Cannings 1969)

The next few routes start from the small ledge (Green Cormorant ledge) that can be reached by an infamous jump from the main platform. It can also be reached by a fairly bold traverse starting from the boulders at the mouth of Great Zawn itself. This is about 5a standard but has a serious feel to it when wet, particularly the first step off the boulder. The cunning can abseil down to the ledge via two 100ft abseils. If twin ropes are used it should be possible to pull them through to give that "committed" feeling. Don't let them jam.

GtZn 6)
Green Cormorant Face 150ft E2 5a, **5c** ⚓
★★
P1) 60ft P2) 90ft
Small Friends, TCUs useful. A short hard sequence is the crux, but is well protected.
(FA J. Deacon, M. Banks 1957. With 1 point of aid P. Littlejohn, F. Cannings alt 1969. FKFA R. Edwards, F. Smith 1975)

GtZn 6a)
Variation to Pitch two 90ft E3 6a
(FA H. Barber, F. Cannings 1974)

GtZn 6b)
Second variation to Pitch two 90ft E3 6a
(FA P. Littlejohn, M. Burgoyne 1985)

GtZn 8)
Déjà Vu 150ft E4/5 5c ☠ ★★★
A magnificent climb. Technically the moves are not at the top end of their grade, but in an exposed position high above protection they can feel harder; the main section is fairly serious and should not be undertaken lightly. Dry conditions are essential. It is possible to split the pitch on the stance of Green Cormorant Face.
(FA H. Barber, F. Cannings 1974)

GtZn 8a)
Variation Start 40ft Hard Very Severe 5a+
Start from inside the zawn via a traverse from the boulder.

GtZn 9)
The Dream (T2) 230ft E3 5a, **6a,** 5c ★★★
P1) 45ft P2) 90ft P3) 95ft
The first pitch (and the variation start) is harder and more serious when wet. Friends of all sizes, small rocks and micros are useful. It is possible to climb up to the first stance from the zawn bed by traversing into the groove from a boulder and climbing directly up to the small ledge.
(FA M. Guilliard, R. Wilson 1968. With three points of aid P. Littlejohn, I. Duckworth. FFA P. Livesey 1976)

Great Zawn - The West Face
Topo 2 (p91)

GtZn 9)
The Dream (T1) 230ft E3 5a, **6a,** 5c ★★★

GtZn 9 + 11)
The Dream/Liberator Combination
★★★★
E3 5a, 6a, 5c **R**
The showpiece of the zawn. The first two pitches of The Dream finishing up Liberator. Exposed, steep, sustained, varied and testing. The slab is now polished. Some spare rocks, Friends, karabiners etc. useful for belays.
(FFA P. Livesey, R. Fawcett various 1976)

Topo 2
The Great Zawn
The West Face

Dream, E3 6a, Bosigran Great Zawn. Climber: Rowland Edwards

GtZn 10)
Canute 215ft E4 5a, 5c, 6a **R**
P1) 40ft P2) 85ft P3) 90ft
(FA M. Fowler, S. Lewis 1982)

GtZn 11)
Liberator (T3) 220ft E4 <u>6a</u>+, 5c **R ★★★**

P1) 120ft P2) 100ft
There is an air of seriousness about this climb. The first pitch is at the top end of its grade and the second is both fairly bold and

*Howling at the Moon E7 6b/c, Paradise Wall.
Climber: Mark Edwards*

strenuous. An excellent climb if you're well established at this grade; but the run-outs, technicality, strenuousness and belays could provoke an uphill struggle, if not an outright epic, for those whose ambitions exceed their abilities.
(FA F. Cannings, P. Littlejohn 1970. FFA R. Fawcett, P. Livesey 1976)

GtZn 12)
Fool's Lode (T3) 210ft E5 6a, 6a ●⃰ ★
P1) 110ft P2) 100ft
This roams the west face incessantly to find difficulties. It succeeds.
(FA P. Livesey, J. Lawrence 1977)

GtZn 13)
The West Face (T3) 180ft E5 5c, **6b**, 5a ★★★
P1) 70ft P2) 80ft P3) 30ft
Once a brutish whack and dangle, this is now a superb free climb. Probably the finest line in the zawn. A spectacular and exciting climb that strenuously crosses some massive overhangs. Let desire outweigh the gravity of the situation.
(FA P. Biven, T. Peck 1957. With one point of aid P. Livesey, J. Lawrence 1975. FFA R. Fawcett 1976)

GtZn 14)
Opium (T3) 180ft E6 5c, **6c**, 4a R ●⃰ ★★★
P1) 70ft P2) 80ft P3) 30ft
"This route is perhaps the most exciting hereabouts and its quality is second to none. It makes 'Dream' appear shabby, hence the name." Steven Haston, Compass West logbook, 1989
The second pitch starts up a groove (2PR), traverses right and then a serious move gains a standing position and a break (Friend 2 and rocks 6, 7 or 8; runners should be extended) in order to make the crux moves over the roof and up to a belay 20ft higher.
(FA P. Biven, I. Howell as Captivator, A1 1970. FFA S. Haston, C. Bull 1989)

Great Zawn - Desolation Row Slab
Topo 3 (p94)

GtZn 11)
Liberator (T2) 220ft E4 **6a+**, 5c R ★★★
P1) 120ft P2) 100ft

GtZn 12)
Fool's Lode (T2) 210ft E5 6a, 6a ●⃰ ★

GtZn 13)
The West Face (T2) 180ft E5 5c, **6b**, 5a ★★★

GtZn 14)
Opium (T2) 180ft E6 5c, **6c**, 4a R ●⃰ ★★★

GtZn 15)
Desolation Row 110ft E2 5b R ★★★
A good introduction to the zawn, a large number of small rocks, and Friends, provide spaced, but reasonable, protection; though determination is required as the route can erode self-assurance.
(FA F. Cannings, P. Littlejohn 1969)

GtZn 16)
Hurricane 120ft E4 6a ☠ ★
Delicate climbing lacking protection. It is possible to move into Candy Man for a side runner to reduce the "bite".
(FA P. O'Sullivan, A. Hall 1990)

GtZn 17)
Candy Man 110ft E2 5c R
(FA R. Edwards, I. Pomfret 1973)

GtZn 18)
Ocean Rain 110ft E2 5b
The crack right of Candy Man.
(FA G. Everett, J. Sonczak 1985)

Great Zawn - The East Face
Topo 4 (p95)

GtZn 19)
Judas 240ft E1 **5a**, 4c, **5b**, 4b R ★
P1) 50ft P2) 50ft P3) 90ft P4) 50ft
(FA F. Cannings, D. Steel, I. Duckworth 1970)

Topo 3
The Great Zawn
The West Face &
Desolation Row
Slab Area

GtZn 19a)
Judas Variation Start 50ft Hard Very Severe 5a.

GtZn 20)
Kubla Khan 200ft E3 6a, 6b ☠ ★★
P1) 100ft P2) 100ft
An intricate line with great exposure at the top, the first pitch is sparsely protected.
(FA R. Edwards, M. Edwards, I. Blake 1984)

**Topo 4
The Great Zawn
The East Face**

GtZn 21)

Xanadu 200ft E2 **5b, 5b**, 5a 🪶 ★★★
P1) 100ft P2) 60ft P3) 40ft
THE route of this face with magnificent position. Large items of protection are useful; the first pitch suffers from seepage, is slow drying and could be climbed with a point of aid or two to reach the upper pitches if required. The walk off, up the overgrown slope, from the top of the final pitch feels quite serious when wet and it may be worth staying roped up and treating it as a pitch.
(FA M. Springett, S. Young 1968. FFA P. Littlejohn, I. Duckworth 1970)

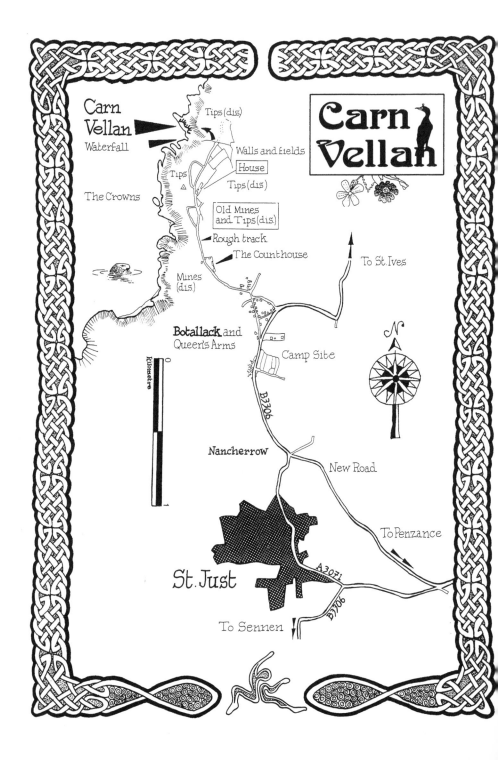

Carn Vellan

COASTGUARD IDENTITY: Carn Vellan.

NEAREST PHONE: ℂ Botallack.

OS REFERENCE: 364 342

TIDAL? The main platform in the amphitheatre is non tidal. To the left of the huge suspended boulder, on the left of the platform along to Fun Curve Factory Cliff, the cliff is tidal. In very rough seas even the main platform can be washed by waves.

ASPECT: South-westerly, it catches the afternoon and evening sun.

CHARACTER: A massive, brooding and threatening cliff; the great roof overhangs by more than is first apparent. The cliff yields its climbs reluctantly, but when it does the rewards are great; the climbing is much better than you would expect at first sight, with small incuts and hidden holds. Friends and TCUs are very useful.

ROCK: Slate.

TYPE OF CLIMBS: Atmospheric and often bold traditional routes on good, sharp holds; mainly in the extreme grades, as good as those at Gurnard's Head. Controversial home to long, very technical, sports routes the equal of any in other areas. These were climbed in the 1990s when there was no policy against bolts on slate. The potential for some of the hardest sports projects in the UK remains on the massive roof.

PROBLEMS: The descent slopes are very fragile (some steps would help limit erosion). The cliff suffers from seepage and sea spray and is slow drying. Care is required in handling brittle rock, particularly on the upper tier. Cut staple bolts on the sports routes.

ENVIRONMENTAL CONCERNS: ❀ SSSI ❀ The slopes leading down to the cliff are extremely fragile and plants such as sea aster and sea spurry are very vulnerable to trampling. Please stick strictly to the described approach. The upper buttresses above the amphitheatre are vegetated and should be handled carefully. Seabirds also nest in the vicinity. Act considerately and don't litter.

PARKING: By the side of the dirt track, as close to Carn Vellan as you dare drive, or in Botallack.

APPROACH: Turn off at Botallack and past the Queen's Arms drive down a road (sign, Mannor Farm) past Botallack mines and some houses, to join a dirt track (but not if you have low suspension). Go down this 700m and park on a grass verge just before a dip and a wall. (Where the road dips down only four-wheel-drive vehicles can continue.) Walk seawards and bear right to pass a wall and so down a hill to a stream; cross this and pick up a path that contours towards a rock headland, and notch for the path to pass. At the headland turn to your left and carefully follow the leading edge of the cliff down until it leads into the amphitheatre at the base. It is important that this approach is kept to. Do not plough up and down the slope. For Fun Curve Factory Cliff follow the path through the rock gap and descend the obvious gully bearing left to rock platforms. At low tide, with calm seas, it is possible to boulder hop and scramble around from the Ziggurat and Zero Gravity areas.

DESCENTS: Walk off the tops of climbs and back down via the approach path. With single pitch routes to the left of My Mule… it is possible to either finish as for that route or to scramble off.

On reaching the main platform the most eye-catching feature is the massively overhanging main roof area bounded on the right by a corner. The first route is the obvious crack just right of this corner. Right again is a short wall. Some potential lines exist but the rock is very brittle.

The Ziggurat Area - Topo 1

CV 1)
Wild At Heart 80ft E6 6b 🌑 ★★
This climbs the obvious crack-line immediately right of the corner. There is some loose rock in the lower section. The meat of this route is gaining, and climbing, the main crack via fierce jamming. You may be prompted to mutter "Oh, for crux sake!" or similar on the crux.
(FA M. Edwards, R. Edwards 1991)

CV 2)
Bridge Of Sies 80ft E? 6b 💀 🌑 ★★★
A line crossing the two prominent overhangs to finish up the corner. It began life as Spaceman Spliff, E6 6b, when P. Craggs crossed the first roof and moved into the Ziggurat belay. Craggs believed he had freed The Lid and took a ground fall on his first attempt, breaking his arm in four places. M. Edwards climbed the entire route free using pegs for protection (E6). For a second ascent P. Twomey replaced the loose and fractured pegs (two were removed by hand) with SS bolts, which have now been cut. Some in situ fixed gear, or a virtually unprotected ascent would now be required. The second roof is the crux. The grade is for the route in its present state.
(FA Spaceman Spliff P. Craggs 1990. Bridge Of Sies M. Edwards, J. Fraela 1991)

CV 3)
Ziggurat 170ft E5 5a, 6a/b, 5b ★★★
P1) 40ft P2) 80ft P3) 50ft
A great natural line in a stupendous position. Although it hangs out over a lot of nothingness it does not offer a vacuous climbing experience. Much may depend on how fit you are. The first ascent took place after a number of earlier attempts, placing protection on the lead and training in order to gain the necessary stamina. Friends would be of use, as would be some pegs for the hanging belay.
(FA R. Edwards, M. Edwards 1980)

CV 4)
Un-named 140ft F8c project ✙ ☹
A severe case of abrupt, arrested development.

Uncompleted. If conquered in the future surely a major addition to Cornish climbing?

CV 5)
1025 60ft F7c ✙ ☹ ★★
The roof and leaning wall above the belay at the end of the traverse on Ziggurat. 1025 is not a year, but a campus board move kindly replicated by nature.
(FA M. Edwards, I. Blake 1992)

CV 6)
The Lid 140ft A3
This climbs the thin crack line in the roof and the corner above (of Ziggurat). But would it, could it, will it go free?
(FA P. de Mengle, A. Mahony 1972)

CV 7)
Monster Munch 140ft F8b+ ✙ ☹ ★★★
The first few feet are obscured behind the boulder. A gigantic dinosaur of a line through the roof and finishing up the leaning wall above with the crux at two-thirds height. Now tranquillised; surely a line that deserves serious consideration?
(FA M. Edwards unseconded 1993)

CV 8)
Nuts Are Not The Only Fruit 130ft F8b
✙ ☹ ★★★
Start obscured. Power and stamina produced a tango with gravity.
(FA M. Edwards unseconded 1991)

CV 9
Blue Sky Lighting 130ft F8a ✙ ☹ ★★
The shock of the new. An intense, searing line. Would it (will it?) have ever seen a flash? A victim of a punitive, puritan, purification purge.
(FA M. Edwards unseconded 1991)

CV 10)
Several Species Of... 100ft E2 5b
A strong, natural fault line, which isn't as good as it looks. A start from the beginning of Monster Munch would be logical, but has yet to be climbed. Friends useful. Its full name is 'Several Species Of Small Furry Animals Gathered Together In A Cave Grooving

Topo 1
Carn Vellan
The Ziggurat Area

Together With A Pict.' ' Hubble' just hasn't the same ring.
(FA P. de Mengle, A. MacFarlane 1971.
FFA P. Craggs 1990)

CV 12)
Life's Moments (T2) 240ft E4 4c, 5b, **6b**, 5c, 5c
P1) 35ft P2) 65ft P3) 40ft P4) 40ft P5) 60ft
(FA R. Edwards, M. Edwards 1993)

CV 13)
Rich Picking (T2) E4 5a, 5c, **6b** ★★★
P1) 20ft P2) 70ft P3) 50ft
Captivating. The first two pitches can be climbed as an E2 5c finishing as for Several Species... Worth doing for a good juggy trip over the roof. Big Friends essential. Expose yourself in the upper groove, which was protected by a PR (removed).
(FA R. Edwards, M. Edwards 1993)

CV 14)
Grand Illusion (T2) 220ft E4 **6b**, 5b, 6a, 5c, 5c
★★★
P1) 35ft P2) 45ft P3) 40ft P4) 40ft P5) 60ft
The longest straight-up route at Carn Vellan. A classic E4 journey with simian roofs, scintillating exposure and continually challenging climbing.
(FA R. Edwards, M. Edwards alt 1993)

Topo 2   Carn Vellan
Zero Gravity Area

Zero Gravity Area - Topo 2

CV 11)
My Mule Don't Like You Laffin' 195ft
Very Severe 4c, 3c, 4c ★
P1) 120ft P2) 40ft P3) 35ft
The rock requires careful handling in places
and good ropework is required. Start
obscured. Climb up a wide groove until you
can break out onto the slab, as depicted.
Follow the fault-line to the top past some
suspect rock. P2, which is not depicted on the
topo, climbs a short wall and scramble
towards a bigger wall. P3. Climb the wall to a
groove which leads to the top. Additional
belays can be found.
(FA W. Carver, M. James 1970)

CV 12)
Life's Moments (T1) 240ft E4 4c, 5b, **6b**, 5c,
5c

CV 13)
Rich Pickings (T1) E4 5a, 5c, **6b** ★★★

CV 14)
Grand Illusion (T1) 220ft E4 **6b**, 5b, 6a, 5c, 5c
💣 ★★★

CV 15)
Monkey Climb 185ft E1 5c
P1) 50ft P2) 135ft
(FA P. Montgomery, K. Lawlor 1981. FFA
M. Edwards, C. Edwards 1992)

CV 17)
The Blimp 110ft E2 5a, **5b** ★
P1) 50ft P2) 60ft
May have changed through rockfall. A 'follow your nose' line with some good climbing, but superseded by later routes. Climb to the break, climb up leftwards to a diagonal crack and follow this rightwards to My Mule... Follow the leftwards slanting crack until able to gain the cosy belay ledge. Two PR used on FA, now rotted out.
(FA A. McFarlane, P. de Mengle 1971)

CV 18)
Hot Rubber 110ft E3 5c **R** ★★
An eliminate based upon The Blimp.
(FA R. Edwards, M. Edwards 1992)

CV 19)
Barnacle 120ft E2 5c
Make sure you tap the barnacles to make them stick with limpet-like tenacity before you step on them! Now what are the ethics of using crustaceans to start a route?
(FA R. Edwards, M. Edwards 1991)

CV 20)
Silver Shadow 120ft E3 5c **R** ★★
Good climbing throughout.
(FA C. Nicholson, A. Gallagher 1980)

CV 21)
Crystal Grazer 110ft E3 6a **R** ★★★
Good exposure, excellent rock and with diverse, continually interesting climbing. This passes three roofs past 2 SS pegs.
(FA R. Edwards, J. Fraela 1991)

CV 22)
Zero Gravity 110ft E3 6a ★★★
Good protection, big holds and an exposed position on an overhanging wall. This pumpy route has a lot going for it. It can be started at high tide via a traverse from the platform on the left (facing in).
(FA R, Edwards, M. Edwards 1980)

CV 23)
Kurtzer 100ft Very Severe 4c
This climbs a prominent diagonal break at the far end of the cliff.
(FA N. Freemantle, S. Shimitzu, D. Cook 1981)

Fun Curve Factory Cliff

The following routes are not shown on the topos. These are on the area of the cliff that joins onto the end of the Fun Curve Sea Arch.

CV a)
Insurance Drain 60ft E3 5c
A wall climb right of Joy Riders.
(FA M. Edwards, M. Barnes 1992)

CV b)
Joy Riders 60ft E3 5c
The groove on the wall right of the chimney.
(FA M. Edwards, I. Blake 1991)

CV c)
Sooty 60ft Severe 4a
A chimney blessed with holds.
(FA M. Edwards, C. Johns 1990)

The sea-arch at the far left-hand end (facing in) of the cliff gives one route.

CV d)
The Fun Curve Factory 70ft E5 6a ★★★
This starts up the rib to the right of the arch before moving out above it. Steep, well protected climbing on good rock in fine position. Bliss out.
(FA M. Edwards and party 1991)

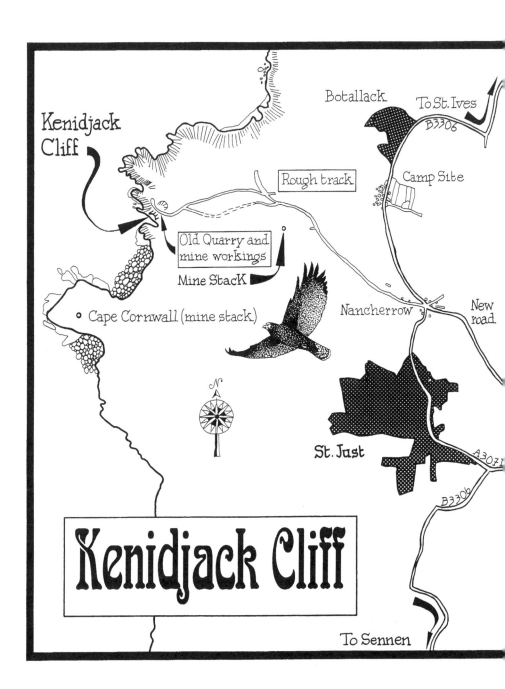

Kenidjack Cliff

Botallack

To St. Ives
B3306

Camp Site

Rough track

Old Quarry and
mine workings

Mine Stack

Cape Cornwall (mine stack)

Nancherrow

New
road

N

St. Just

A3071

B3306

Kenidjack Cliff

To Sennen

Kenidjack

COASTGUARD IDENTITY: Kenidjack Castle.

NEAREST PHONE: ✆ St. Just.

OS REFERENCE 354 326

TIDAL? No, though affected by spray from high seas blown onto the rock. Major storms will move the boulders around!

ASPECT: South, a good afternoon and evening sun trap.

CHARACTER: The finest slab in Penwith, though some will insist it's a wall. Saxon Direct is generally well protected with Friends and rocks, apart from its start and finish; other routes on this slab require boldness and protection can be hard won; often small gear in cracklets. Confidence and competence at the grade required.

ROCK: Slate.

TYPE OF CLIMBS: Technical and thought-provoking slab climbing, often run out.

PROBLEMS: There is the potential for harm from trampling to the heath and some path erosion. Path restoration would help control this.

ENVIRONMENTAL CONCERNS: ❀ SSSI ❀ The slopes and vegetation above the cliff are very fragile; please return to the path as quickly as possible after finishing belaying. There is some wear on the descent path on the right-hand side (facing out) of the cliff and on the top of the Saxon slab. Please stay on the paths, exit climbs cleanly, try and avoid trampling the maritime heath.

PARKING: Parking should be possible at some point on the approach track; take care not to block it for outgoing traffic. There may be a boulder across the track to stop travellers camping, in which case you'll have to walk. See the access notes in Green Pages.

APPROACH: From St. Just - Drive out of St. Just northwards (towards St. Ives) and down a steep hill. At the bottom, in Tregeseal, a concealed left turning by the Nancherrow Farm leads onto a narrow road running down a valley beside a stream. After 1km, just past a farmhouse on the right and an old mine chimney stack on the left, the road forks and becomes two very rough tracks. Go straight on (taking the right-hand branch) past a parking bay and up a hill to reach another fork. This time take the left-hand branch leading around the headland to the small quarries and slopes at the top of the cliff.

DESCENTS:

1) The vegetation on the descent slopes are very fragile. Carefully descend a steep slope (see topo one) until the top of the cliff is reached. Keep to its right (facing out) and scramble down a path to a small ledge and block overlooking the main slab of Saxon. It is possible to abseil from here. Refer to topo; do check no-one is climbing up Gneiss Gnome first! From the block it is also possible to continue scrambling down the slope and downclimb the last 15ft to a ledge.

2) Alternatively, from the small quarry walk onto the spur on the left (facing out) until you can walk, scramble and downclimb the steep slope to join the large boulder at the base of the slab.

Kenidjack Descents - Topo 1

C 4)
Saxon With A Direct Finish (T2) Hard Very
Severe 5a ★★★
K 7)
Thane (T2) E2 5b+ ★★

Kenidjack Main Slab - Topo 2

It is possible to climb virtually anywhere on
the slab at around 5b/5c standard and by
accident or design many variations to routes
have been climbed over the years. Friends,
rocks, small tricams and even microwires are
useful on most of these climbs.

K 1)
Gneiss Gnome 90ft Hard Severe 4b
A good introduction to the slab. Large Friend/
hex useful.
(FA K. Darbyshire, P. Littlejohn 1971)

K 2)
In The Gallery 120ft Hard Very Severe 4c **R**
(FA R. Edwards, M. Edwards 1979)

K 3)
Rockdancer 150ft E1 5a **R** ★★★
Good rock and graceful, captivating
movement produce excellent, pulse-
quickening climbing as protection may be a
vague rumour below you in places. The
amount of protection may depend upon the
level of your skill.
(FA R. Edwards, M. Edwards 1979)

K 3a)
The Wooden Box (Direct Start) 20ft E2 5c **R**
Start about 10ft left of the normal start to Rockdancer. Pull over to the base of a groove. Step right and climb on small holds to the ramp.
(FA P. Williams, S. Bird 1985)

K 4)
Saxon With A Direct Finish (T1) ★★★
150ft Hard Very Severe 5a **R**
One of the finest steep slab climbs in the country. The start and finish are the crux sections, both requiring commitment. Medium size hex's useful for belays on the top. Finishing as for In The Gallery or Saxon Original produces a line at HVS 4c standard. The original route traversed right along the upper faultline to a belay on a block and then finished diagonally leftwards.
(FA P. Littlejohn, S. Jones 1974. Direct finish R. Edwards, M. Edwards 1979)

K 4a)
Saxon Direct Start E1 5a **R**
(FA M. Edwards, C. Edwards 1985)

K 5)
The Shield 130ft Hard Very Severe 4c, 5a **R** ★★
P1) 70ft P2) 50ft
A good introduction to the harder climbs on this side of the slab.
(FA P. Littlejohn, K. Derbyshire 1971)

K 6)
Super Direct 120ft E2 5b+ **R** ★★
(FA R. Edwards, M. Edwards 1979)

K a)
Facedancer 130ft E2 5b
A direct line climbing up onto the boss of rock right of the shield and finishing as for **Super Direct**.
(FA D. Carroll, D. Viggers 1993)

K 7)
Thane (T1) 130ft E2 5b+ **R** ★★
A strong line that would cruelly expose any deficiencies of a leader; it is a continually absorbing climb.
(FA P. Littlejohn, S. Jones 1974)

K 8)
Sunny Cellophane 150ft E1 5a+ **R**
(FA R. Edwards, S. Salmon 1979)

K 9)
Storm Bringer 150ft E3 5c **R**
(FA R. Edwards, S. Salmon 1979)

K 10)
Slanter 140ft Very Severe 4b, 4b
(FA R. Edwards M. Edwards 1979)

K 11)
Diagonal 150ft E2 4b, 5b
(FA R. Edwards, M. Edwards 1979)

K 12)
Short Circuit 150ft E1 4b, 5b
(FA P. O'Sullivan, C. Woodhead 1979)

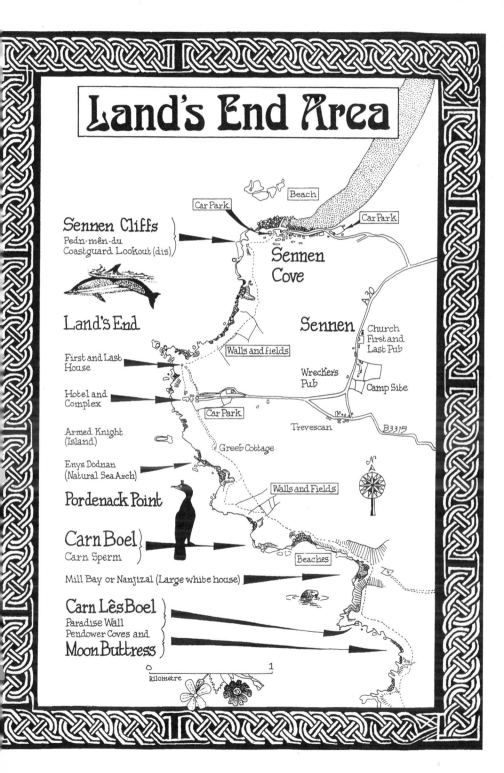

Land's End Area

Beach

Car Park

Car Park

Sennen Cliffs
Pedn-mên-du
Coastguard Lookout (dis)

Sennen Cove

A30

Land's End

Sennen

Church
First and
Last Pub

First and Last House

Walls and fields

Hotel and Complex

Wreckers Pub

Camp Site

Armed Knight (Island)

Car Park

Trevescan

B3315

Greeb Cottage

Enys Dodnan
(Natural Sea Arch)

Pordenack Point

Walls and Fields

N

Carn Boel
Carn Sperm

Beaches

Mill Bay or Nanjizal (Large white house)

Carn Lês Boel
Paradise Wall
Pendower Coves and
Moon Buttress

0   1
kilometre

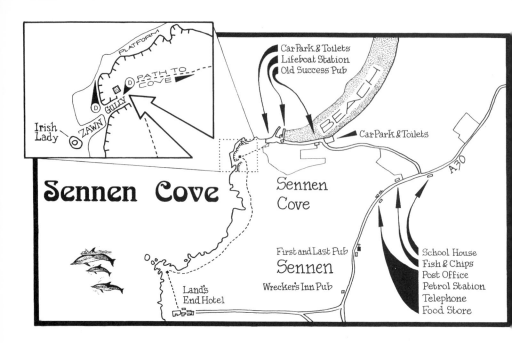

Sennen Cove
& Irish Lady Cove

COASTGUARD IDENTITY: Pedn-Mên-Du. The old lookout is a useful landmark.

NEAREST PHONE: ℂ Sennen Cove. By the lifeboat station.

OS REFERENCE: 347 262

TIDAL? Not tidal on the main sections of the main Sennen Cove cliff apart from the Congo Crack and Black Zawn areas. But the whole of the main cliff can be affected by high seas and the main platform can be wave washed. All of the Irish Lady Cove is tidal.

ASPECT: Westerly and sheltered, a good place for afternoon and evening sun.

CHARACTER: A very friendly short cliff plastered with routes, a favourite with the Diff - HVS climber and only a few minute's walk from a café.

Irish Lady Cove. Less visited; a good place to get away from the crowds but with some gritty rock.

ROCK: A fabulous feast of felsite fascia featuring a fantastic farrago of fractures, flutings, flakes and fins which facilitates a frantic, fingertip fandango.

TYPE OF CLIMBS: Predominantly short, single pitch and often absorbing routes.

PROBLEMS: The main platform can be wave washed in high seas. Beware the blow hole. It can be very busy during the summer months as it is popular with clubs and groups. Tourists have thrown the odd rock from the top.

ENVIRONMENTAL CONCERNS: Nesting birds on a few routes. Some erosion on cliff top and on the descent path. Litter, boulders used as toilets, etc.

PARKING: A car park is at the far end of Sennen Cove, past the Lifeboat station and old roundhouse. Pay as you enter. It's busy in the height of summer.

APPROACH: Refer also to the Sennen Cove and Land's End Area maps. Well-worn paths starting from the car park toilet block lead to the obvious small, stone lookout station on the cliff top.

DESCENTS: Sennen Cove: Abseil entry to the platform is popular, particularly from the Corner Climb area. Anti-social on a busy day. If you wish to walk, to the left of the old lookout are two descent gullies (take the more polished seaward one) leading to a path and scramble (some downclimbing would be required) going rightwards around the base of the cliffs. It is also possible to walk around Forgotten Wall into Black Zawn. Low tide and calm seas are essential. Adepts and locals downclimb easier routes. Remember they probably climbed up them first. Griptight Gully is often wet and has been the scene of several downclimbing accidents.
Irish Lady Cove: Refer to ILC topo one. Scramble down the gully from the lookout and around 10m along the descent path (where it bends sharply) a steep gully falls down away from the path. Scramble down this gully to the start of the climbs.

SENNEN COVE

General View (p110)

SC 16)
Golva (T1,T2) 120ft E2 5c ☺ ★★

SC 20)
Vertical Crack (T1,T2,T3) 75ft Hard Severe 4c ★★

SC 29)
Altar Route (T3) 70ft Very Severe 4c ★★

SC 38)
Sinner's Route (T3) 50ft Moderate ☺ ★★★★

SC 43)
Double Overhang (T4) 65ft Very Severe 4c ★★

SC 45)
Africa Route (T4) 65ft Very Severe 5a ★★★

SC 50)
Staircase (T4) 60ft Difficult ☺ ★

SC 54)
Marionette (T4) 60ft E2 5c ★

SC 56)
Gilliwiggle (T5) 65ft Hard Severe 4b

SC 58)
Main Face Climb (T5) 70ft Difficult ☺ ★

SC 61)

Banana Flake (T5) 85ft Very Difficult ☺ ★★

SC 63)
Left Banana Flake (T5) 80ft Very Difficult

SC 70)
Letterbox (T5,T6) 85ft Hard Severe 4b ★★

SC 73)
Civvy Route (T6) 80ft Severe 4b ★★

SC 76)
Corner Climb (T6) 75ft Difficult+ ☺ ★★

SC 79)
Demo Route (T6) 80ft Hard Severe 4b+ ★★★

SC 83)
Samson (T7) 75ft E4 6a ★

SC 85)
A Swift Flight Of Fancy (T7) 85ft E3 6a ★★★

SC 91)
Amazonia (T8) 75ft E7 6c ★★★

NB. A large number of short pitches have been climbed on the lowest walls that can be seen on this photograph.

The climbs are described from right to left as you approach along the descent path from the

109

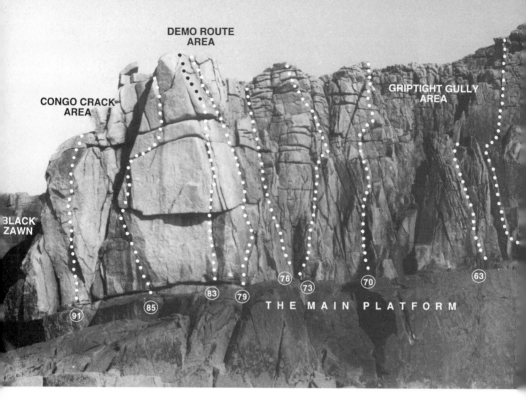

The following labels appear on the image: DEMO ROUTE AREA, CONGO CRACK AREA, BLACK ZAWN, GRIPTIGHT GULLY AREA, THE MAIN PLATFORM, 91, 85, 83, 79, 76, 73, 70, 63.

square lookout on the cliff top. On many of the easier routes it is possible to wander, almost at will, anywhere up the cliff.

The first section of cliff beneath the lookout is a very broken area of slabs, chimneys and cracked towers. Many routes from Very Difficult to E1 have been climbed here but mainly left unrecorded over the years. We leave them to your sense of adventure to rediscover.

About 15m along the approach path from the descent gully, and after the descent to Irish Lady Cove, you reach the Hayloft Area.

The Hayloft Area
Topo 1 (p112)

SC 1)
On Your Marks 100ft Hard Very Severe 5a, 5a.
P1) 30ft P2) 70ft
(FKA M. Edwards and party, 1985, also claimed by T. Warwick, T. Williams, 1989, but starting up the small arête to the right.)

110

SC 2)
Hayloft Cracks 100ft Very Severe 4c, 4c
(FKA M. Edwards and party 1985)

SC 3)
Hayloft Gully 120ft Difficult
P1) 40ft P2) 40ft P3) 40ft
Climb the obvious corner.
(FA Royal Marines 1940s)

SC 3a)
Hayloft Variation Start 35ft Hard Very Severe 5a
(FKA M. Edwards 1984)

SC 4)
Hayloft 150ft Very Severe 3c, **4c**, 3c, 4b **R** ★
P1) 40ft P2) 45ft P3) 35ft P4) 30ft
The 4c pitch is bold and been the scene of several accidents. To finish traverse a ledge leftwards and climb up a short, awkward chimney to the top.
(FA Unknown, possibly Royal Marines 1940s)

AFRICA RIB
AREA

CHURCH WINDOW
AREA

APPROACH

**Topo 26
Sennen Cove
General View**

SC 5)
Slanting Crack 120ft Hard Very Severe 5a+,
4c **R**
The crux is the start, good pro' at 15ft. The
second pitch climbs a flake to join Terrace
Cracks.
(FA R. Edwards, M. Edwards 1976)

SC 5a)
Slanting Crack Variation 35ft E1 5a ☠
(FA M. Edwards 1986)

SC 6)
Terrace Cracks 120ft Hard Very Severe 5a-,
4c ☺ ★
P1) 40ft P2) 80ft
A direct start (as for Baptism?) up the wall is
bold E5 6a.
*(FA R. Edwards, M. Edwards 1976. Direct start
S. Ohly 1994)*

SC 7)
Baptism Of Fire 45ft E6 6b ☠ ★★

Technique required, in abundance. The right
side of the arête, side runners reduce the 'E'
grade.
(FA M. Edwards solo 1988)

SC 8)
Hell Hath No Fear 45ft E7 6c ☠ ★★★
The left side of the arête; a lead that elevates
mind, body and spirit; a fall brings you firmly
back to earth. A side runner reduces it to E6.
(FA M. Edwards solo 1988)

SC 9)
Dolphin Cracks 85ft Hard Very Severe **5a** 4c
R ★★
P1) 25ft P2) 60ft
The first pitch is deceptive, a major climb of
its day. Sling useful.
*(FA P1 T. Genge 1947. P2 R. Goodier, J. Deacon
1955)*

The next two routes start from the ledge above
P1 of **Dolphin Cracks.**

111

Topo 1
Sennen Cove
The Hayloft Area

SC 10)
A Flair For The Theatrical 140ft E4 6a ★★
(FA M. Edwards, I. Blake 1984)

SC 11)
Super Jam (T2) 95ft E5 6b ★★
The crux could involve astral projection though lateral thinking may solve an intractable problem. Masochists will attempt to hand jam it.
(FA M. Edwards, R. Edwards 1984)

SC 12)
Stunted Arête 25ft Hard Very Severe 5a **R**
(FA M. Edwards solo 1985)

SC 13)
The Cut Price Comedy Show 25ft Very Severe 4c **R**
(FA M. Edwards solo 1985)

SC 14)
Smeagol (T2) 100ft Hard Very Severe 5a **R**

SC 15)
Pinch The Egyptian (T2) 90ft ft E6 6c 🦅
☠ ☠ ★

SC 16)
Golva (T2) 120ft E2 5c m 🦅 ★★

SC 18)
Gillian (T2) 110ft E3 5c **R** 🦅 ★★★

SC 20)
Vertical Crack (T2, T3) 75ft Hard Severe 4c
★★

SC 21)
Slim (T3) 70ft Hard Very Severe 5a **R** 🦅
(FA B. Wake, G. Wilson 1962)
The 'seawalls' below the Hayloft area give good bouldering, on slabs and arêtes, at low tide on a calm day.

The Golva Wall
Topo 2 (p114)

SC 11)
Super Jam (T1) 95ft E5 6b ★★

SC 14)
Smeagol (T1) 100ft Hard Very Severe 5a **R**
P1) 40ft P2) 60ft
(FA T. Walker, M. Tighe 1973)

Seabirds often nest on ledges on the next five routes.

SC 15)
Pinch The Egyptian (T1) 90ft E6 6c 🦅 💣
☠ ★★
(FA M. Edwards unseconded 1992)

SC 16)
Golva (T1) 120ft E2 5c ☺ 🦅 ★★
A taxing climb for any simian this crack is strenuously recommended. Large Friend useful near the top.
(FA M. McDermott, S. Bemrose 1964. FFA R. Edwards 1976)

SC 17)
ExSqueeze Me 70ft E5 6b 🦅 💣 ☠
Bicarbonate of soda?
(FTR S. Rourke 1994. FA M. Edwards unseconded 1994)

SC 18)
Gillian (T1) 110ft E3 5c **R** 🦅 ★★★
Cerebral control, long reaches and balancy movement required initially. Micro wires and thin tapes provide protection on the first 25ft, good protection thereafter.
(FA M. Mahoy, P. de Mengel. FFA R . Edwards 1977)

SC 18a)**Gillian Direct Start** 20ft E4 5c

SC 19)
Squeeze Me 75ft E3 6a **R** 🦅
A right to left rising traverse is **Tango In The Night,** 95ft, E3 6b **R**
(FA M. Edwards solo 1988. TITN M. Edwards, I, Blake 1987)

SC 20)
Vertical Crack (T1, T3) 75ft Hard Severe 4c
★★
A popular, enjoyable climb with a hard start. After the initial corner climb· the hidden chimney.
(FA J. Barry 1943)

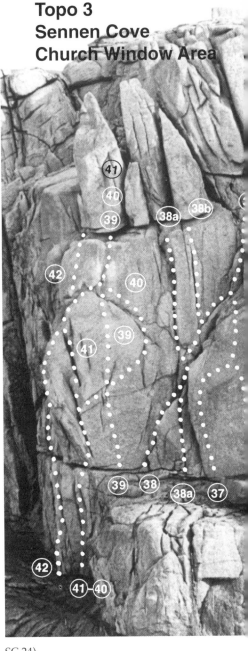

SC 24)
International Groove (T3) 70ft E3 5c **R**
(FA M. Edwards, S. Rourke, S. Stotz 1994)

Church Window Area - Topo 3 (p115)

SC 20)
Vertical Crack (T1, T2) 75ft Hard Severe 4c
★★

SC 21)
Slim (T1) 70ft Hard Very Severe 5a **R**

SC 22)
Monday Face 60ft Very Severe 4b+ **R**
(FA Royal Marines 1940s)

SC 23)
Pots Arête 60ft Hard Very Severe 5a
(FA R. Tewson, S. Salmon, P. Thompson 1983)

SC 24)
International Groove (T2) 70ft E3 5c **R**

SC 25)
Cliff Assault Wing Route 70ft Difficult ☺
(FA Probably Royal Marines 1940s)

SC 26)
Senior's Route 70ft Difficult ☺
(FA Probably Royal Marines 1940s)

SC 27
Overmarked 70ft Severe 4a
(FA M. Edwards 1983)

SC 28)
Tombstone 70ft E1 5b **R**
A direct start is E3 5b
(FA M. Edwards, R. Edwards 1981)

SC 29)
Altar Route 70ft Very Severe 4c+ ★★
P1) 50ft P2) 20ft
Lubricated when wet. A variation is to move
into a crack at 25ft and climb this at VS 4c. A
second pitch finishes up the wide chimney, on
the right, from the terrace; 4c and bold.
(FA Royal Marines 1940s)

SC 30)
Catholic Girls 50ft E1 5c R
Start as for Church Window, climb to the flake
of the Quaker. Move around this and
diagonally right to finish as for Altar Route.
*(FA M. Edwards, C. Edwards, M. McMahon
1985)*

SC 31)
Church Window 70ft Severe 4a R ★
P1) 45ft P2) 25ft
From a boulder, boldly mantleshelf onto a
ledge (small rock). A long step left gains the
leaning corner crack. Climb this into a niche
and gain the terrace by a short groove. At the
back of the terrace, on the right-hand side, is a
slab with a crack (V.Diff.). Climb this.
(FA Royal Marines 1940s)

SC 32)
Church Window Direct 50ft Very Severe 4c+
★
Climb the leaning corner. At the niche move
right and finish up a thin crack leading to the
terrace.
(FA Royal Marines 1940s)

SC 33)
The Quaker 60ft E1 5c
Climb the thin crack to the niche, move right
across a flake and finish leftwards where it
angles back left.
(FA R. Edwards and party 1977)

The wall to the left is home to some hard
eliminates.

SC 34)
Communion Crack 70ft E2 **6a**, 5c
The obvious crack striking up to the niche.
Resist starting from the boulder. Finish up the
slab to the left of the Church Window finish,
bold 5c.
*(FA With aid, unknown. FFA R. Edwards, I.
Pomfret 1972)*

116

SC 35)
Angel's Highway 75ft E2 5c+ R
Climb the thinner crack up to the tiny arête
and a larger crack, move left and climb a slab
to finish. No using the boulders!
(FA R. Edwards, M. Edwards 1978)

The next two routes are not shown on the topo.

SC a)
Knave's Route 60ft E3 6b
Climb faint cracks to cross Angel's Highway
and finish up a corner.
*(FA R. Edwards, A. N. Other 1977. Also claimed
separately by M. Edwards and B. Knight)*

SC b)
Black Widow 60ft E3 6b ☠ ★
Climb to an obvious hand hold, move right
and up then trend back left to finish up the
centre of the wall.
(FA M. Edwards solo 1987)

SC 36)
Messenger From The Furnace 60ft E5 6c/7a
💣☠★★
The logical outcome of developments, the
direct way up the wall.
(FA M. Edwards, R. Southall 1992)

SC 37)
Windows Of Perception 50ft E5 6a ☠
Climb the right-hand side of the arête, hand
traverse the holds of Stairway and finish
direct. It is also possible to continue up the
arête or traverse the wall at half-height at the
same grade
(FA M. Edwards solo 1988)

SC 38)
Sinner's Route 50ft Moderate ☺ ★★★★
An perfect novice route. The start is the crux;
the crack just to the right can also be used.
(FA Unknown, possibly Royal Marines 1940s)

SC 38a)
Variation 1. The crack going straight up can
be joined at half height at Difficult standard.

SC 38b)
Variation 2. The flake crack to the right again
is Very Difficult.

SC 39)

Windows Of Perfection 45ft E5 6b 💣 ☠ ★
Climbs directly up the flake past a black chicken head.
(FA M. Edwards, S. Anson 1989)

SC 40)
Dextrose 50ft Hard Very Severe 5a+ **R** ★★★
Excellent, varied climbing that tests skill, technique, strength and nerve. No sidling onto easy ground on the right for a rest after the traverse. This has a serious feel to it in its upper section and is harder for the short. It packs a punch! Friends, slings, etc. useful.
(FA V. Stevenson, J. Hay 1962)

SC 41)
Dexter 55ft Very Severe 4c ★★
Friends, hex's and slings useful. Harder for the short.
(FA J. Kinnaird and party 1954)

SC 42)
Devotee (T4) 55ft E1 5b **R**
The crux is the final step up onto the slab.
(FA The arête, Devo, M. Edwards solo 1984. Finish M. Edwards, T. Dennell 1993)

The Main Platform
Africa Route Area
Topo 4 (p117)

SC 42)
Devotee (T3) 55ft E1 5b

SC 43)
Double Overhang 65ft Very Severe 4c ★★

Topo 4
The Main Platform
Africa Route Area

DESCENT

The awkward finishing moves provide a challenging crux, Friends useful for belays.
(FA J. Barry 1940s)

SC 44)
White Man's Burden 65ft Hard Very Severe 5a **R**
Finish as for Double Overhang.
(FA D. Roscoe, P. Temple 1976)

SC 45)
Africa Route 65ft Very Severe 5a ★★★
Serendipity. An enchanting pitch. The start and finish are both hard; boulder the former, a good runner can be placed by the big hold, 10ft up.
(FA R. Flemming and party 1955)

SC 46)
Mark Up Another One 65ft E5+ 6a ☾ ☠ ★★
Good protection (TCUs) can be placed in the crack at half height. A bold finish.
(FA M. Edwards, T. Dennell 1993)

SC 47)
Overhanging Corner 50ft Very Severe 4c+ **R** ★
An alternative finish is Overhanging Eliminate, E3 5c, climbing a thin crack beside two black knobbles on the left and finishing direct.
(FA J. Deacon, R. Goodier 1955. Variation Finish P. Twomey, T. Dennell 1993)

SC 48)
Overhanging Wall 75ft Very Severe 4c+ **R** ★
The crack to the left, **Truescrew Crack**, is also 4c.
(FA V. Stevenson, J. Hay 1962. Variation, M. Edwards and party 1980s)

SC 49)
Skewcrack 60ft Severe 4b
(FA S. Salmon, P. Thompson 1983)

SC 50)
Staircase 60ft Difficult 🐦 ☺ ★
Strange, small birds nest in a crack high on the right, be careful where you shove Friends! Protection should be placed to prevent the
118

second swinging off the slab in the event of a fall.
(FA Royal Marines 1940s)

SC 51)
No Number 60ft Very Severe 5a ☺ ★
Large Friend useful.
(FA S. Salmon, D. Hannigan 1983)

SC 52)
No Name 65ft Hard Very Difficult ☺ ★★
(FA Royal Marines 1940s)

SC 53)
No Pack Drill 60ft E2 5c
(FA T. Dennell, S. Rourke, M. Edwards 1994)

SC 54)
Marionette 60ft E2 5c ★
Scores have failed on this but it doesn't deter other suitors; a stern, debilitating jamming crack.
(FA D. Roscoe and party 1974, FFA R. Edwards and party 1976)

The Main Platform Griptight Gully Area
Topo 5 (p119)

SC 55)
Black Slab 80ft Hard Very Difficult 3c ★★
Joyous. A better, but bolder, start is up the slab to the immediate right.
(FA Royal Marines 1940s)

The blowhole in this area, which has drenched many an unsuspecting second, has been climbed at severe standard. It doesn't get many repeat ascents.

SC 56)
Gilliwiggle 65ft Hard Severe 4b
Arduous. Well 'arduous in fact.
(FA J. Paterson, V. Stevenson 1963)

SC 57)
Black Jack 60ft Very Severe 4b
(FA J. Paterson, V. Stevenson 1963)

SC 58)
Main Face Climb 70ft Difficult ☺ ★
(FA Royal Marines 1940s)

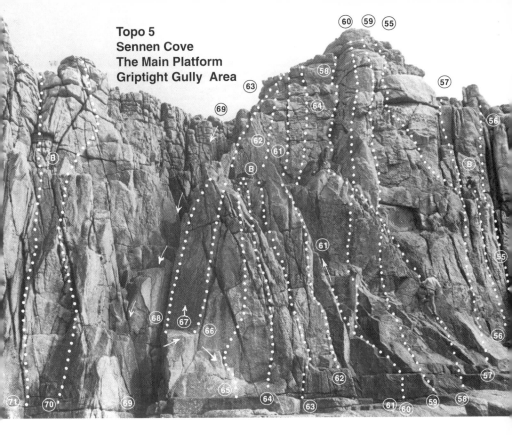

Topo 5
Sennen Cove
The Main Platform
Griptight Gully Area

SC 59)
The Arête 80ft Hard Severe 4a+
(FA V. Stevenson, P. Stevenson 1961)

SC 60)
Banana Split 80ft Hard Very Severe 5a
(FA M. Edwards solo 1985)

SC 61)
Banana Flake 85ft Very Difficult ☺ ★★
Follow the right-hand groove. The left-hand
one is HVD. The fin alone is Severe 4a and
bold.
(FA Royal Marines 1940s)

SC 62)
Orange Slice 85ft Severe 4b **R**
(FA M. Edwards solo 1983)

SC 63)
Left Banana Flake 80ft Very Difficult
Harder for the vertically challenged.
(FA Royal Marines 1940s)

SC 64)
Banana Crack 80ft Hard Very Severe 5b
(FA M. Edwards solo 1983)

SC 65)
The Flakes 80ft E1 5b **R**
A bold reach problem that can frustrate the
short.
(FA R. Edwards, A. N.Other 1978)

SC 66)
Right Hand Pitch 40ft Very Difficult
(FA Royal Marines 1940s)

SC 67)
Centre Pitch 40ft Very Severe 4a **R**
(FA M. Edwards solo 1980s)

SC 68)
Left Hand Pitch 40ft Severe 4a **R**
There is a small rock placement at the start and
nasty fall potential down the gully.
(FA V. Stevenson 1962)

*Banana Flake, Very Difficult, Sennen Cove.
Climber: Sigrid Merc*

The Main Platform
Demo Route Area
Topo 6 (p121)

SC 72)
Post The Postman 75ft Very Severe 4c
(FA M. Edwards solo 1987)

SC 70)
Letterbox (T5) 85ft Hard Severe 4b ★★

SC 71)
Walter's Chimney (T5) 75ft Severe 4a

SC 73)
Civvy Route 80ft Severe 4b ★★
Stimulating. Large Friend useful.
(FA Royal Marines 1940s)

SC 74)
Protein 80ft Very Severe 4c+ **R** ★
A determined approach required. Protection
is hard gained.
(FA W. Morrow 1960)

SC 74a)
Hot Tuna 15ft HVS 4c **R**
A direct finish through the roof.
(FA M. Edwards, I. Blake 1986)

SC 69)
Griptight Gully 80ft Moderate
If descending it is best to cross over the gully
to the block near the bottom. There are a
number of variations on the left wall of
Griptight Gully, most only around Difficult
standard.
(FA Royal Marines 1940s)

SC 70)
Letterbox (T6) 85ft Hard Severe 4b **R** ★★
A perplexing crux, style desirable.
(FA Royal Marines 1940s)

SC 71)
Walter's Chimney (T6) 75ft Severe 4a
Large Friend useful.
(FA Royal Marines 1940s)

SC 75)
Corner Crack 75ft Severe 4a ☺
Little independence.
(FA R. Handley, E. Phillip 1950)

SC 76)
Corner Climb 75ft Difficult ☺ ★★
*(FA Royal Marines 1940s. Originally named Sheer
Corner)*

SC 77)
Andrimne 75ft Severe 4a
(FA S. Young, K. Peterson 1970)

SC 78)
Intermediate Route 75ft Severe 4a ★
(FA Royal Marines 1940s)

SC 79)
Demo Route 80ft Hard Severe 4b+ ★★★
A challenging, varied route that constantly interests and inspires. That many have failed, or fallen, on it only goads others into redoubling their efforts. This should be enjoyed by everyone who has the ability. The chimney is the crux and awkward, though many balk at the moves around the nose. Pass this using underclings (beware rope drag) to gain the slab.
(FA J. Barry 1940s)

SC 80)
Demolition 75ft E6 6a ☠ ★★★
Straight up or on the rocks? Tremble up the 'blank' vertical slab.
(FA M. Edwards, I. Blake 1985)

SC 81)
Samson Arête 75ft E2 5c+ **R** ★★
Very good protection in the break, often dithered on; go on, layback and enjoy it. If you do, the Rock Hopper is the logical finish. This

route and Samson share a common finish.
(FA R. Edwards, I. Pomfret 1974)

SC 82)
The Rock Hopper (T7) 25ft E4 6a **R** 💣
Micros useful.
(FA M. Edwards, S. Rourke 1993)

Congo Crack & Black Zawn Area
Topo 7 (p122)

SC 83)
Samson 75ft E4 6a ★
Break the rules, use a knee! It's also worth taping your fingers. Finish as for Samson Arête.
(FA B. Page, M. McDermott 1957. FFA R. Edwards 1974)

SC 82)
The Rock Hopper (T6) 25ft E4 6a **R** 💣

121

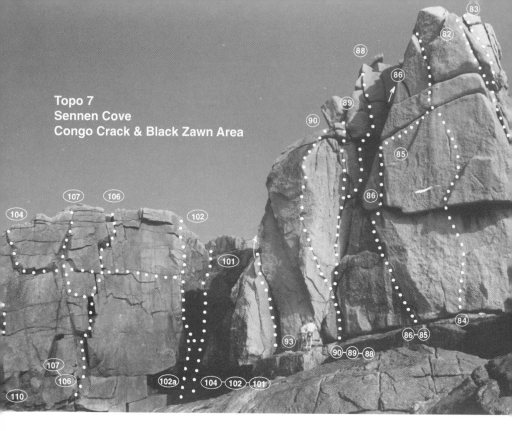

Topo 7
Sennen Cove
Congo Crack & Black Zawn Area

SC 84)
Red Rose TR 6b 💣
The remains of an ultra-controversial sports route on granite that never had a second ascent. Since vandalised and the bolts have cut. The ordinary version dyno'd for the flake; a more direct, harder one climbed directly up to the roof. Claimed at 8b/c.
NB. At the time of writing efforts are being made to restore the route to its original condition.
(FA M. Edwards unseconded 1988, belayed by C. Johns and G. Davis. TR since, A. Pollitt 1989)

SC 85)
A Swift Flight Of Fancy 85ft E3 6a **R** ★★★
A steep, beautiful route with some memorable moves.
(FA R. Edwards, M. Edwards 1984)

SC 86)
Finale 85ft E2 5c
(FA M. Tighe, B. Newton 1973)
122

SC 88)
Meany 75ft Hard Very Severe 5a
(FA R. Edwards, M. Edwards mid 1980s)

SC 89)
Eeny 65ft Hard Very Severe 5a
(FA R. Edwards, M. Edwards mid 1980s)

SC 90)
Let The River Live 75ft E6 6b **R** 💣 ★★
(FA M. Edwards unseconded 1987)

SC 93)
Congo Crack (T8) 80ft E1 5b+ ★★
(FA H. Banner, J. Gosling 1966)

SC 101)
Norge Corner (T9) 70ft Hard Severe 4b+ **R** ★★
A great little route with an exciting finish. There's a hard way and a slightly easier way of doing this. Will you find the latter?
(FA Unknown, probably 1950s)

A Swift Flight of Fancy, E3 6a, Sennen Cove. Climber Rowland Edwards

SC 102)
Ace Of Spades (T9) 85ft E4 5c ☠ ★★

SC 102a)
Direct Start E5 5c ☠
(FA M. Edwards solo 1985)

SC 104)
Thieves Carnival 100ft E6 6b **R** 💣
A traverse of Zig Zag Wall.
(FA M. Edwards, S. Anson 1988)

SC 106)
Zig Zag (T9) 65ft Hard Very Severe 5a+
★★★

SC 107)
Cool Curl 75ft HVS 5b
An alternative, easier, start to Delilah. Finish
direct, or move left along a break below the
top, where an impressive gymnastic move
gains the top.
(FA M. Edwards solo 1987)

SC 110)
Prow (T9) 55ft E4 6b
(FA R. Edwards, M. Edwards 1987)

Black Zawn - Slippery Slab Area
Topo 8 (p124)

SC 87)
Genge's Groove 75ft Hard Very Severe 5a+
★★
Bridge up the final wide groove after
grappling with the start.
(FA T. Genge 1947)

SC 91)
Amazonia 75ft E7 6c 💣 ☠ ★★★
If it weren't for the lack of protection this might
be more popular. An extremely exacting,
exceedingly technical test-piece. Failure could
extinguish a leader's hopes, if not their
existence. One PR, removed.
(FA M. Edwards, R. Edwards 1987)

SC 92)
Rainbow Warrior 90ft E7 6c 💣 ☠ ★
Another exacting test-piece.
(FA M. Edwards unseconded 1990)

Tears of a Clown E7 6b, Sennen.
Climber: Mark Edwards

124

SC 93)
Congo Crack (T7) 80ft E1 5b ★★ 5b+

SC 94)
Much Ado About Nothing 40ft E6 6c/7a
●⃰ ★★

Acrobatic. This takes the roof left (facing in) of the second of two cracks across the roof and a triangular slot. No 4 Camalot useful. Depicted with Dark Comedian, E3 5b, as the finish up the slab. The cracks are two aid routes, both A2, 1960s.
(FA M.A.A.N M. Edwards unseconded 1991, Dark Comedian, M. Hounlow solo 1984)

SC 95)
Congo Route 100ft Very Severe 4c **R** ★
Harder if the opening groove is greasy. A variation finish is up the right to left diagonal ramp, HVS 4c. A mid-height traverse of the slabs is Trip Across The Slip, bold E2 5c.

Last Dancer E4 6b, Land's End.
Climber: Mark Edwards

(FA M. McDermott, B. Berbonne 1961. T.A.T.S M. Edwards solo)

SC 96)
Slippery Slab 70ft Very Severe 5a ★★
Engaging. Small gear useful.
(FA P. Biven, T. Peck, W. Bacon 1955)

SC 97)
Slab Happy 70ft E3 5b ☠
(FA M. Edwards solo 1987)

SC 98)
Slippery Chute 70ft Very Severe 4c+ ★★
Highly reputable climbing.
(FA Unknown, probably late 1950s, early 1960s)

SC 100)
Skid Mark (T9) 70ft E4 6b **R** ●⃰ ★
(FA M. Edwards, J. Fisher 1994)

SC 103)
Tears Of A Clown (T9) E7 6b ●⃰ ☠
★★★★

125

Black Zawn - Zig Zag Area
Topo 9 (p125)

SC 99)
Slight Pause 70ft Hard Very Severe 4c **R**
(FA A. Newton, D. Roscoe 1981)

SC 100)
Skid Mark (T8) 70ft E4 6b **R** 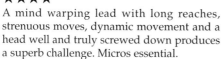 ★

SC 101)
Norge Corner (T7) 70ft Hard Severe 4b+ **R**
★★

SC 102)
Ace Of Spades (T7) 85ft E4 5c ☠ ★★
A very bold, high crux. The blunt arête to the left goes at E5 5c.
(FA M. Edwards, R. Edwards 1982. Arête M. Edwards solo 1985)

SC 103)
Tears Of A Clown (T8) E7 6b ☠ ☀
★★★★
A mind warping lead with long reaches, strenuous moves, dynamic movement and a head well and truly screwed down produces a superb challenge. Micros essential.
(FA M. Edwards unseconded 1986)

SC 105)
29 Palms 70ft E6 6c ★★★
An early sports route that went the same way as Red Rose. First led on mild steel knife blades, replaced with stainless pegs in drilled out placements to provide in situ protection. These were later removed and would need replacing; or, a completely unprotected ascent with the peg sockets filled.
(FA M. Edwards, R. Edwards 1987)

SC 106)
Zig Zag (T7) 65ft Hard Very Severe 5a+
★★★
Gritstone approach desired, Friends useful, elegance optional.
(FA M. Banks 1955)

SC 108)
Delilah 70ft E2 5b ★★
Salacious. A good, enjoyable classic. TCUs and

rocks useful to protect the crux.
(FA J. Deacon, D. Holdroyd 1956, FFA M. White 1973)

SC 109)
High Street Blues 60ft E4 6a ★★
(FA R. Edwards, M. Edwards 1987)

SC 109a)
Variation Finish E4 6a

SC 110)
Prow (T7) 55ft E4 6b

The Forgotten Wall

These routes are not depicted on a topo

This is the leaning black wall facing the sea at the end of Black Zawn.

SC c)
The Forgotten Wall 40ft E5 6a ☠ ☀
The left-hand end of the wall (facing in) has a short clean groove capped by a roof. Starting up the arête is E6 6a.
(FA M. Edwards unseconded 1994)

SC d)
Placa Del Edwards 60ft E7 6c/7a ☠ ☀
Climbs the centre of the overhanging wall starting below a roof. Either traverse from the left, or cross the roof direct, and then power up the upper leaning wall finishing via a shallow groove. Two PR.
(FA M. Edwards unseconded 1994)

Irish Lady Cove

This is the obvious zawn of black rock seen just after the scramble down the gully from the lookout. A prominent small island, The Irish Lady, is just offshore capped by a large perched block. Descent is by carefully scrambling down the gritty gully to the tidal platform. Refer to topo one. Seabirds nest in the vicinity. Please exit climbs cleanly.

Various stories have circulated as to how the cove came by its name. The wildest concerns a Victorian shipwreck, the sole survivor of which was an Irish woman who scrambled onto the island and for three days, whilst the storm raged, beseeched the helpless villagers to save her before finally being swept to her death! A less dramatic one concerns a rich benefactor who bought the headland in the 1920s to save it from developers.

Irish Lady Cove
Commando Crack Area
Topo 1 (p127)

The two cracks to the left of Knight Move have been climbed, the first at Very Severe standard whilst the second, shorter one is a Severe.

ILC 1)
Knight Move 70ft E1 5a
(FA M. Edwards solo 1986)

ILC 2)
Big Blade 65ft E3 5c
FA M. Edwards solo 1985)

ILC 3a)
Direct Start To Six Blade Knife E2 5c
(FA M. Edwards solo 1985)

ILC 3)
Six Blade Knife E1 5b R
(FA M. Edwards, E. Stone 1985)

**Topo 1
Irish Lady Cove
Commando Crack Area**

LOOKOUT ↓

TO SENNEN

DESCENT

ILC 4)
Commando Crack 50ft Very Severe 5a ★
(FA M. Banks, J. Eliot 1950)

ILC 5)
Stone The Crows 50ft E4 6a
(FA R. Edwards, M. Edwards, 1986)

ILC 6)
Commando Corner 50ft Very Severe 4c
Some gritty rock.
(FA Royal Marines 1940s)

ILC 7)
Brain Drain 50ft E2 5c
(FA M. Edwards solo 1987)

ILC 8)
Sky Train 50ft E2 5b
(FA R. Edwards, M. Edwards 1984)

ILC 9)
Chi-Squared 50ft Hard Very Severe 5a
(FA R. Coates, S. Young 1968)

128

ILC 10)
Flexi Toys 50ft E4 6a
(FA M. Edwards, R. Edwards 1984)

ILC 11)
Plastic Edge 60ft E1 5b
Climb cracks in the leaning upper wall should
you fancy a second pitch.
(FA M. Edwards, R. Edwards 1984)

North Wall Area
Topo 2 (p128)

ILC 12)
Speliology 75ft Hard Very Severe 5a ★
*(FA T. Thompson, P. de Mengle 1972. FFA
unknown)*

ILC 13)
Stout Crack 75ft E4 6a
One PR. Dry conditions essential.
(FA M. Edwards unseconded 1991)

ILC 14)
North Wall 100ft Very Severe 5a
Belays can be taken on ledges.
(FA T. Thompson, A . Mahony alt 1972)

ILC 15)
Campanology 75ft Severe 4a ★
(FA T. Thompson, P. de Mengle 1972)

ILC 16)
Dead Ringer 75ft Hard Very Severe 5b ★
(FA M. Edwards, C. Johns 1988)

ILC 17)
Coconut Cove 70ft E5 6b ★★
*(FA M. Edwards
I. Blake 1987)*

ILC 18)
Teleology Hard
Severe 4a
This climbs a
chimney at the
back of the corner
finishing up the
wall above.
*(FA P. Checkland
1969)*

ILC 19)
Face Lift 50ft E3 5c
The arête to the left is Soft Touch, E2 5b,
starting up a crack from the corner.
(FAs M. Edwards solo 1987)

ILC 20)
Dark Lady 75ft E1 5a
*(FA M. Edwards solo 1986, also claimed by S.
Salmon, M. Easterbrook 1989)*

ILC 21)
Christine 60ft Severe 4a
(FA M. Edwards, C. Johns 1987)

*Demo Route
Hard Severe 4b,
Sennen Cove.
Climbers: Morino
Van Joaren and
Burt Halewijon
(p121)*

Land's End

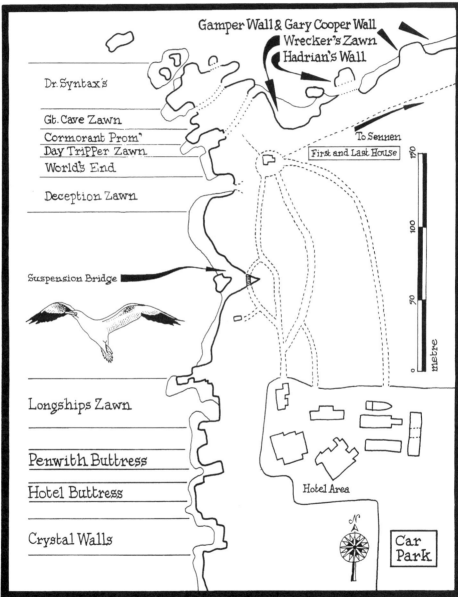

Gamper Wall & Gary Cooper Wall
Wrecker's Zawn
Hadrian's Wall

Dr. Syntax's

Gt. Cave Zawn
Cormorant Prom'
Day Tripper Zawn
World's End

Deception Zawn

To Sennen

First and Last House

Suspension Bridge

Longships Zawn

Penwith Buttress

Hotel Buttress

Crystal Walls

Hotel Area

metre

Car
Park

Land's End

COASTGUARD IDENTITY: Land's End.

NEAREST PHONE: ✆ The tourist complex.

OS REFERENCE: 342 252

TIDAL? Partially; routes starting from the ledges at the base of Dr Syntax's Head, at the World's End Area, Penwith Buttress and Crystal Walls are not affected by tides and can be reached by abseil, with calm seas at high tide. As can the start of Day-tripper. Land's End Long Climb is also not tidal, but caution is strongly advised, as four schoolboys were swept to their deaths from the ledges in this area in the mid 1980s.

ASPECT: Westerly predominantly, though some walls are southerly and others catch the sun reluctantly. A good sheltered place to climb in the winter months if you drop down out of any wind.

CHARACTER: Still much underrated. A challenging, yet accessible, cliff that is tremendously atmospheric and with some routes of major quality. A long, complex cliff with something for everyone; friendly buttresses, steep walls and faces, technical arêtes, adventurous zawns and a Long Climb (take some money for the café at the top).

ROCK: Granite, some of the best and worst to be found in Penwith. It is worth taping up for many of the crack climbs. Good in most places, though some routes have a gritty surface texture; elsewhere the tops can be suspect as are routes whose name begins with the word 'Death'! Additional guidance is given in the text.

TYPE OF CLIMBS: Single and multi-pitch routes of some commitment. It is hoped that the following topos will encourage visits, and new routes.

PROBLEMS: Tides. Rock fall can change the nature of routes after winter storms. Gritty rock and loose finishes require careful handling in places. Committing zawns; an abseil rope is useful

ENVIRONMENTAL CONCERNS: Path erosion and some damage to some cliff edges from climbers topping out and disturbance to nesting birds; it is an important nesting area. Please look for nests before an ascent and avoid any nest or chicks that you encounter. Away from the complex the heathland is susceptible to trampling. We ask that you take care to follow, not create, paths and descents and pre-place abseil ropes to protect cliff edges at the top of routes in Wreckers' Zawn and Day-tripper Zawn. Please refer to the text. Removal of pegs should be via free ascents. The offshore islands are barely worth a visit and have little to offer in the way of new routes; if visited at all this is best left to late summer

PARKING: Major car park two minutes' walk from the cliffs. Do not pay. Tell them you're climbers at the gate and you are admitted free, to climb only.

APPROACH: Refer to the Land's End area map. Drive to Land's End from Sennen and park. Refer to maps, topos and any text at the start of each cliff area for approach details. The cliffs are only a few minutes' walk from the car park..

DESCENTS: An abseil rope is useful. Approaches and descent information is given for each area in the text. Use of the maps and topos in conjunction with the text should get you to where you want to go on this complex cliff. Refer to topos for abseil points.
    The Long Climb (LE 117) area is reached by a walk and scramble down the left side (facing out) of the buttress that lies in front of the left-hand side of the hotel (facing out). The path starts below a small round house and telescopes and is fairly obvious, ie. well worn.

The cliffs are depicted, and described, from left to right as you face them.

Topo 1
Land's End
Gary Cooper Wall

Garry Cooper Wall
Topo 1 (p132)

This area is tidal. Access for Gary Cooper Wall. Walk northwards, toward Sennen Cove, along the coast path for 200m and then branch left down to the cliff edge. Once you have located the bay it is possible to scramble down the prominent ridge to sea level. Refer to topo one.

LE 1)
Route One 30ft Very Severe 4c
(FA R. Edwards solo 1994)

LE 2)
Candy 30ft Hard Severe 4b
(FA R. Edwards solo 1994)

LE 3)
Espron Negro 55ft E3 6a
(FA R. Edwards, J. Andres-Avajas 1988)

LE 4)
Pump It 55ft E2 6a
(FA R. Edwards unseconded 1994)

LE 5)
Yet Again 55ft Very Severe 4c
(FA R. Edwards, E. Edwards 1994)

LE 6)
And Another 55ft Very Severe 4c ✠
(FA R. Edwards, E. Edwards 1994)

LE 7)
Fast Lane 85ft E4 6a ★★
Good, well protected thin crack climbing.
(FA R. Edwards, J. Andres-Avajas 1988)

LE 8)
O.K. Coral 55ft Hard Very Severe 5b
(FA R. Edwards, E. Edwards 1994)

LE 9)
High Noon 50ft E1 5b ★
Good rock and good position.
(FA R. Edwards, E. Edwards 1994)

LE 9a)
High Noon Left Hand Finish 50ft E2 5c
(FA R. Edwards, E. Edwards 1994)

Topo 2
Land's End
Gamper Wall

LE 13)
Bulging Arête (T2) 60ft
Hard Severe 4b ★★
One of the strongest
teams of their time, the
exploratory instinct as
strong as ever.
*(FA J. Deacon, V. Stevenson
1959)*

Gamper Wall
Topo 2 (p133)

This area is tidal. Access
to the starts of routes on
Gamper Wall. Walk
northwards, toward
Sennen Cove, along the
coast path for 200m and
then branch left down to
the cliff edge. Once you
have located the bay it is
possible to abseil from the
top of the buttress. Refer
to topo two.

LE 13)
Bulging Arête (T1) 60ft
Hard Severe 4b ★★

LE 14)
Mind Bubble 80ft Hard

LE 9b)
High Noon Right Hand Finish 50ft Hard
Very Severe 5b
(FA R. Edwards, E. Edwards 1994)

LE 10)
Tumble Weed 50ft Very Severe 5a
(FA R. Edwards, E. Edwards 1994)

LE 11)
Pony Express 50ft Very Severe 5a
(FA R. Edwards, unseconded 1994)

LE 12)
True Grit 55ft E2 5b
Desperate off-width climbing. The size of
one's bust, tum or bum together with style
determines success or failure.
(FA R. Edwards, unseconded 1994)

Very Severe 5a+ 💣
(FA R. Edwards, H. Van Ham 1988)

LE 15)
Sunset Crack 80ft Hard Very Severe 5a
(FA R. Edwards solo 1988)

LE 16)
Fading Into Black 80ft E2 5c 💣
(FA R. Edwards, N. Mooney, V. Van Ham 1988)

LE 17)
Double Take 60ft Very Severe 5a
(FA R. Edwards, J. Andres-Avajas 1988)

LE 18)
The Long Reach 60ft E4 6b ❀ 💣

Escape is possible at half height. Rock suspect at the top.
(FA M. Edwards, R. Edwards 1988)

LE 19)
Looking Over The Edge 120ft E1 5b 🏵 💣
Loose rock at the finish
(FA R. Edwards, J. Andres-Avajas 1988)

LE a)
Children Of Laughter 130ft E4 6b 🏵 💣
★★
Not depicted on the topo. Two PR were used on the FA and 2 BR (replacing pegs used on the FA) should be present. This route takes the obvious arête, behind the pinnacle in the middle of the Zawn and to the left of the cave. Climb the ledges to just below the arête, climb this and continue up to a small roof. Pass this onto the wall and then up the arête to a good ledge. Belay or abseil from here. P2. Continue climbing the short wall to finish up easy ground.
(FA R. Edwards, J. Andres-Avajas 1988)

The pinnacle in the centre of the zawn has two interesting routes on it. One takes the left arête via a crack at E1 5b. The other follows a crack in the face to the right, E1 5b.

Hadrian's Wall
Topo 3 (p134)

This area is tidal. Access to the starts of routes on Gamper Wall. Walk northwards, (toward Sennen Cove) along the coast path for 200m and then branch left down to the cliff edge to identify the bay. For the route Hadrian's Wall, scramble down the left arête to ledges which lead back right to the base of the wall. For the routes on the opposite wall, Caesar's Groove etc., abseil down the arête on the right (facing out) then traverse easily backwards onto the ledges. It can also be gained from Day Tripper Zawn. All climbs are possible from mid to low tides and are all on excellent rock.

DESCENT

Topo 3
Land's End
Hadrian's Wall

APPROACH FROM ABSEIL

→

Wrecker's Zawn
Topo 4 (p135)

This area is tidal and the best time to climb here is during a dry period with a northerly wind. From the First & Last House continue northwards to the first of the deep zawns (past Dr Syntax's Head) cutting into the headland and 25m west of the wooden fence. Scramble to the zawn floor down the slopes either side of the zawn and traverse into Wrecker's Zawn. Or scramble through the cave from Day Tripper Zawn (this may be preferable on first acquaintance). The wall is obvious from here.

Approach before low tide. This will give you about 2 to 3 hours of free passage out of the zawn again.

These climbs, and there is scope for many more, all end at a 10ft band of earth topped by unspoilt grass cornices. Belays at the top of the cliff are not immediately at hand. It has proved possible to climb over the earth band to the top, and extra long pre-placed ropes, stakes or a bolt in a boulder have all been suggested for belays. However, repeated topping out would damage the cliff edge in a very short time. A few abseil/lower-off points just beneath the earth band would enable the climbs to be enjoyed without destroying the environment; we leave this for you to mull over. In the meantime pre-place an abseil rope or hang a karabiner over the edge on a spare rope as a lower-off.

LE 20)
Hadrian's Wall 50ft Very Severe 4c ★
(FA J. Deacon, V. Stevenson 1959)

LE 21)
SPQR 50ft E3 5c ★
(FA M. Edwards, R. Edwards 1982)

LE 22)
Hadrian's Nose 50ft E1 5b
(FA R. Edwards, M. Edwards 1981)

LE 23)
Cassio 110ft E2 5c
(FA R. Edwards, M. Edwards 1982)

LE 24)
Brutus 110ft Hard Very Severe 5b
(FA R. Edwards, M. Edwards 1982)

LE 25)
Caesar's Groove 110ft E2 5c
(FA M. Edwards, R. Edwards 1982)

LE 26)
Infinite Design 185ft E4 6a ❀ ● ★★
(FA R. Edwards, M. Edwards 1988

135

LE 27)
A Winking Crack 185ft E4 6a, 5a- ✿ ●
★★
(FA R. Edwards, H. Van Ham 1988)

Dr Syntax's Head: North Side
Topo 5 (p136)

Walk to Dr Syntax's Head (refer to the map and topo five) and locate the abseil points.

LE 28)
April Fool 70ft E2 5b
(FA R. Edwards solo 1988)

LE 29)
Exit Visa 70ft Hard Severe 4b
(FA R. Edwards, M. Edwards, A. Wingham 1984)

LE 30)
Copy Cat 70ft Very Severe 4c
(FA R. Edwards, M. Edwards, A. Wingham 1984)

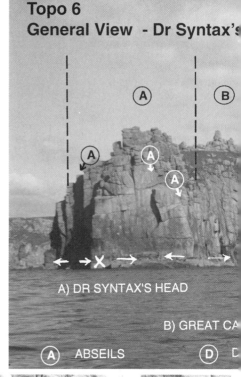

Topo 6
General View - Dr Syntax's

A) DR SYNTAX'S HEAD

B) GREAT CA

Ⓐ ABSEILS   Ⓓ D

Topo 5
Dr Syntax's Head Ⓐ
North Side

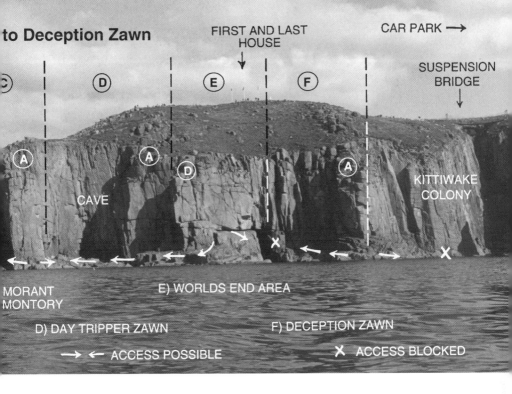

to Deception Zawn

FIRST AND LAST HOUSE

CAR PARK ⟶

SUSPENSION BRIDGE

Ⓒ Ⓓ Ⓔ Ⓕ

Ⓐ Ⓐ Ⓓ Ⓐ

CAVE

KITTIWAKE COLONY

MORANT MONTORY

E) WORLDS END AREA

D) DAY TRIPPER ZAWN

F) DECEPTION ZAWN

⟶ ← ACCESS POSSIBLE

✕ ACCESS BLOCKED

LE 31)
Perfect Prescription 70ft E3 6a ★
Fine, thin crack climbing with small rock protection.
(FA M. Edwards, R. Edwards 1984

LE 32)
Soloer's Paradise 160ft Severe 4b
Belays can be taken on ledges.
(FA M. Edwards solo 1984)

LE 32a)
Variation Severe 4a

Dr Syntax's Head to Deception Zawn
Topo 6 - General View

Dr Syntax's Head: West Side
Topo 7 (p138)

Walk to Dr Syntax's Head (refer to the map and topos six and seven) and locate the abseiling points.

LE 33)
Born Free 70ft Very Severe 4c
(FA M. Edwards, R. Edwards 1983)

LE 34)
Easy Way Out 70ft Very Difficult
(FA R. Edwards solo 1987)

LE 35)
New Release 75ft E2 5c 💣 ★★
A well defined groove.
(FA R. Edwards, C. Edwards, I. Blake 1990-

LE 36)
Second Chance 85ft HVS 5a ★★
Good, strenuous crack climbing that leads to a surprising finish.
(FA R. Edwards, M. Edwards 1986)

LE 37)
Recycled 70ft Very Severe 5a
(FA R. Edwards, M. Edwards 1987)

LE 38)
Time Out 75ft E3 5c ★★

Good bold climbing with an interesting groove to finish.
(FA R. Edwards, M. Edwards 1983)

Originally there were a further eight routes on this buttress, but they vanished in a winter storm.

LE 39)
Land's End Micro Climb 70ft Hard Very Severe 4c **R**
Start just left of the arête then move onto the south face and follow the obvious crack.
(FA M. Edwards, R. Edwards 1983)

Dr Syntax's Head: Great Cave Area
Topo 8 (p139)

This area is very atmospheric with a feeling of commitment. Walk to Dr Syntax's headland (refer to the map and topos six and seven) and locate the abseil points on the west side of Dr Syntax's Head.

Approach by a 50ft abseil down the west side and an easy traverse follows to the Great Cave. A step across a wide crack leads to ledges at the foot of the wall. Refer also to topo eight.

LE 40)
Blitzkrieg 140ft E1 5b
(FA R. Edwards, M. Edwards 1985)

LE 41)
New Waves 150ft Hard Very Severe 5b
(FA R. Edwards, M. Edwards 1985)

LE 42)
Edge Of Time 145ft E4 5c, **6b** **R** ●⁕ ★★★
P1) 45ft P2) 100ft
A powerful and serious route. It can be done as one pitch thus avoiding the difficult belay.
(FA R. Edwards, M. Edwards 1985)

LE 42a)
Heritage Of Follies 145ft E5 5c, **6b** **R** ●⁕
★

138

**Topo 8
Dr Syntax's Head
Great Cave Area**

Topo 9
Cormorant Promontory
West Side

DAY TRIPP
ZAWN

51a

43
44
45
46
47
48
49
50

P1) 45ft P2) 105ft
An even more powerful variation of Edge Of Time. After the first pitch climb up to the roof, cross this and pass two BR (replaced pegs, may be missing) to rejoin the parent route.
(FA M. Edwards, R. Edwards 1988)

LE 43)
Irish Whiskey (T9) 80ft Hard Very Severe 5a 🕊️ 💣
Other routes have been claimed in this area, but the exact lines are unknown.
(FKA R. Edwards, N. Mooney 1990)

LE 44)
Hors d'oeuvre (T9) 80ft Very Severe 4c, 4b 🕊️
P1) 50ft P2) 30ft
(FA J. Deacon, V. Stevenson alt 1959)

Cormorant Promontory: West Side
Topo 9 (p140)

Refer to the map and topos six and nine. Walk to Day Tripper Zawn and Dr Syntax's Head. The Promontory juts out, dividing the two. Descent is as for Day Tripper Zawn or by abseil directly from the top of the routes, where a large perched block can be used as an anchor. Many routes on Cormorant Promontory are also regular nesting sites. Visual inspection prior to an ascent and strenuous efforts to avoid eggs or chicks on the top are advised. The best vantage point is the opposite side of Day Tripper Zawn from the Promontory.

LE 43)
Irish Whiskey (T8) 80ft hard Very Severe 5a 🕊️
Start obscured in cleft, refer to topo eight.

LE 44)
Hors d'oeuvre (T8) 80ft Very Severe 4c, 4b 🕊️

LE 45)
Magnet Fever 95ft E6 6b R 🕊️ 💣 ★
(FA M. Edwards, R. Edwards 1990)

LE 46)
Syncromatic 95ft E4 6a 🕊️ 💣 ★★
Two PR. Start below the slanting crack 10ft left of Technotronic.
(FA R. Edwards, S. Jones 1990)

LE 47)
Technotronic 95ft E4 6a+ 🕊️ 💣 ★★
One PR. This climbs the left arête of Lindy.
(FA R. Edwards, S. Jones 1990)

LE 48)
Lindy 95ft E3 5b 🕊️ ☠️
Climb the obvious groove to finish up a chimney.
(FA E. Grindley, G. Higginson 1973)

LE 49)
A Sudden Splash 95ft E3 5c 🕊️ ★
(FA R. Edwards, C. Edwards, V. Van Ham 1988)

LE 50)
Cormorant Slab 80ft Severe 4a 🕊️ ★
Thoughtful protection, pleasant climbing.
(FA D. Holroyd, A. Blackshaw, J. Deacon 1957)

LE 51)
Cormorant's Ben 80ft E2 5b R 🕊️ ★
(FA S. Dougherty, M. Nicholson 1981)

LE 51a)
Cormorant's Ben Direct Finish 80ft E2 5b 🕊️
(FA M. Edwards, R. Edwards, R. Barker 1981)

LE 52)
Lost Souls (T10) 95ft E4 6b R 💣 🕊️ ★★
One PR should be in place.
(FA M. Edwards, R. Edwards 1985)

Day Tripper Zawn
Topo 10 (p142)

Approach. Refer to the map and topos six, ten and eleven. Strike out rightwards (facing out) from the car park towards the suspension bridge. Cross this and continue along the path for a short while until the cliff dramatically drops into a zawn to the left of the path's edge. This is Day Tripper Zawn. Descent is usually by abseil. Looking west into the Zawn a small

Topo 10
Day Tripper Zawn

WAY OFF

DR SYNTAX'S HEAD

headland is on the left (facing out) or south side of this. This is the top of the World's End Area. Abseil from here to the ledges and boulders at low tide. Other abseil points are available around the zawn (50m rope useful). There is also a downclimb from World's End,

see topo eleven.

Many routes on the Cormorant Promontory, which forms the northern end of the zawn, are also regular nesting sites. Visual inspection prior to an ascent and strenuous efforts to avoid eggs or chicks on the top are

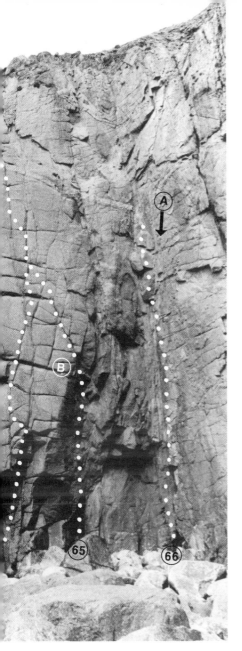

LE 52)
Lost Souls (T9) 95ft E4 6b R 🌑 ⚡ ★★
One PR should be in place.
(FA M. Edwards, R. Edwards 1985)

LE 53)
The Cormorant's Bill 90ft Hard Very Severe
5b ⚡ ★★
Pure, unadulterated fun. Good position, fine climbing, excellent rock and more than adequate protection.
(FA J. Deacon, C. Fishwick 1971. FFA P. Littlejohn 1972)

LE 54)
Last Dancer 125ft E5 6c ⚡ ★★★
P1) 30ft P2) 95ft
Four PR should be in place; it finishes up The Last Dance.
(FA M. Edwards, R. Edwards 1985)

LE 54a)
The Last Dance 90ft E4 6b 🌼 ⚡ ★★★
Two PR. One of the best routes at this grade in Penwith. The start of the route, at the base of Cormorant's Bill, can be reached by abseil at high tide. After a bold start, from the triangular ledge, protection can be arranged. The lichen should be treated carefully but makes little practical difference to the climbing.
(FA R. Edwards, M. Edwards 1985)

LE 55)
Split Minds 120ft E1 5b, 5b ★
P1) 30ft P2) 90ft]
On the upper part, climb a crack system on the left of the wide groove. Friend 4 useful.
(FA R. Edwards, M. Edwards 1981)

LE 56)
Johnstone's Route 90ft Severe 4a, 4a ★
P1) 45ft P2) 45ft
On the upper part, climb the right-hand corner before moving left to finish up a crack. Some gritty rock near the top.
(FA J. Deacon, D. Holroyd 1957)

advised. The best vantage point, from which to check the nesting situation, is the opposite side of Day Tripper Zawn from the promontory.

LE 57)
Backlash 115ft E1 5b, 5a 🌼 ☠
The top part of this route should be avoided as it is covered in lichen and plants. Please pre-place an abseil rope for a descent.
(FA E. Grindley, I. Roper, G. Higginson alt 1972)

Edge of Light E2 5b, Land's End. Climber: Rowland Edwards on FA. Photo: Tim Dennell

LE 58)
Witch Hunt 115ft E2 5c 🌸
This route follows a line just right of Backlash and should be avoided due to its extensive coverage of lichens and plants.
(FA P. Littlejohn, D. Roberts 1977)

LE 59)
Edge Of Light 115ft E2 5b ★★
Small Friends, TCUs and rocks essential. Good protection, care required in placing it. A clean finish.
(FA R. Edwards, C. Edwards 1994)

LE 60)
Black Power 115ft E2 5b R 🌸 💣 ★
The vee-groove is earthy and poorly protected.
(FA E. Grindley and party 1972)

LE 61)
Oliver Twist 115ft Hard Very Severe 5a 🌸
(FA J. Deacon, V. Stevenson 1959)

LE 62)
Dancing On Crystals 80ft E5 6b 🌸 💣 ★★
Granite Flamenco. This route finish on the sloping ledge of Tide Race. Escape could be made up the final vegetated ledges, but in order to avoid damaging the vegetation it is advisable to pre-place an abseil rope in order to descend back to the base of the route. Small rocks, micros, TCUs useful.
(FA R. Edwards, M. Edwards, S. Rourke 1994)

LE 63)
Tide Race 80ft Very Severe 4b+ R 🌸' 🪓
Good if gritty climbing. The final 20ft are very vegetated and unstable, in order to avoid damaging it, we advise pre-placing a second abseil rope to belay off and descend back to the base. Check there are no nesting birds prior to an ascent.
(FA J. Deacon, M. McDermott 1959)

LE 64)
Day Tripper 130ft E3 6a, 4c 🌸 ★★★
P1) 110ft P2) 20ft
One of the classic crack climbs of the area. A pre-placed abseil rope would prevent environmental damage to the top of this cliff. The short second pitch is for those who must

reach the top, but is best avoided.
(FA R. Edwards, M. Edwards 1981)

LE 65)
A Bridge Too Far 150ft E5 **6b**, 6a, 4c 🌸 💣 ★★★
P1) 50ft P2) 70ft P3) 30ft
The first pitch is one of the most unique, unusual and entertaining around involving reversing along the hanging groove and around the roof. Two PR. It is possible to take a hanging stance off a single large rock after pulling out onto the face, otherwise rope drag will be a problem. The second pitch traverses into Day Tripper and finishes as for this. Large rocks and medium Friends useful.
(FA R. Edwards, C. Edwards 1994)

LE 66)
Flash Control 75ft E3 5c+ 🌸 💣 ★★
A good, popular wall climb; both sustained and technical. Five SS pegs in situ. TCUs useful. A final pitch has been climbed at E2 5a+, ⚕, but is very unstable. Current practice is to lower off the twin pegs from the ledge. NB: Pegs stripped 1996.
(FA R. Edwards, S. Jones, N. Mooney 1990)

Day Tripper Zawn and World's End Areas
Topo 11 (p147)

Approach. Refer to the map and topos six, eleven and twelve. Approach from the First & Last House and walk down the slope to a small rock outcrop. Walk slightly northwards until you are above a small promontory (this forms the southern end of Day Tripper Zawn) and scramble down to reach its top. From here either climb down the wide crack on the left (Diff) or arrange an abseil.

LE 67)
Currying Favour 100ft Hard Very Severe 5a
Large Friends, hex's and rocks useful.
(FA R. Edwards, S. Jones 1990)

LE 68)
Edge Control Two 100ft E5 6b R 💣 ☠
★★★

145

Flash Control E3 5c+, Land's End. Climber: Mark Edwards

Bold, strenuous climbing. Three PR.
(FA R. Edwards unseconded 1988)

LE 69)
Virgin On A Crisis 100ft E6/7 6c   ☠
★★★
Lack of confidence could lead to a feeling that
an ascent could end in tragedy or is this just a
sensation of purity in a turmoil? Steep cracks
and a fierce wall topped by a very bold run-
out. Two PR, the upper peg is stacked in a
flared crack.
(FA M. Edwards, R. Edwards 1985)

Right of 'Virgin' is a very loose corner; this was
soloed, on sight, by Svetio Polacek of
Czechoslovakia in 1986 who left it un-named.
It is ☠ ⚓ and has not been repeated.

LE 70)
The Prodigal's Return 95ft Hard Very Severe
5a
(FA J. Deacon, A. Alvarez, C. Fishwick 1971)

LE 71)
Black Wednesday 95ft E5 6b   ★★★
A superb, thin crack climb. One bolt replaces
a peg used on the first ascent. Friends 1$^{1/2}$ and
2 useful.
(FA M. Edwards, R. Edwards, I. Blake 1991)

LE 72)
Strongbody (T12) 50ft Hard Very Severe 5a
(FA P. Gordon, I. Duckworth, G. Morgan 1971)

LE 75)
The Dawning (T12) 75ft E4 6a ★★

LE 76)
It's A Square World (T12) 90ft E4 6c

LE 77)
World's End (T12) 85ft E1 5a ★★★

147

World's End Promontory
Topo 12 (p149)

Approach. Refer to the map and topos six, eleven and twelve. Approach from the First & Last House and walk down the slope to a small rock outcrop. Walk slightly northwards until you are above a small promontory (this forms the southern end of Day Tripper Zawn) and scramble down to reach its top. From here either climb down the wide crack on the left (Diff) or arrange an abseil.

LE 72)
Strongbody (T11) 50ft Hard Very Severe 5a

LE 73)
Procyon 70ft Very Severe 4c
(FA I. Duckworth, A. McFarlane alt 1972)

LE 74)
Sunset Wall 85ft E3 5c ☠ ⚔
A direct start to World's End. Bold climbing. Micros useful.
(FA M. Edwards, R. Edwards 1985)

LE 75)
The Dawning (T11) 75ft E4 6a ★★
A hard, sustained lead. Micros useful.
(FA M. Edwards, R. Edwards 1984)

LE 76)
It's A Square World (T11) 90ft E4 6c R
One BR. A very tough crux. The route was initially called Means To An End.
(FA M. Crocker, M. Ward 1987)

LE 77)
World's End (T11) 85ft E1 5a R ★★★
HVS for an E1 leader, E1 for a HVS leader! A charming, impressive pitch and a leading climb of its day. There is protection after a bold start, thereafter things depend on how strong you are.
(FA J. Deacon, D. Holroyd, A. Day 1957)

LE 78)
The Outside Man 75ft E1 5b
(FA R. Edwards, M. Edwards 1984)

LE 79)
Zawn Face Route 80ft Hard Very Severe 4c ★★
A very worthwhile, enjoyable expedition offering varied climbing that is nicely exposed after an undignified and bold start.
(FA D. Holroyd, J. Deacon 1957)

LE 80)
Time Lord 100ft Hard Very Severe 5a
(FA P. Rigg, K. Marsden, N. Metcalf 1977)

Black Wednesday E5 6b, Land's End.
Climber: Mark Edwards

LE 81)
Echoes (T13) 100ft E3 5c **R** ★★
One PR. Shags have recently begun nesting on ledges.
(FA M. Edwards, R. Edwards 1985)

LE 82)
Voices (T13) 100ft E3 5b **R** ★★
Good climbing, although rock falls have changed it significantly since its first ascent. Shags have recently begun nesting on ledges.
(FA P. Littlejohn, D. Roberts 1977)

LE 84)
Edge Control (T13) 90ft E3 5c ☠

LE 86)
Nineteen Eighty Four (T13) 90ft E2 5c

LE 87)
The Maiden (T13) 90ft Hard Very Severe 4c ⊕

(FA P. Littlejohn, F. Cannings 1971)

LE 88)
Deception (T13) 90ft Very Severe 4c ⊕

Deception Zawn
(AKA Abseil Point Area)
Topo 13 (p150)

On the northern or right-hand (facing out) end of the suspension bridge leave the path and bear seawards following faint paths to reach a promontory. Descent is by abseil. Refer to topos six and thirteen.

LE 81)
Echoes (T12) 100ft E3 5c **R** ★★

LE 82)
Voices (T12) 100ft E3 5b **R** ★★

LE 83)
The Parasite 90ft E2 5b **R**

Still has a bite.
(FA J. Deacon, V. Stevenson 1959. FFA P. Littlejohn, D. Roberts 1977)

LE 84)
Edge Control (T12) 90ft E3 5c ☠ ★
There's the odd, uninspiring runner hazily beneath one on the first half of this route.
(FA R. Edwards, M. Edwards 1985)

LE 85)
Initiation 90ft E2 5b ★
(FA M. McDermott, J. Deacon 1959. After rockfall R. Edwards, M. Edwards 1979)

LE 86)
Nineteen Eighty Four (T12) 90ft E2 5c
Good crack climbing.
(FA R. Edwards, M. Edwards 1985)

LE 87)
The Maiden (T12) 90ft Hard Very Severe 4c ⊕

LE 88)
Deception (T12) 90ft Very Severe 4c ⊕
(FA M. McDermott, J. Deacon 1959)

LE 89)
Silent Shadow 90ft E5 6b
(FA R. Edwards, M. Edwards 1995)

LE 90)
Piton Route 85ft Hard Very Severe 5b
(FA J. Deacon, V. Stevenson 1959. FKFA R. Edwards solo 1994)

LE 91)
Sabre Cut 80ft Hard Very Severe 5b 💣
(FA R. Edwards, T. Dennell 1995)

LE 92)
This Year's Model Very Severe 4c 💣
(FA R. Edwards, T. Dennell 1995)

LE 93)
Old Generations 80ft Hard Very Severe 5a

(FA R. Edwards, T. Dennell 1995)

LE 94)
Motivation 80ft E2 5b ★
(FA R. Edwards, M. Edwards 1987)

LE 95)
Hidden Secret 80ft E2 5c+ ★
The bulge at the start is taken direct, the rock-over is the crux. Micros useful.
(FA R. Edwards, T. Dennell 1995)

LE 96)
Land's End Short Climb 85ft E1 5b
(FA J. Barry, D. Nicholls 1976)

LE 97)
Down The Line 80ft E2 5b
This climbs a crack, hidden on the topo, on the rounded nose of the arête starting from its right-hand side.
(FA R. Edwards, M. Edwards 1985)

LE b)
Come To My Aid 95ft E5 6a
Around the arête just past the previous route

is a slender groove leading to wall and roof. Climb up to this and traverse right to finish up a thin crack.
(FA M. Edwards, R. Edwards 1987)

The cliff area between Deception Wall and Longships Zawn has poor rock and a colony of kittiwakes. Some routes have been climbed here including the inspiringly named **Death Rattle Gulch**, XS 5a, ✠ which is for Black-church aspirants only, but not included here.

General View of Longships Zawn to Hotel Buttress
(At low tide)
Topo 14 (p151)

LE 110)
Atlantic Ocean Wall (T16) ★★★★

LE 114)
Rock Star (T17) ★

LE 115)
Rude Awakening (T17)

Topo 14
Land's End Longships Zawn and Long Climb Areas

LE 116)
Castaways (T17)

LE 117) (p156)
Land's End Long Climb ★★★

Longships Zawn
Longships Wall
Topo 15 (p152)

Refer to the map and topos fourteen and fifteen. Approach from the photographers' signpost on the north side of the Hotel. Descend the steep hillside heading rightwards (facing out) until you are above a promontory which juts out into the sea. One the south side of this is Longships Wall. Scramble easily out onto the promontory to abseil points. A descent at the end of the promontory (see topo fifteen) is also an escape route (Difficult). It is only possible to use this for one or two hours before and after low tide so you can easily be cut off. As a precaution it's best to leave an abseil rope in place down Longships Wall.

LE 98)
Pyjamarama 65ft E4 6b ★★★
A powerful crack climb.
(FA M. Edwards, R. Edwards 1986)

LE 99)
Imagination 70ft Severe 4a
(FA M. McDermott, J. Deacon 1959)

LE 100)
All's Wall That End Wall 75ft E5 6c ★★
A fine line up the middle of the wall. Side runners reduce the 'E' grade.
(FA M. Edwards, R. Edwards 1988)

LE 101)
Antenna 85ft E4 5c ★★★
A fine, sustained pitch.
(FA P. Littlejohn, I. Peters 1977)

LE 101a)
Bongo Wall (Antenna Direct Start) 85ft E4
6a ★★
Follows the natural line for Antenna. The short
may have to use levitation to help jump start
the opening moves.
(FA R. Fawcett, A.N. Other 1978)

LE 102)
Longships Wall 75ft E3 6a ★★★
One of the classics of the area. Steep, satisfying
climbing that should be enjoyed to the full by
anyone who has the ability.
*(FA J. Deacon, M. McDermott 1959. With one pt
aid E. Grindley and party 1973. FFA P. Littlejohn,
I. Peters 1977)*

LE 103)
New Editions 100ft E4 6b ★★★
Good climbing in keeping with its neighbours.
One PR.
(FA R Edwards, M. Edwards 1986)

LE 104)
Blade Runner 85ft E7 6b ★★
Stimulate the senses. This climb can be made
less 'necky' by using the peg runner in New
Editions.
(FA R. Edwards unseconded 1984)

LE 105)
Southern Belle 80ft E2 5c ★★
A route dominated by its neighbours but still
good. Climb the corner to reach the hanging
crack. Continue as depicted.
(FA S. Foster, M. Rhodes, R. Fawcett 1978)

To the right of Southern Belle is a large scar. It
is all that remains of the famous route **Yankee
Doodle** which vanished during the huge
storms of 1989/90. It now lies amongst the
large boulders at the bottom of the Zawn. Two
routes have been climbed on the freshly
uncovered rock.

LE 106)
Glory (T16) 80ft E5 6a ♁ 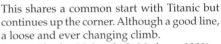 ★
Good climbing marred by poor rock in the
upper groove.
(FA M. Edwards, R. Edwards 1990

LE 106a)
Well, That's Just Dandy (T16) 80ft E3 5b ♁
A climb taking the obvious arête, but spoilt
by loose rock. Bold throughout.
(FA M. Edwards, R. Edwards 1990)

Longships Zawn
The Atlantic Ocean Wall Area Topo 16 (p154)

Approach and descend as for Longships wall.

LE 106)
Glory (T15) 80ft E5 6a ★

LE 106a)
Well, That's Just Dandy (T15) 80ft E3 5b ♁
The arête to the right has some very suspect
rock. Bold throughout.
(FA M. Edwards, R. Edwards 1990)

LE 107)
Lucinda 130ft E2 5a ♁
This shares a common start with Titanic but
continues up the corner. Although a good line,
a loose and ever changing climb.
(FA E. Cleasby, M. Lynch, R. Matheson 1981)

LE 108)
Kingdom Of The Deep 210ft E7 6b, 6b
P1) 110ft P2) 100ft
Takes a line out left from the hanging belay of
Titanic. Very serious for both leader and
second with some loose rock.
*(FA using 2 BR 1988. FFA 1989 both ascents M.
Edwards, R. Edwards)*

LE 109)
Titanic 210ft E8 6b, 6c ★★★
P1) 110ft P2) 100ft
Verticality abounds. Continually difficult wall
climbing with mind distorting exposure,
precarious moves and scant rests that have to
be fused into an integrated whole. A fall on
P2 may not result in collision with ground
zero, but could be uncomfortably close. This
theory has yet to be empirically tested
however.
*(FA M. Edwards, R. Edwards 1986. FFA M.
Edwards, R. Edwards 1994)*

Topo 16
Longships Zawn
Atlantic Ocean Wall

required; this is also useful on the final crack (two may be more reassuring). The FA utilised only pegs and efforts have been made to both provide non-corrodible bolt belays and to dispense with them. The current situation seems to be fairly stable but abseil inspection may be advisable. If thinking of re-placing belays please think tit-anium. Friends are very useful though were not available for the FA. A better start, particularly if the normal start is wet, is up the first two pitches of Astrodome.
(FA M. Edwards, R. Edwards alt 1981)

LE 111)
Astrodome 255ft
E5 3b, 5c, **6b**, 5b
⬤ ☠ ★★★
P1) 20ft P2) 95ft
P3) 85ft P4) 55ft

LE 110)
Atlantic Ocean Wall (T14) ★★★★
225ft E5 3b, 6a, 6b, 6a **R**
P1) 20ft P2) 25ft P3) 80ft P4) 100ft
A spectacular and exciting challenge and one of the finest routes found at this grade. At present the following is in place for belays. The second belay: 1 poor peg, 1 SS peg. The third belay: 2 BB (slide a rock over the heads of the bolt). On the first belay, a large Friend is

Seven ordinary peg placements were used on the FA, since removed by an unknown climber. A BB on Atlantic Ocean Wall was also used and is now a SS peg. Pegs would need replacing for a subsequent ascent, or an unprotected lead.
(FA R. Edwards, M. Edwards 1988)

LE 112)
The Great Green Wave 100ft E7 6b+ ☠ ⬤

154

This climbs the black seam right of the top pitch of Atlantic Ocean Wall finishing up the wall to avoid the vegetated groove. It is started by a traverse from about halfway down the buttress that forms the right-hand (facing in) end of Longships Zawn. One poor SS peg should be in place. This is a very serious route with friable rock in places.
(FA M. Edwards, R. Edwards 1991)

LE 113)
Hands Across The Ocean 200ft E6 6a, 6a
💣 ☠ ★★
P1) 100ft P2) 100ft
A very serious traverse for both leader and second alike. It traverses the wall at the back of the zawn, following the obvious break starting from the top of Lucinda and finish-

Topo 17
Penwith Buttress

114 115 116

ing up Atlantic Ocean Wall. On the FA two pegs on Kingdom Of The Deep were clipped and runners stacked by a loose block on Titanic. A sling was draped over a hollow spike on the Atlantic Ocean Wall pedestal before a foot traverse led into Atlantic Ocean Wall. Finish as for this "To all seconds, don't do it, or die! I wouldn't rest on any runner, far less fall on it." Steve Anson, 1989.
(FA M. Edwards, S. Anson 1989)

A small buttress protrudes from the southern end of Atlantic Ocean Wall and holds three routes: **Western Approaches**, VS; **Rap City In Blue**, V. Diff; and **Farewell To Friends**, VS all climbing obvious cracks and grooves. *(FKAs T. Dennell, P. Birchell, var 1995)* To the right again is a futuristic smooth wall marred by poor rock. After this is Penwith Buttress.

Penwith Buttress
Topo 17 (p155)

Refer to the map and topos fourteen and seventeen. This area lies between the two headlands of Hotel Buttress in the south and Longships Wall to the north. Though tidal it can be visited shortly after the tide begins to fall. It can be reached in two ways. 1) From the hotel patio walk down the steep hillside between the two headlands until a black sewage pipe can be seen (this leads to the Urinal Zawn, Ugh!). Penwith Buttress is to the north of the pipe. Abseil down from the cliff top. 2) Scramble down the north side of Hotel Buttress and make your way northwards over easy ledges until you reach the entrance of the zawn. Climb down and across boulders to the base of the wall. All routes are of excellent rock and unaffected by its unpleasant neighbour.

LE 114)
Rock Star (T14) 85ft E3 5c **R** ★
(FA R. Edwards, M. Edwards 1984)

LE 115)
Rude Awakening (T14) 85ft E2 5c
(FA R. Edwards, M. Edwards 1984)

LE 116)
Castaways (T14) 85ft Hard Very Severe 5a
(FA M. Edwards, R. Edwards 1984)

Hotel Buttress Area
See Topo 14 (p151)

A non-tidal area of rock although big swells can reach well up the cliffs. Be warned! The most worthwhile route here is Land's End Long Climb. Other routes have been put up here but nature is now regaining a foothold and these routes should probably be left alone.

Refer to the map and topo fourteen. Walk from the photographers' signpost on the south-west side of the Hotel, towards the summit rocks of Hotel Buttress. Walk down the south side of these rocks until a gap in between two large boulders with a cemented heap of rocks is reached. Go over these and down the steep rocks at the bottom, well above sea level. Traverse north (right, facing out) to

the foot of the broken buttress (this approach also leads to Penwith Buttress a further 25m on). Land's End Long Climb takes a natural line up the centre of the broken buttress. Start just to the right of the large corner which can be seen high up (this is taken by the 'Elbow Crack')

LE 117)
Land's End Long Climb (T14) ★★
225ft Very Difficult+ (or 4a) **R**
P1) 50ft P2) 25ft P3) 55ft P4) 35ft & P5) 15ft - 4a P6) 45ft - 4a
A splendid, enjoyable, varied route on good rock; a good expedition. Many finish after pitch 4 but it is worth continuing with the final two. The chimney pitch is bold, but amenable to bridging.

P1) 3c Climb short walls to reach a crack leading to a ledge below a prominent corner crack.
P2) 3c+ Climb the corner 'elbow' crack with increasing difficulty. Precarious footholds are on the left wall and medium sized Friends and hex's are useful.
P3) 3b Climb the short slab on the right (facing in), descend its back, step across a wide crack and climb a short wall to the pinnacle.
P4) 3c Move round behind the pinnacle and bridge up the gap between the pinnacle and cliff. A final hard move right and up gains a spacious ledge. It is possible to walk off from here.

The next two pitches are harder than the first four. Competence required by both leader and second.

P5) 4a Move right (facing in) and traverse around an arête (large Friend useful) and climb down to ledges leading to the other side of the gully. The gap across the gully can be jumped and is part of Marine training - at the cost of some broken legs.
P6) 4a Friends useful. Climb large blocks to gain a short, slabby seaward face. Climb this to a hard finishing move. Block belay.
(FA Royal Marines 1946)

*Virgin on a Crisis E6/7 6c, Land's End
Climber: Mark Edwards*

LE 117a)
Pinnacle Route 100ft Hard Very Severe 4b, <u>4c</u> **R**
P1) 50ft P2) 50ft

*White Eagle E4 6b, Paradise Wall,
Carn lês Boel.   Climber: Rowland Edwards*

A more direct, and harder version of the Long Climb. Start 10ft right of this below a groove. Belay as for P2 of Land's End Long Climb. Climb a rising line to the right, step around

the arête and follow flakes to the top. Finish as for the parent route.
(FA M. Edwards, F. Keegan 1985)

About 15m to the right (facing in) of Land's End Long Climb buttress is a shorter buttress with a prominent vein, or jagged spine, of quartz running up its lower wall. This provides **The Vein**, 90ft Very Difficult, which boldly climbs the 'dragon's backbone' to a belay and then the corner above. Good practice for the direct start to Terrier's Tooth.
(FA Probably Royal Marines 1940s)

Crystal Walls
Topo 18 (p157)

The rock here is mainly good but heavy seas affect this area badly and it is tidal. Approach: refer also to the map and topo fourteen. On a falling tide as for the Hotel Buttress. Once at the foot of the gully turn south and scramble over ledges until, after approx. 35m you reach the walls. The tops of the walls can also be reached by continuing the walk, down from the Hotel Buttress approach. Abseil from their tops or scramble down on its south side. The rock is very rough in places.

LE 118)
Spare Rib 80ft Very Severe 4c
A pitch has been climbed on the upper buttress but is best left undisturbed.
(FA R. Edwards, M. Edwards 1984)

LE 119)
Picador 100ft Hard Very Severe 5a
(FA R. Edwards, M. Edwards 1984)

LE 120)
Silly Old Moo 100ft Hard Very Severe 5a
(FA M. Edwards, C. Johns 1984)

LE 121)
Aberdeen Angus 95ft E1 5b ★
(FA R. Abbas, T. Mawer 1977)

LE 122)
Iron Hand 95ft E2 5c ★
(FA R. Edwards, M. Edwards 1984)

LE 123)
Desert Hawk 95ft E6 6b 💣 ★★
(FA M. Edwards unseconded 1985)

LE 124)
Birds Of Prey 95ft E2 5c ★
(FA R. Edwards, M. Edwards 1984)

LE 125)
Cactus Crack 95ft E1 5b ★
(FA M. Edwards, R. Edwards 1984)

LE 126)
Diamond Life 100ft E7 6c ☠ 💣 ★★★
A prime, serious line offering quality of rock and climbing. One PR.
(FA M. Edwards, R. Edwards 1988)

LE 127)
Crystal Fingers 100ft E3 6b 💣 ★★★
A superb climb with some committing moves. Two pegs were used on the first ascent and are still in place; they may be in poor condition.
(FA R. Edwards, M. Edwards 1984)

LE 128)
Gemstone 100ft E5 6a 💣
(FA M. Edwards unseconded 1995)

LE 129)
Dynosaurus 95ft E3 6c ☺ 💣 ★
Friends and reach useful.
(FA M. Edwards unseconded 1995)

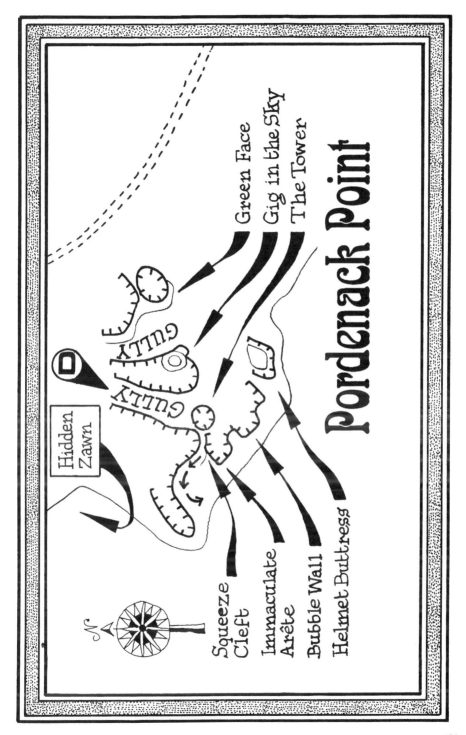

Pordenack Point

Green Face
Gig in the Sky
The Tower

Hidden Zawn

GULLY

GULLY

D

Squeeze Cleft
Immaculate Arête
Bubble Wall
Helmet Buttress

N

159

Pordenack Point

COASTGUARD IDENTITY: Pordenack Point.

NEAREST PHONE: ℂ Land's End tourist complex.

OS REFERENCE: 347 242

TIDAL? Yes, but if high seas are running, even at mid to low tide, the first pitches can be wave-washed. In high seas the starts of some second pitches can be started from the descent path.

ASPECT: Westerly.

CHARACTER: A slightly poorer relation to Chair Ladder, but with some excellent lines.

ROCK: Granite.

TYPE OF CLIMBS: Multi-pitch classic routes in the lower grades, marred by ease of escape and a little gritty rock. Harder single-pitch test-pieces on the lower tier.

PROBLEMS: Gritty rock on some pitches.

ENVIRONMENTAL CONCERNS: ❀ SSSI ❀ Please stick strictly to established tracks. The maritime heath on the headland is susceptible to damage from trampling. Please avoid any nests and areas of lichen on the upper buttress.

PARKING: Land's End car park.

APPROACH: Refer to the Land's End area map (p107). Follow the coast path south from Land's End for 10 minutes (approx.) to the first major headland. The islands shown on the map (Armed Knight and Enys Dodman) are useful landmarks.

Pordenack Point
Hidden Zawn

DESCENTS: Refer to Pordenack

1) For all main areas. Walk down the most seaward gully. Just before the bottom, where it widens, is a large tower on the right and a small gap leading to a steep narrow passageway. Follow this (breath in) to reach a path leading steeply down (some may wish to use a rope on sections of this) and traverse back left across to ledges at the start of the climbs. Again, some may wish to rope up for the traversing. It's not hard but can feel committing in places. In high seas the start of some second pitches can be started from the steep path.

2) To reach Gig In The Sky walk down the gully and bear right until beneath the tower of Helmet Ridge; the roof and perched block of Gig In The Sky is distinctive.

3) To reach Hidden Zawn walk down the north side of the headland (the other side from the descent gully) and begin scrambling right (facing out) into the small bay between Pordenack and Land's End to reach the Zawn. The Zawn cannot be seen from the approach path from Land's End.

Pordenack Point
Hidden Zawn (p160)

These routes are numbered separately from those on the main cliff. The best time to visit is during a warm dry spell in the summer on a falling tide.

HZ 1)
On The Loose 70ft Severe 4a
(FA M. Edwards solo 1993)

HZ 2)
Loose Feelings 80ft Hard Severe 4b
(FA M. Edwards solo 1983)

The next five routes all start from the other side of the zawn via a traverse.

HZ 3)
Freewheeling 100ft Very Difficult 3c ★
(FA R. Edwards, M. Edwards 1993)

HZ 4)
Smear On Sight 100ft E4 5c ◆
This is very slow drying.
(FA M. Edwards, R. Edwards 1993)

HZ 6)
Step On A Cloud 100ft E3 5c ◆
(FA R. Edwards, M. Edwards 1993)

HZ 7)
Empty City 90ft E2 5b ◆
(FA R. Edwards, M. Edwards 1993)

HZ 8)
Star Turn 90ft E3 5c ◆
(FA R. Edwards, M. Edwards 1993)

Northern Area
Topo 1 (p162))

PP 1)
Slagroom 50ft Severe 4b
To the left are some obvious grooves. Climb these.
(FKA R. Edwards, ISR Course Members 1984)

PP 2)
The Harp 50ft Very Severe 5a
FKA R. Edwards, ISR Course Members 1984)

PP 3)
Chopper Chimney 60ft Very Difficult
(FA S. Salmon and party 1977)

PP 4)
Little Trapeze 35ft Very Severe 4c
(FKA R. Edwards and party 1979)

PP 5)
Little Trapeze - Right Hand 35ft Very Difficult
(FKA R. Edwards and party 1979)

PP 6)
Exit Climb 35ft Difficult
(FKA R. Edwards and party 1979)

PP 7)
Blood On The Rocks 45ft Very Severe 5a
(FKA M. Edwards, M. Adams, J. Cooke, J. Mas 1985)

PP 8)
Halfway House 45ft Hard Severe 4b
(FKA R. Edwards and party 1979)

161

**Topo 1
Pordenack Point
Northern Area**

PP 9)
Full House 50ft Severe 4a
(FKA R. Edwards and party 1979)

PP 10)
Little Ned 60ft Very Difficult **R**
(FKA R. Edwards and party 1979)

PP 11)
Big Ned 60ft Hard Very Difficult
(FKA R. Edwards and party 1979)

PP 12)
Whisky 80ft Very Difficult
(FA A. Andrews 1940s)

PP 13)
Teetotal 80ft Severe 4a
(FKA R. Edwards and party 1979)

PP 14)
Intermediate Slab 50ft Difficult
(FKA R. Edwards and party 1979)

PP 15)
Economists' Climb (T2) Hard Very Difficult+ ★
The upper pitches.

The Main Cliff
Topo 2 (p164)

PP 15)
Economists' Climb (T1) 200ft Hard Very Difficult+ ★
P1) 70ft P2) 45ft P3) 35ft P4) 50ft
Both the first and last pitches require a steady approach and the most should be made of protection possibilities.
(FA Royal Marines 1940s)

PP 16)
A Pocketful Of Quartz 65ft Hard Very Severe 4c ✛
💣
Climbing the wall to the scoop on the left is A Pocketful Of Crystals, E3 5b. Both routes cross rock with a seemingly short half life.
(FA M. Edwards solo 1982)

PP 17)
Hiroshima Mon Amour 75ft Hard Very Severe 5b
(FA C. Parker, J. Mathews 1982)

PP 18)
Little Cracker 75ft Severe 4a
(FA R. Edwards and party 1980)

PP 19)
Nut Route 70ft Severe 4a
(FA Royal Marines 1940s)

PP 20)
Towerful 45ft Very Severe 4c
(FKA M. Edwards and party 1980)

PP 21)
Swiss Route 120ft Hard Severe 4a, 4b
P1) 60ft P2) 60ft
(FA P1 H. Grey 1956. P2 S. Westmacott, B. Seiffert 1973)

PP 22)
Vietnamerica 70ft E1 5b **R** ★
Small rocks useful and care required in handling the rock in some sections.
(FA M. Edwards, the Peplow brothers 1981. Also claimed after being cleaned by G. Gibson and party 1982)

PP 23)
Zeke's Route (T3) 65ft Hard Severe 4b+ ★★★
The first of a number of exquisitely technical climbs. Care needed with protection in the lower section; will you find all the hidden holds?
(FA J. Deacon, R. Goodier 1955)

PP 24)
King Crab Crack (T3) 70ft Very Severe 4c
(FA H. Banner, R. Wilson, J. Saunders 1961)

PP 25)
Stone Boom (T3) 105ft E2 5b, **5c** ★★★
P1) 60ft P2) 45ft
A striking line and gratifying climbing, the upper grooves particularly so. A number of small rocks useful on the second pitch
(FA R. Edwards, R. Perriment 1980)

PP 26)
Telegraph Road (T3) 50ft E3 6a ★
A direct start to Stone Boom.
(FA R. Edwards, M. Edwards 1983)

PP 27)
Biceps Wall (T3) 85ft Very Severe 5a
(FA V. Stevenson,, B. Wake 1961)

PP 28)
Sea Fury (T3) 80ft Hard Very Severe 5b ★
(FA B. Biven, T. Peck, P. Biven 1955. FKFA R. Edwards, I. Pomfret 1972)

PP 29)
Immaculate Arête (T3, T4) 115ft E4 6a
★★★

First-rate strenuous, technical climbing. The first ascent utilised a mild steel peg, later replaced with a SS bolt. Removed in favour of an artificially created Friend placement by unknown climbers.
(FA R. Edwards, M. Edwards 1981)

PP 29a)
Immaculate Arête Direct Start (T3, T4) E4 6a
(FA M. Edwards, C. Edwards 1987)

PP 30)
New Editions (T3, T4) 105ft E4 6b

The Immaculate Arête Area
Topo 3 (p166)

PP 23)
Zeke's Route (T2) 65ft Hard Severe 4b+
★★★

164

PP 24)
King Crab Crack (T2) 70ft Very Severe 4c

PP 25)
Stone Boom (T2) 105ft E2 5b, <u>5c</u> ★★★

PP 27)
Biceps Wall (T2) 85ft Very Severe 5a

PP 28)
Sea Fury (T2) 80ft Hard Very Severe 5b ★

PP 29)
Immaculate Arête (T2, T4) 115ft E4 6a
★★★

PP 29a)
Immaculate Arête Direct Start (T2) E4 6a

PP 30)
New Editions (T2, T4) 105ft E4 6b
(FA R. Edwards unseconded 1989)

Zeke's Route Hard Severe 4b, Pordenack Point. Climber: Thor Veen

Topo 3
Pordenack Point
Immaculate Arête
Area

Nothing Much
(T4) 100ft Hard
Very Severe 5a,
3c
P1) 80ft P2) 20ft
(FA D. Wiggett,
A. Smythe 1965)

PP 33)
Friends (T4)
125ft Hard Very
Severe **5a**, 4c
☺ ★
(FA M. Edwards,
S. Peplow 1981)

PP 34)
Wrist Climb
125ft
Very Difficult ★
P1) 60ft P2) 45ft
P3) 20ft
(FA R. Goodier, R.
Shepton, R. Bisley
1955)

PP 35)
Bubble Wall
(T4) 75ft
E5 6b/c ★
A direct start is
E6 6c
(FA R. Edwards,
C. Edwards 1987)

PP a)
Pop! 75ft E7 6c
Just to the right
of Bubble Wall a
poorly protec-

PP 31)
Cain (T4) 100ft E3 6a ☺ ★★★
A draining pitch up a very strong line; sucked
dry of strength, some have fallen by the
wayside on reaching easier ground. Good gear
but you use energy placing it; advanced
practice in resting.
(FA P. Littlejohn 1978)

PP 31a)
Cain Direct Start (T4) E4 6a
(FA Direct Start R. Edwards, C. Edwards 1987)
PP 32)

ted, fiercely technical line fights up a slight
depression in the wall to a vein.
(FA M. Edwards unseconded 1987)

Cain Area
Topo 4 (p167)

PP 29)
Immaculate Arête (T2, T3) 115ft E4 6a
★★★

PP 29a)
Immaculate Arête Direct Start (T2, T3) E4 6a

Topo 4
Pordenack Point
Cain Area

PP 30)
New Editions (T2, T3) 105ft E4 6b

PP 31)
Cain (T3) 100ft E3 6a ☺ ★★★

PP 31a)
Cain Direct Start (T3) E4 6a

PP 32)
Nothing Much (T3) 100ft Hard Very Severe 5a, 3c

PP 33)
Friends (T3) 125ft Hard Very Severe <u>5a</u>, 4c ☺ ★

PP 35)
Bubble Wall (T3) 75ft E5 6b/c ★

PP 36)
Ruby Nails 70ft E3 5c ★★★
(FA R. Edwards unseconded 1988)

PP 37)
Rubber Neck 70ft E3 5c
(FA R. Edwards unseconded 1988)

PP 38)
Siân (T5) 70ft Very Severe 4c
(FA C. Bartlett, A. Mahony 1972)

PP 39)
Dépêchez Vous (T5) 70ft Very Severe 5a
(FA M. Edwards and party 1985)

PP 40)
Love Drive Me Crazy (T5) 70ft Very Severe 4c
(FA M. Edwards, C. Heyl 1985)

Southern Area
Topo 5 (P168)

PP 38)
Siân (T4) 70ft Very Severe 4c

PP 39)
Dépêchez Vous (T4) 70ft Very Severe 5a

PP 40)
Love Drives Me Crazy (T4) 70ft Very Severe 4c

PP 41)
On The Loose 75ft Very Severe 4c ★
(FA R. Edwards, C. Edwards 1987)

PP 42)
Veedy 75ft Very Severe 4c ★
(FA D. Wiggett, A. Smythe 1966)

PP 43)
Helmet Ridge Direct 70ft Very Severe 4b
(FA R. Flemming, A. Mitchell 1954)

PP 44)
Sauraman 70ft Hard Severe 4b
(FA M. Springett, P. Gordon 1967)

PP 45)
Gandalf 80ft Severe 4a
(FA P. Gordon, M. Springett 1967)

PP 46)
Helmet Ridge 110ft Difficult
(FA Unknown)

168

Green Face Area

The next route is not depicted on a topo. Refer to approach description and photograph.

PP b)
Gig In The Sky 95ft E2 6a, 2b ☺ ★★
P1) 75ft P2) 20ft
Climb the short wall to the roof (climbing a crack to the side is better protected) and tackle the roof crack with boundless enthusiasm; jam or layback? Tape up, grab a large Friend and enjoy. Photogenic.
(FA M. Edwards, R. Edwards 1981)

To the right of this climb are a number of faces and buttresses on which around ten lines have been climbed, included the once aptly named **Green Face**, severe. Apart from the odd line that has been cleaned by the passage of climbers over the years these areas are very 'hairy' and probably best left undisturbed.

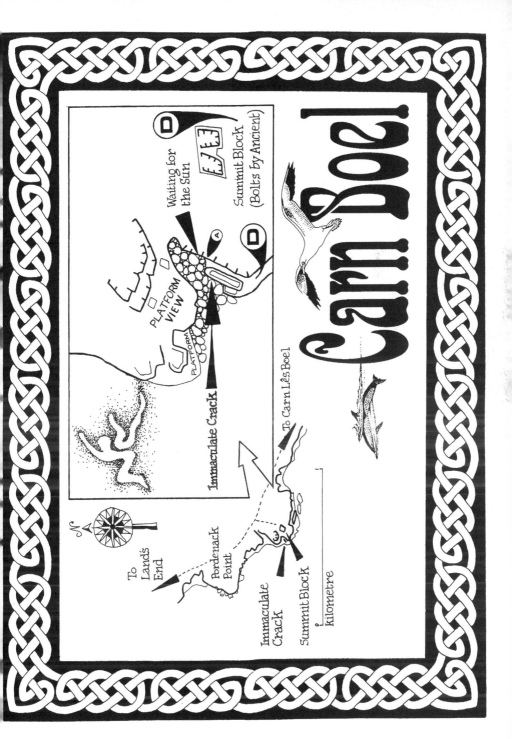

Carn Boel

Waiting for the Sun
E·E·E
Summit Block
(Bolts by Ancient)

D

D

A

PLATFORM
VIEW

PLATFORM

Immaculate Crack

To Carn Lês Boel

To Lands End

Pordenack Point

Immaculate Crack

Summit Block

kilometre

Carn Boel
Immaculate Crack Area

COASTGUARD IDENTITY: Carn Boel.

NEAREST PHONE: ℰ Land's End tourist complex.

OS REFERENCE: 349 239

TIDAL? Yes, best visited at low tides with calm seas.

ASPECT: North-westerly, best visited at low tides during afternoons and evenings.

CHARACTER: A feeling of remoteness and isolation despite being so near Land's End. Stunningly beautiful with excellent rock and climbing.

ROCK: Granite

TYPE OF CLIMBS: Quality, multi-pitch extreme routes.

PROBLEMS: The tides. In situ protection. Lightning strikes have removed blocks from the top of this cliff and may have altered these routes.

ENVIRONMENTAL CONCERNS: ❀ SSSI ❀ This headland is very, very unspoilt and should be treated very gently. Please follow the faint paths through the maritime heath rather than ploughing up and down the slopes and avoid climbing through areas of lichen, gardening, disturbing nests or leaving litter.

PARKING: In the Land's End car park.

APPROACH: Refer to the Land's End area map (p107 also p169)). It is the first major headland after Pordenack Point. Walk south from the car park towards Greeb Cottage to join the coast path. Go straight on, rather than bearing right to Pordenack Point, cross a small stream and continue walking south and then bear right to the headland. Two major rocky outcrops come into sight. The right-hand one (facing out) is Carn Sperm, the left-hand one Carn Boel. Walk to Carn Boel and drop down the left-hand side of a prominent summit block on the headland. (Some nice lines from VS to E2.) Scramble round the headland (the short walls in this area hold some pleasant pitches) to reach the platform by the starts of the routes. Once you have your bearings it should be possible to set up an abseil descent.

DESCENTS: Walk off the top of the cliff and back around to the base. Or by abseil. Refer to the map.

NB. Three SS bolts replaced mild steel pegs used on the first ascent of Total Eclipse as belays and since removed. Other routes were equipped with SS pegs which have been stripped in the belief that they were in drilled placements. This is firmly denied by the first ascenders. The text below details fixed gear used on the first ascent. Its presence should not be assumed and it may be worth taking some SS pegs, if thought necessary, in order to complete an ascent.

CBo 1)

Total Eclipse 165ft E5 5b, 6b, 5c   ★★
P1) 30ft P2) 50ft P3) 85ft
The first belay utilised one peg, the second two pegs; later replaced with SS bolts, now removed.
(FA R. Edwards, C. Gearon 1986)

CBo 2)

Waiting For The Sun 165ft E4 5b, 6b, 5b
★★

P1) 30ft P2) 85ft P3) 50ft
One PR used on the first ascent.
(FA R. Edwards, C. Gearon 1986)

CBo 3)

A Leap In The Dark 175ft E4 5b, 6a, 5b ★★
P1) 30ft P2) 85ft P3) 60ft
(FA R. Edwards, C. Gearon 1986)

po 1
arn Boel
maculate
ack Area

LOW TIDE

CBo 5)
The Immaculate Crack 115ft E2 5c, 3b
☺ ★★★
P1) 100ft P2) 15ft
Wonderfully steep, strenuous climbing. Brute strength useful. An unknown climber has traversed out from this route along the obvious break. The pendulum potential is quite good.
(FA R. Edwards, M. Edwards 1980)

CBo 6)
Spirit Of Summer 115ft E6 6b/c 💣 ★
P1) 100ft P2) 15ft
Sun, sea, sand, surf and ...rock! Climb the heavenly crack, creep up the tombstone-like wall, then bask in delight.
(FA M. Edwards, R. Edwards 1990)

CBo 4)
Walking On The Light Side 160ft E5 5b, 6b
💣 ★★
P1) 30ft P2) 130ft
No drilled pegs were placed on this route, yet all 3 pegs were subsequently removed.
(FA R. Edwards, M. Edwards 1987)

CBo 7)
Adios Kernow 115ft E4 6a
P1) 100ft P2) 15ft
And good-bye hands if you don't tape up for this gnarly crack.
(FA M. Edwards, S. Jones 1990)

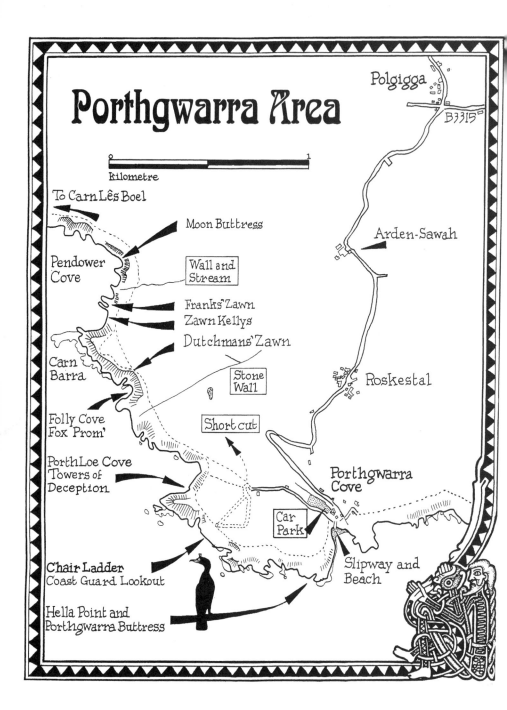

Porthgwarra Area

Polgigga

B3315

kilometre

To Carn Lês Boel

Moon Buttress

Arden-Sawah

Pendower Cove

Wall and Stream

Franks' Zawn
Zawn Kellys
Dutchmans' Zawn

Roskestal

Carn Barra

Stone Wall

Folly Cove
Fox' Prom'

Short cut

Porth Loe Cove
Towers of Deception

Porthgwarra Cove

Car Park

Chair Ladder
Coast Guard Lookout

Slipway and Beach

Hella Point and
Porthgwarra Buttress

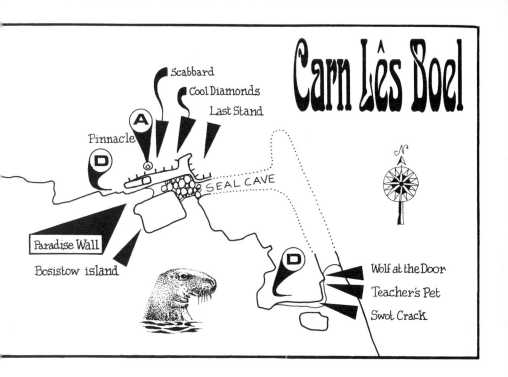

Carn Lês Boel

COASTGUARD IDENTITY: Carn Lês Boel.

NEAREST PHONE: ⊘ Porthgwarra. (Land's End is a slightly longer walk.)

OS REFERENCE: 357 232.

TIDAL? Not on Paradise Wall but the routes described start very close to the sea and can be affected by choppy seas. Look before you leap. The gap between the cliffs and island is small and can funnel waves into quite large sizes. The Badlands Area is tidal. The Seal Cave Area is the cliff to the right (facing out) of the Badlands Area, next to the prominent cave that gives the area its name, and is not wholly tidal but requires calm seas.

ASPECT: Southerly, a good sun trap in the afternoon.

CHARACTER: Paradise Wall and the Seal Cave areas are large and intimidating, and routes have an air of commitment to them. Take heart, protection is generally good, particularly with Friends. The island is for those seeking adventures unlike others in this book.

ROCK: Granite, generally excellent.

TYPE OF CLIMBS: Best known for powerful, technical lines in atmospheric position with strenuousness as a backbeat. Excalibur and The Scabbard offer a good introduction and a reason for the middle grade climber to visit.

PROBLEMS: Lower pitches affected by heavy seas. Cracks are slow drying. Environmentally sensitive due to birds, seals and vegetation. Excalibur and Paradise Wall are best visited after July 1st, but do check visually for any nests from the abseil point after this date. Bositow Island is best visited from August 1st onwards through to March 1st.

ENVIRONMENTAL CONCERNS: 🏵 SSSI 🏵 The maritime heath on the headland is susceptible to trampling. Please stick to the paths and exit climbs cleanly. Some routes regularly attract nesting birds and the island is a major nesting site for gulls. Excalibur, Scabbard, Hot Line, Cool Diamonds, Howling At The Moon, Badlands etc. are all popular nesting sites. Please refrain from climbing these in spring and early summer if birds are present. (We suggest visual pre-inspection and avoidance if necessary between March 1st and July 1st) and avoid any chicks after this. We also suggest avoiding climbing on the island between March 1st-July 1st. Seals inhabit the great cave. Please do not enter Seal Cave for any reason at all; the seals pup in autumn and cormorants nest inside it in spring.

PARKING: Porthgwarra car park.

APPROACH: Refer to maps for the Porthgwarra area (p172), Pendower Coves area (p182) and Land's End area (p107). It is a 20-minute walk from the car park. From the rear of the car park walk up the small road and at a sharp bend join the track going northwards towards Land's End. After a gentle 10 minutes' walk you'll pass a prominent ragged dry stone wall. A further five-minute walk bring you to a headland giving a majestic view of Pendower Cove. Carn Lês Boel is the headland on the northern end of this. On the approach Paradise Wall is hidden from view behind Bositow Island.

DESCENTS: For Excalibur scramble down the line, shown on the right of topo one, to reach a ledge at the start of the route. Paradise Wall: abseil down Modern Images from the pinnacle. An alternative abseil can be found down the wall itself. For Badlands etc. please avoid abseiling down the chimney to the base of the zawn; this will strip away vegetation. Avoid abseil point A2 during the nesting season as it is a popular spot. If the abseil bolt is defunct an alternative can be found, but you have to return to collect your gear.

For Seal Cave area refer to both map and topo four. Walk southwards from Paradise Wall for around 50m to a small depression in the headland and descend the slopes to the left (facing out) to skirt round to the cave entrance. Or: from the northern end of Pendower Cove by going over the top of the cave and either setting up an abseil or scrambling down.

Paradise Wall

Topo 1 (p175)

CLB 1)
Excalibur 110ft HVS 4b, 5a R 🪨 ★★★
Worth seeking out. Topo shows the second 2nd pitch. Excalibur starts at the base of the descent gully by stepping onto a wall from a ledge and traversing right and up (4b and bold but above water) to a good ledge and belay. The crux pitch climbs the corner to gain the top of the pinnacle and finishes up a short wall.
(FA J. Deacon, D. Holroyd, A. Day 1957)

The belay shown on the topo is also the start of the next two routes.

CLB 2)
Motivator 60ft E3 5c
(FA R. Edwards, M. Edwards 1984)

CLB 3)
Generator 60ft E1 5b
(FA R. Edwards, M. Edwards 1984)

CLB 4)
The Scabbard (T2) 100ft HVS 5a 🪨 ★★
Best if combined with the direct start.
(FA M. Springett, R. Hodgson 1967. FFA H. Banner, W. Hill 1967)

CLB 4a)
The Scabbard Direct Start (T2) 25ft Hard Very Severe 5a
Best reached by abseil.

CLB 5)
Modern Images (T2) 120ft E2 5c
(FA M. Edwards, R. Edwards 1982)

CLB 6)
Fantasy Crack (T2) 130ft E3 5c
(FA R. Edwards, M. Edwards 1982)

CLB 7)
Interspace (T2) 130ft E4 6a ★★★★
It may feel like outer space 'out there' on an immaculate wall.
(FA R. Edwards, M. Edwards 1982)

Topo 2
Carn Lês Boel
Paradise Wall

EASY START

Cool Diamonds E5 6b, Carn Lês Boel. Climber: Stefan Glowacz

CLB 8)
Burning Gold (T2, T3) 140ft E4 6b ★★★
The line of the wall with a good, old style, classic feel to it (and that also means hard!). This route follows the obvious deep crackline. Six BR and five PR used on first aid ascent. Climbed entirely free on the FFA; most fixed protection removed after a second free ascent by R. Edwards who also replaced one with a SS BR. Bolder if you ignore it.
(FA Unknown. FFA P. Littlejohn, C. King 1978)

CLB 8a)
Variation Start 50ft E3 6a
(FKFA R. Edwards, M. Edwards 1982)

The first pitches of the following routes can be avoided by an easy scramble to a large ledge (refer to topo) from where the upper pitches can be started. Route No 10 starts from here.

CLB 9)
White Eagle (T2) 180ft E4 6b ★★★
First of the modern wall climbs that leaves the crux to the end.
(FA R. Edwards, M. Edwards 1982)

CLB 10)
Howling At The Moon (T2, T3) 180ft E7 6b/c 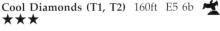 ★★★
A haunting journey. Don't stray too far from the path. Named after a triumphant cry of success. Excellent rock with a splendid roof.
(FA M. Edwards, M. Barnes 1992)

CLB 11)
Hot Line (T2, T3) 160ft E4 6b 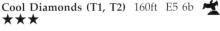 ★★
Too hot to handle? Only you know the answer.
(FA M. Edwards, R. Edwards 1982)

CLB 12)
Cool Diamonds (T2, T3) 160ft E5 6b 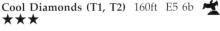 ★★★
A real gem requiring 'cool' on the final crack.
(FA R. Edwards, M. Edwards 1982)

Paradise Wall Area
Topo 2 (p176)

CLB 4)
The Scabbard (T1) 100ft HVS 5a 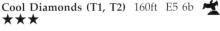 ★★

178

CLB 4a)
Direct Start (T1) 35ft HVS 5a

CLB 5)
Modern Images (T1) 120ft E2 5c

CLB 6)
Fantasy Crack (T1) 130ft E3 5c

CLB 7)
Interspace (T1) 130ft E4 6b ★★★★

CLB 8)
Burning Gold (T1, T3) 140ft E4 6b ★★★

CLB 9)
White Eagle (T1) 180ft E4 6b ★★★

CLB 10)
Howling At The Moon (T1, T3) 180ft E7 6b/c
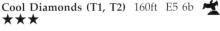 ★★★

CLB 11)
Hot Line (T1, T3) 160ft E4 6b 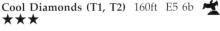 ★★

CLB 12)
Cool Diamonds (T1, T3) 160ft E5 6b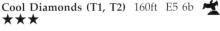
★★★

Badlands Area
Topo 3 (p179)

CLB 8)
Burning Gold (T1, T2) 140ft E4 6b ★★★

CLB 10)
Howling At The Moon (T1, T2) 180ft E7 6b/c 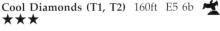 ★★★

CLB 11)
Hot Line (T1, T2) 160ft E4 6b 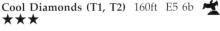 ★★

CLB 12)
Cool Diamonds (T1, T2) 160ft E5 6b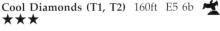
★★★

The next three routes can be reached by an abseil from an (occasional) bolt. Once the rope has been pulled through total commitment is guaranteed. A traverse into the zawn can also be made at a bold 6a+ standard, harder than

CLB 15)
Last Stand 160ft
E3 6a
Two SS BB on the
hanging belay.
*(FA M. Edwards,
R. Edwards 1982)*

Seal Cave Area
Topo 4 (p180)

This wall is left of the large cave, at the northern end of Pendower Cove. It faces north-east and catches the morning sun. Nesting birds occasionally use the area. Please check visually first and do check the ledge at the climb's start as well. Seals use the cave and breed in September and October. Cormorants nest inside the cave and it is very important that they are not disturbed. Please do not attempt to enter Seal Cave

Topo 3
Carn Lês Boel
Badlands Area

the actual routes. Abseiling down the chimney at the back could be very damaging to the top of the cliff.

CLB 13)
Badlands 160ft E1 5c
(FA M. Edwards, R. Edwards 1982)

CLB 14)
No Place For Cowboys 160ft E1 5b
(FA R. Edwards, M. Edwards 1982)

for any reason nor disturb any swimming seals.

CLB SC 1)
Top Of The Class 90ft Hard Very Severe 5a
(FA R. Edwards, M. Edwards 1983)

CLB SC 2)
Late Developer 90ft Hard Very Severe 5a
(FA R. Edwards, M. Edwards 1983)

CLB SC 3)
Swot Crack 90ft Hard Very Severe 5a
(FA M. Edwards, R. Edwards 1983)

Topo 4
Carn Lês Boel
Seal Cave Area

CLB SC 4)
Teacher's Pet 90ft E2 5b  ★★
A striking line. Gulls may nest on ledges.
(FA P. Littlejohn, A.N. Other 1979)

CLB SC 5)
Rock Citadel 150ft E4 6a ★★
Three SS pegs should be in place. Good rock throughout.
(FA R. Edwards, S. Jones 1990)

CLB SC 6)
Wolf At The Door 130ft E6 6b 🌀 ★★★★
Named after an art gallery, a stroll up this is equally as entertaining and imaginative, if on the avant-garde side of things. Five SS pegs should be in place. A Friend 2 and small TCUs are of considerable use.
(FA M. Edwards unseconded 1990)

CLB SC 7)
The Cornishman 180ft E6 6b, 6b+ 🌀
P1) 80ft P2) 100ft
A major line. Rockfall (not shown on topo), however, has removed the belay point and there has not been a subsequent ascent, some mild steel pegs were used on the first ascent and have been removed by the first ascenders. Abseil inspection advised.
(FA M. Edwards, R. Edwards 1990)

CLB SC 8)
Cerberus 80ft E6 6b/c 🔺 🌀
An alternative first pitch to The Cornishman.
(FA M. Edwards unseconded 1990)

Bositow Island

This route is not depicted on a topo

The North Face 230ft Hard Very Severe A2
🔺 ★
P1) 40ft - A1 P2) 50ft - A2 P3) 35ft -A2 P4) 110ft - A2 & HVS 5a
A great expedition giving some exciting positions and a great feeling of remoteness. The route can feel much more serious should sea conditions suddenly change. Do allow plenty of time for an ascent. On one the climbers were marooned for nine hours until the seas subsided enough to allow a retreat across the lower tyrolean. All equipment should be in place but also use rocks and Friends. First led on pegs, a later ascent replaced some of these with SS bolts. The route essentially circumnavigates the island before finishing up a crack on the north face to reach the summit. Access can be gained by a tyrolean crossing. Retreat: an old length of rope has been tied around blocks on the summits. This may need replacing. Either abseil back down to the first tyrolean used to reach the island or, before starting, tie the end of a ball of twine to the end of a rope and hurl the twine across the summit of the island. One end of the rope should be firmly anchored to the cliff top. When you get to the summit, pull the twine so bringing across the rope. Fix this to the summit and cross to the mainland. If the first person across takes over one end of a climbing rope it is now possible to arrange the ropes so they can be pulled through when the last person is safely back. This departure is advised should heavy swells be running.
(FA R. Edwards, M. Edwards, P. Rogers 1983

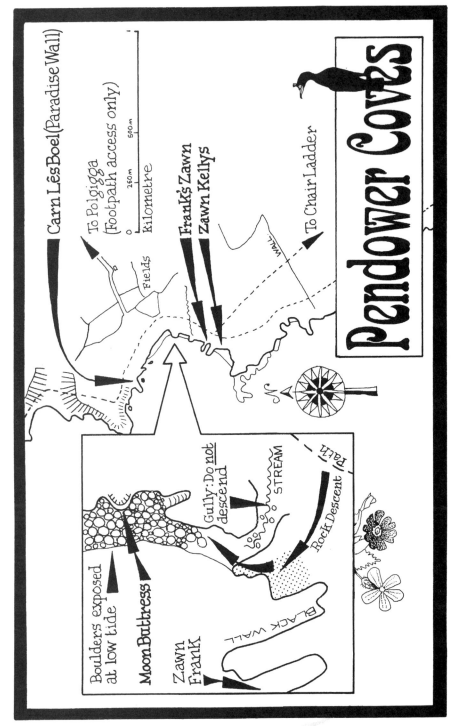

Pendower Coves

Carn Lês Boel (Paradise Wall)

To Polgigga
(Footpath access only)

Frank's Zawn
Zawn Kellys

To Chair Ladder

WALL

Fields

Kilometre

0   250m   500m

Boulders exposed
at low tide

Moon Buttress

Zawn
Frank

BLACK WALL

Gully: Do not
descend

STREAM

Rock Descent

Path

Pendower Cove

COASTGUARD IDENTITY: Pendower Coves.

NEAREST PHONE: ✆ Porthgwarra.

OS REFERENCE: 361 230.

TIDAL? Yes, best visited during low tides, when the sea isn't rough. When the sea is calm it can be approached across the boulder beach at around two hours after high tide.

ASPECT: South-westerly, a good sun trap.

CHARACTER: A large, beautiful and isolated cove. Carn Lês Boel and its Seal Cave area is just to its right (facing out). The quality of routes and rock is variable; some are marred by poor quality rock on the upper pitches, but have good first pitches.

ROCK: Granite.

TYPE OF CLIMBS: Cracks, grooves and corners. Isis is the best known, but others are entertaining.

PROBLEMS: The upper pitches of these routes and the cliff-top edge are fragile and likely to be easily eroded by the passage of climbers. Please do not abseil down the cliffs but use the described approach. SS pegs may be in place as lower-offs (refer to topos) so you can enjoy the good first pitches and avoid harming the upper pitches. Attempt to check visually first; if they're not in place we suggest that you do not climb here. The choice is yours.

ENVIRONMENTAL CONCERNS: ❀ SSSI ❀ The maritime heath on the cliff top can be damaged by trampling and the upper parts of the cliff damaged by the passage of climbers. There is potential for erosion on cliff-top edges and environmental degradation on upper pitches which are fragile. SS pegs may be in place as lower-offs. Visual confirmation advised. If not, we suggest that you do not climb here. Please refer to the topos. This is solely our suggestion. There are some nesting birds in spring and early summer. Look out for nests or chicks before you climb. Please do not attempt to enter Seal Cave and so avoid disturbing the seals; they pup in the autumn, so avoid any seals on the boulder beach in September and October. The gully is very sensitive to disturbance and contains rare plants so do not attempt to go down it but use the described approach.

PARKING: Porthgwarra car park.

APPROACH: Refer to the Porthgwarra area (p172) and Pendower Coves maps. From the rear of the car park walk up the small road and at a sharp bend join the track going northwards towards Land's End. After a gentle ten minutes' walk you'll pass a prominent ragged dry stone wall. A further five-minute walk brings you to a headland giving a majestic view of the large semi-circular cove. It is the first major cove reached after passing Carn Barra. A large rectangular cave (Seal Cave) is a prominent feature on the opposite (right-hand, facing out) side of the bay. Between the headland and Pendower Cove is another small cove on its left side (facing out). Walk past this to a wall and stream in a small valley. The descent begins here.

DESCENTS: Refer to the Pendower Coves map. At the left-hand end of Pendower Cove a stream crosses the path and disappears down a lush gully. Do not descend this. Walk down the slope left of the stream to reach a black and reddish slab that is often damp. Go easily down this to a large ledge and scramble down to the boulder beach. This can be scrambled over around the base of the buttresses.

Topo 1
Pendower Cove
Moon Buttress

placed above the roof and has since been removed. The route has been unrepeated since though Friend placements may exist in the crack below the roof. A bolt lower-off was placed at the start of the easy slabs for the same reason as that on Isis. It has also been removed. *(FA M. Edwards, R. Edwards 1987)*

PC 2)
Isis 150ft E4 6a, 4a
❀ ★★
P1) 70ft P2) 80ft
Some gritty rock in the crux crack, but good protection. The route was first climbed on sight with no in situ protection. A bolt lower-off was later placed for use on both Isis and Space Cruiser which preserved the vegetation on the easy finishing pitch. This led to a small struggle of attrition between 'purist' and 'conservationist' with at least 3 bolts now having been placed and removed by various parties. Environmental organisations are now monitoring the cove. *(FA M. Edwards, R. Edwards 1986)*

Moon Buttress
Topo 1

At the time of writing a SS peg has been placed in the centre of the buttress as a lower-off for the following routes.

PC 1)
Lunatic Owl 140ft TR 7a ❀ ●⁚ ☠
To start the wall hidden by the arête. E5 6b on FA, but many now be 7a as holds have broken off on a repeat ascent. One protection bolt was

PC 3)
Space Cruiser 150ft E3 6a, 4a ❀ ★
Good crack climbing.
P1) 70ft P2) 80ft
(FA R. Edwards, M. Edwards 1986)

Halfway Buttress
Topo 2

A SS peg has been placed in the centre of the buttress (1996) as a lower-off for the following routes.

PC 6)
Awksberg 50ft Hard Very Severe 5a ✿
Care required at the top of the crack, traverse left to the arête.
(FA R. Edwards, N. Mooney, I. Blake 1991)

PC 7)
Right Edge 50ft Very Severe 4c ✿
(FA R. Edwards, N. Mooney, I. Blake 1991)

PC 8)
Fatal Attractions 50ft Very Severe 4c ✿
(FA R. Edwards, N. Mooney, I. Blake 1991)

**Topo 2
Pendower Cove
Halfway Buttress**

PC 4)
Shadow On A Wall 160ft E3 6a, 4a ✿ ★★
P1) 110ft P2) 50ft
Even better crack climbing.
(FA R. Edwards, M. Edwards 1986

PC 5)
Time Starts Now 150ft E2 5b, 4b ✿
P1) 100ft P2) 50ft
Strenuous, overhanging crack climbing.
(FA R. Edwards, M. Edwards 1986)

PC 9)
Seal Crack 50ft Very Severe 4b+ ✿
(FA R. Edwards, N. Mooney, I. Blake 1991)

PC 10)
The Edge 50ft E3 5c ✿ ● ☠
Little protection on the upper slab.
(FA R. Edwards, N. Mooney, I. Blake 1991)

Pendower Buttress
Topo 3

A SS peg has been placed in the centre of the buttress (1996) as a lower-off for the following routes allowing you to enjoy the route and abseil back down without touching the fragile upper areas. Please look out for nesting birds first.

PC 11)
Pendower Direct Hard Very Severe 5a+ ✿
(FA R. Edwards, M. Edwards 1982

PC 12)
Time Tavern 100ft Very Severe 4c ✿
(FA R. Edwards, M. Edwards 1989)

PC 13)
Blue Kazoo 90ft Hard Very Severe 5a ✿
(FA R. Edwards, M. Edwards 1982)

PC 14)
Kooky Crack 90ft Very Severe 4c ✿
(FA R. Edwards, M. Edwards 1989)

186

PC 15)
Stackolee 100ft Hard Very Severe 3b, 4a ✿
P1) 35ft P2) 65ft
(FA V. Stevenson, P. Stevenson 1963)

PC 15a)
Direct Finish Severe 4a ✿

PC 16)
Seal Chimney 100ft Hard Severe 4b ✿
(FA M. Edwards, R. Edwards 1989)

PC 17)
Sabre Cut 100ft Very Severe 4c ✿
(FA R. Edwards, M. Edwards 1989)

PC 18)
The Cut (T4) 100ft Severe 4a ✿
(FA R. Edwards, M. Edwards 1989)

PC 19)
Demelza's Arête (T4) 100ft E2 5c ✿
(FA M. Edwards, R. Edwards 1989)

Pendower Buttress
Topo 4

PC 18)
The Cut (T4) 100ft Severe 4a ❀

PC 19)
Demelza's Arête (T4) 100ft E2 5c ❀

PC20)
Pendower Grooves 100ft Very Severe 3b, 4c, 4a ❀ ★
P1) 30ft P2) 30ft P3) 40ft
(FA V. Stevenson, A.N. Other 1963)

PC 21)
Demelza 100ft Very Severe 3b, 4c ❀
P1) 30ft P2) 70ft
(FA M. Vallance, K. Vickers 1976)

PC 22)
Dour Cracks 90ft Hard Severe 4b ❀
(FA V. Stevenson, P. Stevenson 1990)

PC 23)
Return Ticket 100ft hard Very Severe 4c ❀
(FA R. Edwards, M. Edwards 1989)

PC 24)
One Way Ticket (T4) 125ft E2 5c ❀
Some loose, pebbly rock, good protection.
(FA R. Edwards, M. Edwards 1982

Frank's Zawn & Zawn Kellys

COASTGUARD IDENTITY: Zawn Kellys.

NEAREST PHONE: ℰ Porthgwarra.

OS REFERENCE: 358 227.

TIDAL? Frank's Zawn isn't wholly tidal, but at high tide an abseil entry is required. Zawn Kellys is tidal. The base of the cliffs can be wave-swept during a low tide in rough seas; it is best visited on a falling tide. Avoid the area if the seas are rough.

ASPECT: Franks's Zawn - north-westerly. Zawn Kellys - westerly.

CHARACTER: Frank's Zawn - a steep, dark cleft with intense good climbing. Zawn Kellys - a deceptive cliff offering great adventures and a classic.

ROCK: Granite, gritty in places but generally sound. American Dream is of the sound variety.

TYPE OF CLIMBS: Technical, adventurous routes.

PROBLEMS: The sea, some gritty rock and fragile finishes on some routes.

ENVIRONMENTAL CONCERNS: ❀ SSSI ❀ The heath on the cliff top is fragile. Stick to tracks, exit climbs cleanly, take litter home and act considerately.

PARKING: Porthgwarra car park.

APPROACH: Refer to the maps for the Porthgwarra area (p172) and Pendower Coves (p182). Zawn Kellys is immediately after Carn Barra and the headland on the southern end of Pendower Cove. From the rear of the Porthgwarra car park walk up the small road. At a sharp bend join a rough track going northwards towards Land's End. After a gentle 10 minutes' walk you'll pass a prominent ragged dry stone wall. A further five minutes' walk leads to a small headland overlooking the great Pendower Cove. (A rectangular cave on the opposite side of the cove is an obvious landmark.) Here the path curves rightwards to follow the curve of the coast. Zawn Kellys lies at the base of the left-hand side of this small headland. If you carry on walking and cross a stream then you've gone too far. Frank's Zawn is to the immediate right (facing out) of Zawn Kellys.

DESCENTS: Refer to diagram and topo. Frank's Zawn - by abseil. A small through cave from Zawn Kellys also leads into Frank's Zawn. Zawn Kellys - by abseil from the boulders and small buttresses on the top. It is worth leaving this in place in case retreat is prompted by a rising tide, and they come in quite quickly. If caught out by the tide it is also possible to escape up a gully and stream that runs down the southern corner of the cliff, but you'll get your feet wet.

At high tide American Dream can be started via a traverse from a small ledge reached by an abseil.

Frank's Zawn

This is depicted by a diagram

This zawn still has good scope for new routes. Shags have recently started nesting on ledges on the first two routes. Visual inspection is easily obtained from the opposite side of the zawn. Please leave an ascent until after the nesting season if they are there.

FZ a)

Funeral For A Friend 100ft E6 6b ★★

Named in memory of Frank Harvey who was swept to his death by a wave whilst climbing near Cribba Head. His body was never found. This climbs the black groove and overhanging crack left (facing in) of the sea arch. Start up the crack just to the left of the arch until it is possible to step right into an overhanging crack, PR. Climb the crack and shallow groove to the top. Steep, well protected and in good position.

(FA M. Edwards, E. Stone 1984)

FZ b)

Farewell To Stone 100ft E5 6a R

Diamond Life E7 6c, Land's End.
Climber: Mark Edwards

Frank's Zawn

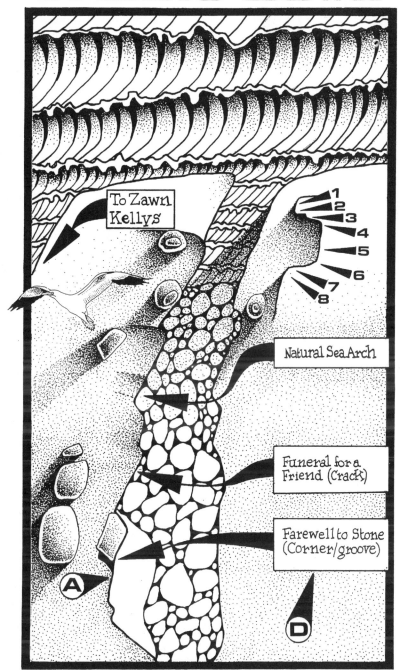

To Zawn Kellys

1
2
3
4
5
6
7
8

Natural Sea Arch

Funeral for a Friend (Crack)

Farewell to Stone (Corner/groove)

A

D

Reflections on the Sea E3 6a, Dutchman's Zawn. Climber: Richard Greaves

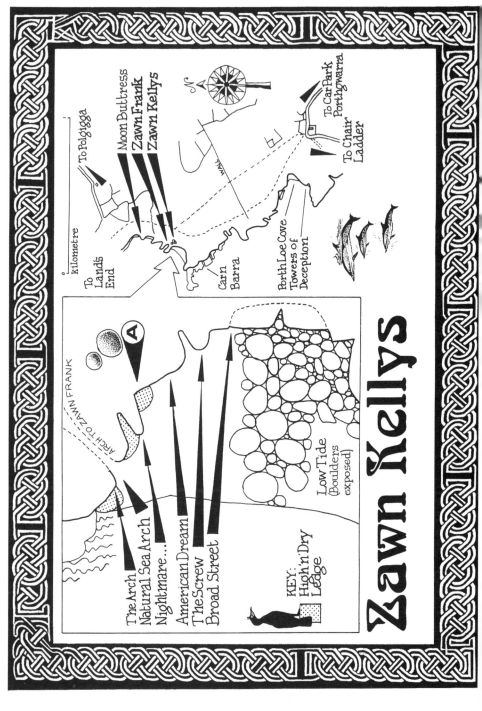

Zawn Kellys

★★★

Named in memory of Ed Stone who fell to his death whilst soloing a Welsh winter route in 1992. A fine route on steep rock. Start on the dry ledge left of the sea arch. Climb the big groove until it is possible to break left and up to a hanging groove to finish.
(FA M. Edwards and party 1993)

The northern side of the zawn has a broken area of rock near its mouth which holds a number of easier routes. Descent is by scrambling down ledges.
The most obvious feature is a small bay. On its right (facing in) is a good arête, undercut at about 20ft. Paul's One Lines climbs the left-hand side of this whilst William's Formula One climbs cracks in its right wall.
To the right of the bay is a short wall. (1) **Pick It**, E1 5b, climbs this. The arête immediately right is (2) **Lick It**, E1 5c. To the right of this is a short undercut groove which gives (3) **Roll It**, Severe 4b. Right again is a juggy red wall giving (4) **Flick It**, Moderate.

At the back is a chimney bordered on the right by a slab. The left-hand side of this gives (5) **Lil' Bitty Gritty**, Difficult. The slabby corner to the right is (6) **Lil' Bitty Groove**, Moderate.
(FAs all M. Edwards, T. Dennell, various 1995)

Two more substantial routes are on the walls either side of the arête. Both start at the base of the prow under the overhang.

7)
Paul's One Lines 50ft Very Severe 4c+ ★
Paul Williams was master of the dry one line. Climb to the overhang, pass this on the left and climb the left side of the arête to the top.
(FA M. Edwards, T. Dennell 1995)

8)
William's Formula One 50ft Very Severe 4b
Climb to the overhang and then the face to the right of the arête following breaks and a diagonal crack.
(FA M. Edwards, T. Dennell 1995)

Topo 1
Zawn Kellys

Zawn Kellys

To the left of Omega Man is a line at Difficult standard and which could be used as an escape route. **Club Route**
(FA LECC members 1979)

ZK 1)
Omega Man 80ft Hard Very Severe 5a
(FA R. Edwards, M. Edwards 1983)

ZK 2)
The Arch 80ft E1 5b ★
(FA R. Edwards, M. Edwards, M. Peplow 1980)

ZK 3)
A Nightmare Of Nightmaidens 80ft E1 5b
✛ ●

Some suspect rock, particularly in the upper section. In 1994 a route called Anglo-American Nightmare was climbed covering similar ground. The similarity in names says something about the quality of the rock.
(FA M. Edwards, P. Williams, J. Fisher 1993. AAN A. Cotton and D. Lacey)

ZK 4)
American Dream 120ft E1 5b+ ★★★
A sustained route with a big feel to it passing a number of small overhangs. A varied selection of rocks and Friends useful. Belay well back.
(FA R. Edwards, C. Bryan 1980)

ZK 4a)
High Tide Start To American Dream 125ft E1 5b

The slab to the left of American Dream has been climbed at a loose E2 5a ✛ standard.

ZK 5)
Second Skin 120ft E2 5b
(FA R. Edwards, M. Edwards 1983)

ZK 6)
The Screw 125ft E3 6a ★
(FA R. Edwards, M. Edwards 1980)

ZK 7)
Broad Street 130ft E4 6b ★★
This requires dry weather for the upper slab to dry. Good climbing past two PR.
(FA R. Edwards, M. Edwards, E. Stone 1984)

*Crack in the Sky
E1 5b,
Carn Barra.
Climber:
Mark Edwards*

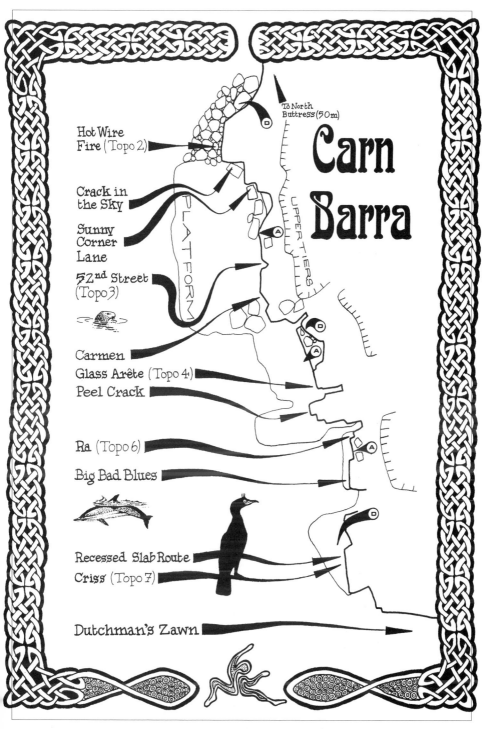

Hot Wire
Fire (Topo 2)

Crack in
the Sky

Sunny
Corner
Lane

52ⁿᵈ Street
(Topo 3)

Carmen

Glass Arête (Topo 4)

Peel Crack

Ra (Topo 6)

Big Bad Blues

Recessed Slab Route

Criss (Topo 7)

Dutchman's Zawn

To North
Buttress (50m)

Carn
Barra

PLATFORM

UPPER TIERS

Carn Barra

COASTGUARD IDENTITY: Carn Barra.

NEAREST PHONE: ✆ Porthgwarra.

OS REFERENCE: 359 226.

TIDAL? Partially - though all areas can be affected by high seas. Non-tidal areas are the Northern Platform, Glass Arête and Central Wall areas. Criss Cross face is partially tidal. Look before you abseil in.

ASPECT: South-westerly, a real sun trap on hot afternoons and evenings, a very good cliff for climbing on in winter.

CHARACTER: Popular for a range of quality routes, predominantly in the HVS - E4 range. Not much visited by those leading below this; which is a shame because there are enough routes, on Criss Cross face in particular, to warrant a visit.

ROCK: Granite, with Attitude!

TYPE OF CLIMBS: Single pitch test-pieces, up steep slabs, walls, corners and arêtes.

PROBLEMS: Affected by high seas even at low tide. Gritty rock in places, particularly on some cracks and corners. The gully traditionally used to descend to the cliff from the cliff top is starting to become worn and the tops of the climbs are becoming badly worn. This is potentially very damaging. Some remedial action such as laying stone steps and path maintenance would be welcome.

ENVIRONMENTAL CONCERNS: ❀ SSSI ❀ There is an agreement between the BMC, National Trust and English Nature that the lichenous upper buttresses should be avoided by climbers. There is some erosion of the maritime heath along the tops of climbs and at the base of the main descent gully. This guide is suggesting an alternative approach to relieve pressure on the gully; this is likely to be only a short term solution. Any remaining old pegs on routes should be eliminated by free ascents.

PARKING: A car park is at Porthgwarra Cove.

APPROACH: Refer to the maps for Porthgwarra area (p172) and Franks Zawn & Zawn Kellys (p190) and to Topo One for Folly Cove (p209). From the rear of the car park walk up the small road. At a sharp bend join a rough track going northwards towards Land's End. After a gentle ten minutes' walk you'll pass a prominent ragged dry stone wall. One hundred and fifty metres after this the coast path drops into a small depression. This is the back of Folly Cove and Fox Promontory. On the right (facing out) side of this cove drop down rightwards and follow a faint path around the hillside, passing through a small gap and under small buttresses, until it joins the base of a large gully and brings you out on top of the Central Wall area (topo six). It is also possible to descend a path down the main gully from the cliff top, but this is earthy and should be avoided. From here it is easy to follow the path over the tops of all routes and areas (map p193).

DESCENTS: By abseil. It is worth leaving the abseil rope in place. It is also possible to reach the North Buttress via a broken rock descent around the northern end.

Routes at Carn Barra are depicted from left to right as you face the cliff.

Far North Buttress
Topo 1 (p195)

(This topo is numbered separately from the other Carn Barra topos.) This cliff is tidal and best approached two hours either side of low tide. Approached from the northern platform area, this buttress lies north of the descent and is very obvious. There is some suspect rock on

some of these routes but they should clean up in time.

FNB 1)
Time Maker 50ft E1 5b
(FA R. Edwards, M. Edwards 1988)

FNB 2)
Cheap Thrills 50ft E1 5b
(FA R. Edwards, M. Edwards 1988)

FNB 3)
Hidden Gems 50ft VS 4c
(FA R. Edwards, M, Edwards 1988)

FNB 4)
Empty Spaces 50ft E2 5c
(FA M. Edwards, R. Edwards 1988)

FNB 5)
Mental Breakdown 50ft E1 5b
(FA R. Edwards, M. Edwards 1988)

Sunny Corner Lane Area
Topo 2 (p196)

CBa 1)
Raindancer 80ft E3 5c
(FA M. Edwards, M. Barnes 1992)

CBa 2)
Hot Wire Fire 80ft E7 6b/c **R** 💣
(FA M. Edwards, M. Barnes 1992)

CBa 3)
Just Another Inquisition 80ft E7 6b 💣
(FA M. Edwards, R. Southall 1992)

CBa 4)
Crack In The Sky 80ft E1 5b ★★★
Engaging, a good introduction to the Carn Barra extremes.
(FA R. Edwards, M. Edwards, C. Bryan 1980)

CBa 4a)
Crack In The Sky Direct Start 35ft E1 5c **R**
(FA R. Edwards solo 1991)

195

Topo 2 Carn Barra. Sunny Corner Lane Area

CBa 5)
Amen Corner 85ft E1 5a **R** ⚑
Climbs the obvious corner with some very poor rock in the upper part.
(FA R. Goodier, J. Deacon alt 1955)

CBa 6)
Reflection On A Mirror 90ft E5 6a ★★★
The first in a series of fine wall climbs.
(FA R. Edwards, M. Edwards 1986)

CBa 7)
Mean Street 90ft E4 6b ★★★
(FA R. Edwards, M. Edwards 1984)

CBa 8)
Psychosis 90ft E5 5c ☠ ★★★
Don't let a Freudian slip. The pegs may not be in place.
(FA M. Edwards, R. Edwards and led without pegs 1984. Claimed later that year as Arc Of A Diver by S. Boyden and P. Harrison with pegs.)

CBa 9)
Sunny Corner Lane 100ft E3 6a- ★★★
Small rocks and large Friend useful.
(FA R. Edwards, M. Edwards 1980)

CBa 10)
Crazy From The Heat 90ft E5 6a **R** ★
(FA M. Edwards, R. Edwards, R. Greaves 1985)

CBa 11)
Powerflex 100ft E4 6a ★★★
(FA M. McDermott, D. Bateman 1966. FFA R. Edwards, M. Edwards 1980)

CBa 12)
Gland Plage, Left Hand Start E4 5c ★
(FA R. Edwards, M. Edwards 1980)

CBa 13)
Scary Route 85ft E6 6b **R**
(FA M. Edwards unseconded 1988)

CBa 14)
Grand Plage 90ft E3 6a **R** ★★★

Justly popular, offering absorbing climbing.
(FA R. Edwards, M. Edwards 1980)

CBa 15)
The Consul 90ft E4 6a **R** ★
(FA R. Edwards, M. Edwards 1985)

CBa 16)
Golden Brown 90ft E3/4 6a **R** ★★
Start as for Grand Plage onto the slab, then
follow the slab rightwards.
(FA G. Gibson, P. Gibson 1982)

CBa 17)
Footless Madness (T3) 90ft E5 6b **R** 💣
★★
A tantalising line to tempt the powerful, or
foolish. A steep little number. Footwork on the
overhanging wall is optional.
*(FA M. Edwards, R. Edwards, R. Greaves 1985.
1PR removed)*

CBa 18)
Comedy Of Errors (T3) 90ft E6 6b/c 💣 ☠
(FA M. Edwards and party 1992)

CBa 19)
Geireagle Two (T3) 90ft E2 5b ★★
Small rocks useful. Easier for the tall.
(FA R. Edwards, M. Edwards 1980)

Dog Town Area
Topo 3 (p197)

CBa 17)
Footless Madness (T2) E5 6b ★★

CBa 18)
Comedy Of Errors (T2) E6 6b/c 💣 ☠

CBa 19)
Geireagle Two (T2) E2 5b ★★
Small rocks on wire useful.

CBa 20)
Big Guns E4 6a
(FA R. Edwards, M. Barnes 1992)

CBa 21)
52nd Street 80ft E2 5c

Topo 3
Carn Barra. Dog Town Area

Climb the obvious corner groove.
(FA R. Edwards, M. Edwards 1980)

CBa 22)
Marisco Striptease 80ft E1 5b
This takes an obvious diagonal line across the face starting as for 52nd Street.
(FA R. Edwards, M. Edwards 1980)

CBa 23)
At Home 80ft E5 6a **R** ★★
This climbs the lower half of the arête, moves onto Marisco Striptease and finishes up Dog Town. There are runners; look round the arête. If the arête is continued direct to the top then it continues up Pig City.
(FA N. Dixon solo)

CBa 23a)
Pig City 70ft E5 6a ★★
Reasonable protection with rocks and a Friend after At Home.
(FA M. Edwards, R. Edwards 1987)

CBa 24)
Dog Town 80ft E5 6a
(FA M. Edwards, R. Edwards 1984)

CBa 25)
Fine And Dandy 70ft Hard Very Severe 5b
(FA C. Bryan, M. & R. Edwards 1980)

CBa 26)
Silent Sleeper 70ft E2 5b ★
(FA R. Edwards, M. Edwards 1985)

CBa 27)
Carmen 70ft E5 6b **R** ★★★
Sustained, challenging and steeply inclined.
(FA M. Edwards, R. Edwards 1985)

Touch of Glass Area
Topo 4 (p199)

CBa 28)
Great Chimney 50ft Difficult
Climbs the obvious chimney to the left. It's also a possible descent.
(FA Unknown 1950s)

CBa 29)
Holiday Tripper 50ft E1 5b
(FA R. Edwards, M. Edwards, D. Allport 1985)

CBa 30)
Five Year Itch 50ft E3 6b ★
This grade is for bone dry conditions.
(FA M. Edwards unseconded 1987)

CBa 31)
Sock It To Me 50ft Hard Very Severe 5b ★
(FA M. Edwards, R. Edwards, D. Allport 1985)

CBa 32)
Socket Arête 50ft Hard Very Severe 4c **R** ★
(FA R. Edwards, M Edwards 1983)

CBa 33)**Cumbelloe** 50ft Hard Severe 4b+ **R**
(FA B. Wilkinson, A. Gallagher 1977)

CBa 34)
Socket Wall 45ft Severe 4b ★
Surprisingly tiring in its lower section. A popular descent is to abseil down this wall.
(FA R. Goodier and party 1955)

CBa 35)
Broken Hearts 50ft E3 5c
(FA M. Edwards, R. Edwards 1991)

CBa 36)
The Lurch 55ft Very Severe 4c
Gain the ledge and step left into the crack. Finish direct or rightwards.
(FA B. Wilkinson, S. Riggs, P. de Mengle 1971)

CBa 37)
Slant Crack 75ft Very Severe 4c
This follows the obvious crack and is often wet.
(FA R. Goodier, R. Shepton 1955)

CBa 38)
Smash And Grab 100ft E2 5c
This follow the diagonal quartz vein.
(FA R. Edwards, M. Edwards 1983)

CBa 39)
Eye Of The Crystal 90ft E7 6c/7a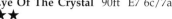
★★
A powerful and committing lower wall climbed on mono digit holds followed by

Topo 4
Carn Barra
Touch of Glass Area

technical balance climbing up the headwall.
TCUs useful.
(FA M. Edwards unseconded 1992)

CBa 40)
Touch Of Glass 90ft E4 6b **R** ★★
Fine, strenuous crack climbing with
demanding protection. One old PR.
(FA R. Edwards, M. Edwards 1983)

CBa 41)
Between The Sheets 90ft E5 6a **R** ★★
Thin, fingery climbing.
(FA M. Edwards, R. Edwards 1991)

CBa 42)
Glass Arête 90ft E3 5c **R** ★★★
Exquisite. Small Friends/TCUs useful.
(FA R. Edwards, M. Edwards 1983)

CBa 43)
Dexter's Groove 70ft Very Severe 5a
The stepped grooves to the right of Glass
Arête.
(FA R. Edwards, M. Edwards 1981)

CBa 44)
Glass Of Sweet Wine 60ft E3 5b, 6a
(FA M. Edwards, R. Edwards 1991)

CBa 45)
Sleazy Corner 50ft Very Difficult
(FA Unknown, early 1950s)

CBa 46)
Peel Crack (T6) 50ft Hard Very Difficult ★★
An excellent, if short crack climb.
(FA F. Peel, R. Flemming, R. Goodier 1955)

CBa 47)
Spring Squill Salad 50ft E5 5c ☠
(FA A. Popp, A. Mutter, N. Dixon 1987)

Razor & Central Wall Area
Topo 5 (p200)

CBa 48)
Weekend Treat 50ft Hard Severe 4b
The chimney to the left is taken by **Weekend Retreat**, Very Severe 4b **R**.
(FA S. Salmon, S. Richards 1983. Weekend Retreat. FA M. Edwards solo 1983)

CBa 49)
Razor (T6) 50ft Hard Very Severe 5a ★★
Climb the large corner then move left to the prominent crack.
(FA B. Wilkinson, C. French 1975)

CBa 50)
Sewing Machine Man (T6) E5 6a ☠ ★★
A very serious, technical arête. A fall doesn't bear thinking about.
(FA M. Saunders, P. Hayes, R. Rogers, G. Pearson 1984)

CBa 51)
Nelson's Eye 60ft Hard Very Severe 5a ★
Pleasant climbing, worth searching out.
(FA A. Newton, K. Griffith, A. Renshaw 1987)

CBa 52)
The Sigh 60ft Very Severe 5a
(FA B. Wilkinson, D. Gregson 1971)

CBa 53)
In Touch E2 5c
(FA R. Edwards, M. Edwards 1989)

CBa 54)
Last Gasp E5 6a **R**
(FA M. Edwards, R. Edwards 1989)

CBa 61)
Axis (T6) 70ft Very Severe 5a ★★
Climb the steep groove directly up centre of the wall.

Topo 6
Carn Barra
Central Wall & Ra Area

CBa 62)
Exodus (T6) 85ft Very Severe 5a
Climb Axis into the corner and to a fault line.
Traverse this rightwards to a crack. Finish up
this and the groove above.

CBa 63)
Cold Hands (T6) 70ft E3 6a
A variation on Wet Barnacle.
(FA R. Edwards, M. Edwards 1987)

CBa 64)
Wet Barnacle (T6) 70ft E3 6a ★
(FA G. Gibson and party 1982)

CBa 65)
Cruising For A Bruising (T6) 70ft E2 5c+ ★
(FA P. Rogers, K. Rogers 1984)

CBa 66)
Big Bad Blues (T6) 70ft E4 6a ★
(FA R. Edwards, M. Edwards 1987)

CBa 67)
Kicking Steps 70ft Hard Very Severe 4c **R**
(FA A. Newton, I. Clarke 1987)

Central Wall & Ra Area
Topo 6 (p201)

CBa 46)
Peel Crack (T4) 50ft Hard Very Difficult ★★

CBa 49)
Razor (T5) 50ft Hard Very Severe 5a ★★

CBa 50)
Sewing Machine Man (T5) 60ft E5 6a ★★

CBa 55)
Bottle Throttle 60ft E4 6a ★
(FA C. Nicholson, B. Wilkinson 1985)

CBa 56)
Ra 70ft Hard Very Severe 5a ★

Troublesome crack climbing. Large Friends and hex's useful. Gritty rock near the top that is cleaning up with passing trade.
(FA P. de Mengle, C. Bartlett, B. Hocken 1972)

CBa 57)
Illustrated Man 70ft E2 5c ★★★
Reassuring protection once the main crack is gained. Sustained difficulties that suffer premature termination immediately after the crux section below the top.
(FA R. Edwards, M. Edward 1979)

CBa 58)
Dialectic Left Hand Hard Very Severe 5a+ ★
(FA C. Nicholson, A. Gallagher 1979)

CBa 59)
Dialectic 70ft Hard Very Severe 5b ★
Gear has to be worked for. The crux is the first 20ft.
(FA I. Duckworth, A. McFarlane 1972. FFA R. Edwards, M. Edwards 1980)

CBa 60)
Dialectic Right hand 70ft Hard Very Severe 5b
(FA R. Edwards, M. Edward 1978)

CBa 61)
Axis (T5) 70ft Very Severe 5a ★★
Enjoyable climbing with the main difficulties in the lower section. Climb the steep groove directly up centre of the wall.
(FA A.McFarlane, I. Duckworth, B. Hocken 1972)

CBa 62)
Exodus (T5) 85ft Very Severe 5a
Start as for Axis into the corner to a fault line. Traverse this rightwards into a groove. Finish direct.
(FA R. Edwards, M. Edward 1979)

CBa 63)
Cold Hands (T5) 70ft E3 6a

CBa 64)
Wet Barnacle (T5) 70ft E3 6a ★

CBa 65)
Cruisin For A Bruisin (T5) 70ft E2 5c+ ★

CBa 66)
Big Bad Blues (T5) 70ft E4 6a ★

CBa 68)
Twisting By The Pool 90ft E3 5c ★
This start is gained at a low tide, with a very calm sea, by approaching from Criss Cross face to reach a ledge. The line is a rising traverse and only the last half of the route is show.
(FA P. Rogers, K. Rogers 1985)

Criss Cross Face Area
Topo 7 (p203)

CBa 69)
Thin Highway 80ft Hard Very Severe 5b
(FA R. Edwards and party 1979)

CBa 70)
Recessed Slab Route 80ft Very Difficult
(FA A. Imrie, R. Goodier 1952)

CBA 71)
Criss 80ft Hard Severe 4b ★
(FA R. Goodier, A. Imrie, M. Banks 1955)

CBa 72)
Iron Cross 80ft Very Severe 4c
(FA B. Wilkinson, J. Wilkinson 1975)

CBa 73)
Winged Victory 80ft E2 5b/c
(FA R. Edwards and party 1994)

CBa 74)
Niche Wall 80ft Hard Severe 4b ★
(FA R. Goodier, J. Lawton 1955)

CBa 75)
Niche Wall Variation Start Very Difficult

CBa 76)
Sea Wolf 80ft Hard Very Severe 4c R
(FKA R. Edwards, A.N. Other 1983)

CBa 77)
Air Tripper 75ft Hard Very Severe 5a
(FA R. Edwards and party 1981)

CBa 78)
Weasle 75ft Very Severe 4c ★★

No weasel words here; pure ermine. Be sure
to ferret it out.
(FA B. Wilkinson, G. Hollyman 1976)

CBa 79)
Rapido 75ft E1 5a
*(FA R. Edwards 1982 and again in 1990 after it
collapsed)*

CBa 80)
Life's Moments 70ft E3 5c
*(FA M. Edwards 1982 and again in 1990 after it
collapsed)*

Around a corner to the right is a square recess
holding three pleasant routes.

CBa a)
Sabre 70ft E1 5b
The back wall is climbed direct to a block and
finishes up and rightwards.
(FA M. Edwards 1982)

CBa b)
Sea Fox 70ft Hard Severe 4a
Climb the cracks in the right-hand corner
passing ledges and finish leftwards.
(FA D. Bateman, D. Brown, G. Morgan alt 1969)

CBa c)
Pedantics 70ft Difficult
Start below a deep chimney, climb a wall to
gain this and climb to a ledge. Climb the right-
hand wall to a groove. Finish leftwards.
(FA D. Bateman, D. Brown, G. Morgan 1969)

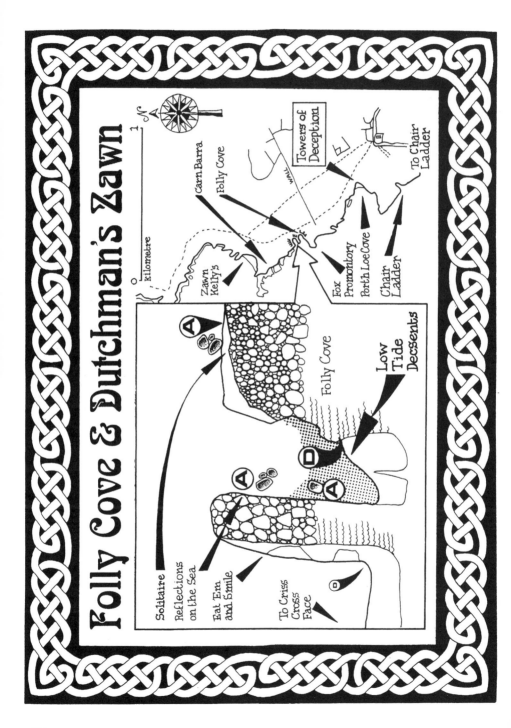

Folly Cove & Dutchman's Zawn

Dutchman's Zawn

COASTGUARD IDENTITY: Near Folly Cove.

NEAREST PHONE: ℂ Porthgwarra.

OS REFERENCE: 361 224.

TIDAL? Yes.

ASPECT: North-westerly, best visited in late afternoon. Eat 'Em And Smile catches the sun from mid morning onwards.

CHARACTER: A small zawn with adventurous routes.

ROCK: Granite.

TYPE OF CLIMBS: Bold walls and slabs, but some cracks too.

PROBLEMS: Avoid when wet after rain. Tidal.

ENVIRONMENTAL CONCERNS: ❀ SSSI ❀ Few, but the cliff-top heath is fragile. Please stick to established paths, avoid nests and exit climbs cleanly.

PARKING: At Porthgwarra car park.

APPROACH: Refer also to the Porthgwarra area map (p172). From the rear of the car park walk up the small road. At a sharp bend join a rough track, the coastal path, going northwards towards Land's End. After a gentle ten minutes' walk you'll pass a prominent ragged dry stone wall. One hundred and fifty metres after this the coast path drops into a depression. This is the rear of Folly Cove; Dutchman's Zawn is the small hidden zawn on the right-hand side (facing out) of Folly Cove.

DESCENTS: On the right-hand (facing out) side of Folly Cove is a rib. Scramble halfway down this to a large boulder then bear right to broken rock and abseil into the zawn. Refer to the topos. It can also be approached from Carn Barra's Criss Cross face, at low tide, via boulder hop and traverse.

The North Side (Photo p206)

DZ a)
Eat 'Em And Smile 130ft E6 7a
 ★★★

This route is not shown on a topo. Eat 'em or what? A steep little number; if completed award yourself scones and cream, eat 'em and smile. A direct version of a route called Eat 'Em (E6 6c) protected by 6 SS pegs. A bolt has been reported on the route but none was placed before or after the first ascent. A Friend 1 is vital in a break at 100ft and rocks 1-7 will be of use.

Start from a large boulder next to a short groove. Move off the boulder into the groove and move left across a rising horizontal break to a PR. Climb directly up the wall past PRs to a horizontal break. Dyno for a small flake and move left on poor holds until a mantelshelf gain easier ground and belays - Friends and rocks.
(FA M. Edwards, R. Edwards, I. Blake 1987)

Eat 'em and Smile, First ascent. E6 7a Dutchman's Zawn. Climber: Mark Edwards

Dutchman's Zawn

The South Side

DZ 1)
A Walk On The Dark Side 200ft E3 4b, 6a

P1) 100ft P2) 100ft
Two PR on the second pitch.
(FA R. Edwards, M. Edwards 1987)

DZ 1a)
Variation Finish 60ft E1 5b
(FA R. Edwards, M. Edwards 1987)

DZ 2)
Reflection On The Sea 200ft E3 4c, 6a
P1) 75ft P2) 95ft
The second pitch has 2 SS pegs. Belay well
back.
(FA R. Edwards, D. Body 1987)

DZ 3)
Second Time Around 170ft E3 4c, 6a
Celebrating a fiftieth birthday in some style.
(FA R. Edwards, M. Edwards 1987)

Folly Cove

COASTGUARD IDENTITY: Folly Cove.

NEAREST PHONE: ✆ Porthgwarra.

OS REFERENCE 361 224.

TIDAL? Yes. It is possible to abseil down Solitaire to boulders for a high tide start. Everything else requires a low tide.

ASPECT: South-westerly, it catches the sun from mid morning onwards.

CHARACTER: A quintessential small Cornish cove with some pleasant climbs.

ROCK: Granite, 'sugary' in places.

TYPE OF CLIMBS: Striking lines; quite bold climbs up cracks, grooves and walls.

PROBLEMS: Tides. Finding belays on the tops of climbs; a pre-placed rope is useful.

ENVIRONMENTAL CONCERNS: ❀ SSSI ❀ Few, but the cliff-top heath is fragile. Please stick to established paths, avoid nests and exit climbs cleanly. Avoid any seals encountered on the beach in autumn.

PARKING: Porthgwarra car park.

APPROACH: Also refer to the Porthgwarra area (p172) and Dutchman's Zawn/Folly Cove maps (p204). From the rear of the car park walk up the small road. At a sharp bend join a rough track going northwards towards Land's End. After a gentle ten minutes' walk you'll pass a prominent ragged dry stone wall. One hundred and fifty metres after this the coast path drops into a depression. This is the rear of Folly Cove.

DESCENTS: Refer to the topo. a) Abseil from the pinnacle at the top of Solitaire. b) A rib separates Dutchman's Zawn and Folly Cove on the right-hand (facing out) side of the cove. Scramble down the centre of the rib then bear left (facing out) to gain the boulder beach at the bottom on a falling tide.

Folly Cove
Topo 1

FC 1)
Initiation 80ft Hard Very Severe 5a
This climbs the very left edge of the wall.
(FA R. Edwards, C. Gearon 1986)

FC 2)
A Hollow Man 100ft E4 6a 💣
The blunt arête to the right of Initiation is climbed past ledges, moving rightwards in the upper part. The first ascent utilised SS pegs and a mild steel peg. A BR replaced this and has been removed, as have other pegs. Pegs would need replacing prior to an ascent, or wholly free one.
(FA R. Edwards, M. Edwards, D. Body 1987)

FC 3)
Solitaire 170ft Hard Very Severe 5a, 5a
★★
P1) 85ft P2) 85ft
A striking line and gracious climbing slightly marred by crunchy rock. This will probably clean up in time. The centre of the impressive wall is split by an obvious crack high up.
  1) Climb the centre of the wall trending leftwards to a ledge belay.
  2) The crack in the centre of the wall is followed to the top.
(FA R. Edwards, C. Gearon 1986)

To the right is an obvious crack-line.

FC 4) **Sky Highway** 160ft Hard Very Severe 4b, **5a**
P1) 40ft P2) 120ft

1) Climb the wall to a ledge.
2) Climb the crack passing a roof to reach a series of grooves leading to the top.
(FA R. Edwards, C. Gearon 1986)

FC 5)
Technicolour Dream (T2) 130ft E2 5b-
★★

Folly Cove
Topo 2

FC 5)
Technicolour Dream (T1) 130ft E2 5b-
★★

A good line that provides a fine outing.
(FA R. Edwards, M. Edwards 1986)

FC 6)
The Bush man 175ft Hard Very Severe 4a,
4c R ☀

P1) 85ft P2) 95ft
(FA R. Edwards, S. Masters 1986)

FC 7)
Hidden Glories 165ft E3 4b, 5c **R** ☀
P1) 70ft P2) 90ft
Takes the flying arête with sparse protection
(FA R. Edwards solo 1987)

FC 8)
Computer Commuter 175ft E2 5a, **5b**
P1) 50ft P2) 125ft
Climb the steep corner crack then up right to grooves in the headwall.
(FA R. Edwards, M. Edwards 1986)

FC 9)
Sun Lord 175ft E4 5b, 6a ☀ ★
P1) 50ft P2) 125ft
Climb a direct line up small grooves in the arête.
(FA R. Edwards, S. Masters 1987)

Topo 2
Folly Cove

FC 10)
The Inquisition 165ft E2 5a, **5c** 💣
P1) 50ft P2) 115ft
(FA R. Edwards, M. Edwards, S. Jones 1987)

FC 11)
Dream Machine 175ft E3 4a, 6a 💣 ★
P1) 35ft P2) 140ft
(FA R. Edwards unseconded 1987)

FC 12)
The Music Man 170ft E2 5c, 3c 💣 ★
P1) 110ft P2) 50ft
(FA R. Edwards, S. Masters, C. Gearon 1986)

FC 13)
Joy Rider 110ft E1 5b 💣 ★
(FA R. Edwards, C. Gearon 1986)

FC 14)
Folly Groove 110ft Very Severe 5a
(FA M. Edwards, R. Edwards 1981)

Fox Promontory

COASTGUARD IDENTITY Black Carn/Folly Cove.

NEAREST PHONE: Ⓒ Porthgwarra.

OS REFERENCE: 361 223.

TIDAL? Yes, for the north face.

ASPECT: North-westerly.

CHARACTER: A black sheet of solid rock, split by a great number of cracks and veins; competence required as protection can be hard earned on some climbs.

ROCK: Granite.

TYPE OF CLIMBS: Face and crack climbing following lines of weakness. Some are quite bold. The climbs can feel more serious if the rock is wet, but on a hot, dry day this is a very pleasant place to climb; a good venue for compulsive route tickers.

PROBLEMS: Tidal, slippery rock when wet.

ENVIRONMENTAL CONCERNS: ❀ SSSI ❀ Please follow established tracks. The heathland on the approach is fragile. Avoid any nesting birds or chicks.

PARKING: Porthgwarra car park.

APPROACH: Refer to the Porthgwarra area (p172) and Dutchman's Zawn & Folly Cove maps (p204). From the rear of the car park walk up the small road. At a sharp bend join a rough track going northwards towards Land's End, to join the coast path. After ten minutes' walk you'll reach a prominent ragged dry stone wall. One hundred and fifty metres after the wall, the path drops into a depression; this is the rear of Folly Cove and Fox Promontory forms the far end of the left side (facing out) of this. A good view of it is obtained from here or Criss Cross face at Carn Barra. Refer to the topo regarding gaining the abseil points.

1)   Go out onto the left-hand (facing out) headland and descend a short gully to reach a small (first) pinnacle. Pass this on its right and descend a short gully to a second pinnacle. Pass this on its left, via blocky ledges, to reach the top of the promontory and abseil points. The notch can be jumped across.

2)   Walk and scramble down the left-hand (facing out) south side of the headland. Cross a slot via the first large jammed boulder. From the boulder climb a short chimney to reach ledges. Fifty feet further along the ledges is a wide gap (notch). Climb the left arête (V. Diff.) to gain the top and abseil points. Other lines to the top, at around VS standard, can be found by climbing up the south side. At low tide it is possible to walk around the ledges at the base of the promontory, once they've been reached by abseil.

DESCENTS: To the climbs, by abseil from the top of the promontory. Refer to the topo.

The North Face

FP 1)
The Blade 60ft E3 5b ☠ ★
A sling can cunningly be used as the only runner.
(FA R. Edwards, C. Munsch, C. Baron 1986)

FP 2)
Second Blood 60ft Hard Very Severe 5b
(FA R. Edwards, C. Baron, C. Munsch 1986)

FP 3)
Foxblood 90ft Severe 4a ★
(FA B. Wilkinson, G. Hollyman 1976)

FP 4)
Droplove 110ft Severe 4b
(FA R. Edwards, A. & E. Timmer, R. Meyer 1986)

FP 5)
Tower Direct 110ft Very Severe 4c

Climb up the wall right of the central cracks of Foxblood.
(FA R. Edwards solo 1990)

FP 6)
Folly Corner 90ft Very Difficult
(FA M. Ridges, J. Lilly 1951)

FP 7)
Vixen's Crack 120ft Very Difficult
Start as for Route 6. Climb up passing ledges to a steep pillar to the right of the arête. Climb the pillar to an obvious crack. Follow this to a short slab and ledge (possible belay) then climb the pinnacle to the top.
(FA R. Edwards, C. Baron, C. Munsch 1986)

FP 9)
Tiptoe 110ft E1 5a ★
(FA R. Edwards, A. & E. Timmer, R. Meyer 1986)

FP 10)
Pilgrims 100ft Hard Very Severe 4c
(FA R. Edwards, R. Meyer, A. & E. Timmer 1986)

FP 11)
Mistaken Identity 110ft Very Severe 4c
(FA R. Edwards 1990)

FP 12)
Cuboid Corner 80ft Hard Severe 4b
There are two alternative finishes to this route, both 4b. The left-hand one climbs the thin rib on the left and finishes direct. The right-hand finish moves right at the roof, around the arête, to a niche and then follows a chimney to reach easy scrambling.
(FA R. Edwards, R. Meyer, A. & E. Timmer 1986)

FP 13)
Rough Rider 100ft Hard Severe 4b
(FA R. Edwards, R. Meyer, A. & E. Timmer 1986)

FP 14)
The Huntsman 80ft Very Severe 4c
(FA A. Gallagher, B. Wilkinson 1978)

FP 15)
Reynard's Revenge 80ft Hard Severe 4b **R**
(FA P. Vaughan, E. Herbert 1966)

FP 16)
Quest 80ft Hard Severe 4b ★
Start as for route 17 until a ledge on the left can be reached, then climb a good crack in the centre of the wall to a small roof. Surmount this to gain the top.
(FA R. Edwards, A. & E. Timmer 1986)

FP 17)
Sunshine Cracks 80ft Hard Severe 4b ★
(FA J. Deacon, A. Blackshaw 1956)

FP 18)
Dark Denizen 90ft Very Severe 4a
(FA R. Bennet, M. Dunning 1980)

FP 19)
Probe 90ft Severe 4a
(FA R. Edwards solo 1986)

FP 8)
Square Chimney 120ft Severe 4a
Start at the foot of the triangular niche below the overhang. Climb the slab, then the chimney to the roof. Pass this to gain a ledge then climb cracks in the wall to the left to finish up a slab.
(FA R. Edwards solo 1986)

FP 20)
Reveille 90ft Hard Severe 4b **R** ★★
(FA J. Deacon, A. Blackshaw 1956)

FP 21)
The Curtain Raiser 85ft Hard Very Severe 5a **R** ★★
(FA V. Stevenson, D. Bateman, D. Brown 1963)

FP 22)
Octopus 90ft E1 5a ☠
(FA P. Pasquil, G. Penketh 1968)

The Nose
This is not depicted on a topo.

The front face of the promontory is known as The Nose. Facing in, the left side of The Nose had an **Aggressive Edge** and a very good crack climb. However, like all good **Hallucinations**, they vanished in winter storms (1994). What is left leaves **Disappointment Arête** 100ft E1 5b *(FA R. Edwards solo 1994)* and **Second Class Slab** 100ft Severe 4a *(FA R. Edwards solo 1994)*. Two very good routes, however, remain.

FP 23)
The Muzzle 85ft Hard Very Severe 4c **R** ★★
Good, varied climbing. This climbs the slender slab and groove on the right-hand side (facing in) of The Nose to a sloping ledge, moves left and climbs a central crack to an overhang. Traverse left to pass this and finish up the wall to the right of the left-hand (facing in) arête. A direct start is Hard Very Severe 5b
(FA D. Blackshaw, J. Deacon alt 1956)

FP 24)
The Whisker 85ft Very Severe 4c ★
Enjoyable. This climbs the slender slab and groove on the right-hand side (facing in) of The Nose to a sloping ledge, then climbs up and rightwards slightly before moving around the arête onto a slab. Follow this to a block, gain the top of this and climb cracks in the right (facing in) side of the little arête to the top.
(FA V. Stevenson, D. Bateman, D. Brown 1963)

Magical Motions E4 6a, Porth Loe Cove. Climber: Rowland Edwards on the FA

Porth Loe Cove
The Towers of Deception

COASTGUARD IDENTITY: Porth Loe.

NEAREST PHONE: ✆ Porthgwarra.

OS REFERENCE: 364 219.

TIDAL? No, but it is best to avoid the area when seas are really rough.

ASPECT: North-westerly and a little gloomy in the morning, but it brightens up considerably when it catches the afternoon sun.

CHARACTER: Large towers with powerful lines, for adventurers who like a magical atmosphere and sea stack types of challenges.

ROCK: Granite, sound in places, very loose in others. The depicted routes are on generally good rock.

TYPE OF CLIMBS: Deceptively good, but not a place for the faint hearted. Blackchurch graduates may be interested.

PROBLEMS: The grittiness on some climbs, lack of protection on others. Refer to the text.

ENVIRONMENTAL CONCERNS: ❀ SSSI❀ The descent gully is fragile. Avoid the plants. Skirt any seals on the boulder beach in September or October.

PARKING: Porthgwarra car park.

APPROACH: Refer to the Porthgwarra area map (p172) and the Chair Ladder (p218) one. From the rear of the car park walk up the narrow road; at a sharp bend join a rough track going northwards towards Land's End. After a few minutes you'll pass a slope, leading down to the top of a small rocky cove and a prominent reed bed. The descent gully is the sandy one the stream from the reed bed takes. From Chair Ladder, it is the next cove northwards from Zawn Rinny as you walk towards Land's End. The descent gully is at the foot of the first small 'valley' reached after Chair Ladder with a large reed bed at its lowest end.

DESCENTS: To the cove: An obvious small, earthy gully (take care of plants, and yourself) leads to the boulder beach, a boulder hop leads to The Towers. **From The Towers:** Two drilled pegs provide abseil anchor points. Best to check their presence visually from the cliff top first. If you have to leave tat behind be discreet in your choice of colours.

The Towers of Deception
Topo 1

PLC 1)
Scandals 75ft (F7c) ◗⁘
Climb the roof left of the tower past 3 BR to a lower-off, all removed by first ascenders. The wall above has also been climbed. Still awaits a bolt free ascent.
(FA M. Edwards, S. Anson 1989)

PLC 2)
Magical Motions 120ft E4 6a ◗⁘ ★★★
Good climbing reminiscent of Barbarian at Tremadog.
(FA R. Edwards, M. Edwards 1989)

PLC 3)
A Broken Mirror 80ft E1 5b ◗⁘ ★
(FA R. Edwards, S. Anson, N. Mooney 1989)

PLC 3a)
Direct Finish 80ft E2 5b+ **R**
(FA R. Edwards, S. Anson, N. Mooney 1989)

PLC 4)
Two Of A Kind 85ft Very Severe 4b
(FA R. Edwards, N. Mooney 1989)

PLC 5)
Jack The Ripper 85ft E1 <u>5a</u>, 5b ◗⁘ ★★
P1) 35ft P2) 50ft

215

A spectacular route.
(FA R. Edwards, C. Baron 1989)

PLC 6)
Sweeney Todd 85ft E4 6a- **R** ★★
Bold and technical with patches of
interesting rock.
(FA R. Edwards, S. Anson 1989)

PLC 7)
Kellogg's Crack 85ft E2 5c ●⁕ ✟
Good crack climbing but rather flaky
rock.
(FA R. Edwards, M. Edwards alt 1989)

Sweeney Todd E4 6a,
Porth Loe Cove.
Climber:
Steve Anson

Topo 2
Porth Loe Cove

The Tower of Deception
Topo 2

PLC 8)
Star Touch 120ft E2 5b 💣 ★
(FA R. Edwards, S. Anson, M. Edwards 1989)

PLC 9)
The Shining 120ft E2 5c 💣 ★
(FA R. Edwards, C. Baron 1989)

PLC 10)
Into A Looking Glass 120ft E2 5c 💣 ★
Two SS Peg runners may be in place.
(FA R. Edwards, S. Anson 1989)

Chair Ladder

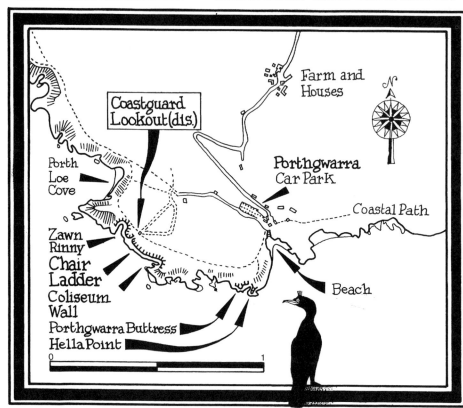

Chair Ladder

COASTGUARD IDENTITY: Gwennap Head.

NEAREST PHONE: ℓ Porthgwarra.

OS REFERENCE: 366 215.

TIDAL? Yes, the base of the whole cliff can only be gained for around two hours either side of low tide. At high tide, or during choppy seas, it is possible to abseil to the starts of the second pitches of some routes; refer to topos. During rough seas you may get wet even on these so avoid during very rough seas. With a very calm sea it is possible to start Terrier's Tooth at high tide.

ASPECT: South-westerly, the cliffs catch the afternoon and evening sun.

CHARACTER: A gentle giant offering a large number of popular climbs of great quality, predominantly in the low to intermediate grades.

Its name comes from local legends about a witch from a St. Leven coven who sat in a stone 'chair' on the cliff 'ladder' and lured ships onto the rocks below. Wrecking was practised in Cornwall and witches were doubtless a useful scapegoat. Legends about giants and witches sitting in stone 'chairs' are also attached to other cliffs in the area such as Logan Rock.

ROCK: Solid, friendly, bubbly granite.

TYPE OF CLIMBS: Multi-pitch routes with corners, slabs, chimneys and cracks a speciality.

PROBLEMS: Tidal, affected by high seas even at low tides. Difficulty in getting bearings on a first visit; even the gullies are not obvious without a little exploration. Abseil rope useful.

ENVIRONMENTAL CONCERNS: ❀ SSSI ❀ There has been erosion in gullies and there is a need to preserve lichen on upper blocks and towers. The maritime heath on the headland supports many flowers and can be damaged by trampling. Please stick to existing paths. There has been path-repair work in the Pinnacle gully, by climbers, so please use it. Please avoid nesting birds in spring and early summer; the main cliff in particular is a popular, important nesting site, but it is usually possible to 'pick and mix' pitches if it is necessary to go round them. We suggest that Pendulum Chimney is avoided between March 1st and August 1st as the number of birds nesting in it is diminishing. Please also exercise restraint by not climbing up heavily lichenous areas of rock.

PARKING: A car park is at Porthgwarra.

APPROACH: Refer also to the Porthgwarra area (p172) and the Chair Ladder maps. From Porthgwarra car park head towards the sea via a road past coastguard cottages. Follow it where this bends sharply leftwards. The eagle eyed will spot a small path leading directly up to the coastguard station. The rest will follow the road to reach the same point, directly above main cliff.

NB. At the time of writing, the coastguard station has closed and it is thought the building may be demolished.

DESCENTS: Refer also to both map and topos. For the right-hand (facing out) sections of the cliff, such as Bulging Wall (e.g. Pegasus, etc.) follow a path around the rim of Zawn Rinny (topo one) and scramble and downclimb steeply heading towards a giant jammed boulder that forms a bridge over to sea level ledges. These are accessible for about two hours either side of low tide. From here it is also possible to boulder hop and scramble along the base of the cliff to reach the Main Cliff area. For other areas an abseil rope is useful. The starts of the second pitches of South Face Direct and Pendulum Chimney can also be reached, at high tide, by a 70ft abseil down the chimney of East Chimney (route CL 38) starting from the side of Ash Can Gully. Refer to topo six. The last 30ft of Ash Can Gully can be downclimbed (Difficult+) or abseiled to reach the starts of routes on Main Cliff and Wolf and Bishop Buttresses. By descending Pinnacle gully (topo nine) and setting up an abseil on the left side (facing out) of the pinnacle, the starts of routes on Wolf Buttress, Bishop Buttress, The Pinnacle (Flannel Avenue, Terrier's Tooth etc.) and Coliseum Wall can be gained. If you abseil in for Terrier's Tooth and find the tide too rough for you to start, a good escape route is to climb a narrow ramp, starting about 5m to the right of Terrier's Tooth, to a ledge and then to climb cracks, starting from the right-hand end of this, to regain the gully. This is much better than attempting to climb the damp chimney that many abseil down.

The routes at Chair Ladder are depicted from left to right as you face the cliff.

General View
Topo 1 (p220)

Key	Z	=	Zawn Rinny
	G	=	Great Gully
	AC	=	Ash Can Gully
	D	=	Dead End Gully
	P	=	Pinnacle Gully
	HW	=	High Water
	LW	=	Low Water

CL 7)
Overhanging Chimney (T4) Very Severe 4c

CL 9)
Seal Slab (T3) Very Severe 4c

CL 12)
Pegasus (T4) Hard Severe 4c

Topo 1
Chair Ladder General view

MAIN CLIFF

BULGING WALL

ZAWN RINNY APPROACH

LW

CL 24)
The Red Tower (T5, T6) E4 6a

CL 32)
Pendulum Chimney (T7) Severe 4b

CL 43)
Original Route (T6, T7) Very Difficult

CL 47)
Corporal's Route (T8) Hard Severe 4b

CL 48)
Aerial (T8) Very Severe 4c

CL 50)
Caliban (T8) E4 6b

CL 51)
The Tempest (T8) E5 6b

CL 52)
Rats In A Rage (T8) E6 7a

CL 55)
Flannel Avenue (T8, T9) Severe 4b

CL 57)
Diocese (T8, T9) Hard Very Severe 5a

CL 63)
Bishop's Rib (T9) 195ft E1 **5b**

Amazonia E7 6c, Sennen.
Climber: Mark Edwards

Silver Shadow E3 5c, Carn Vellan. Climber: Mike Barnes
Rich Pickings E4 6a, Carn Vellan. Climber: Rowland Edwards

WOLF BUTTRESS   BISHOP BUTTRESS   White Slab

THE PINNACLE

CL 70)
Terrier's Tooth With A Direct Start (T9, T10)
Hard Severe 4a

CL 70a)
Terrier's Tooth (T9, T10) Very Difficult 3c+

Zawn Rinny
Topo 2 (p222)

CL 1)
The Naked Edge 175ft E5 5a, 6a, 6b ★★★
P1) 50ft P2) 65ft P3) 60ft
Dynamic movement in atmospheric position.
Two stainless steel pegs on the top pitch. A
bolt belay replaces mild steel pegs.
(FA R. Edwards, I. Blake 1987)

CL 2)
The Groove 175ft E2 4b, 5c
P1) 90ft P2) 85ft
Harder when wet. To exit the climb follow the
line shown. A pre-placed rope useful for belay.
(FA R. Edwards, F. Smith 1976)

CL 3)
Aquiline 160ft E1 5a **R**
P1) 50ft P2) 110ft
(FA R. Edwards, F. Smith 1976)

CL 4)
Rinny Wall 170ft Hard Very Severe 4b, 5a **R**
P1) 50ft P2) 120ft
(FA R. Edwards, F. Smith 1976)

Topo 2
Zawn Rinny

P1) 65ft P2) 65ft P3) 40ft
(FA M. Edwards, R. Edwards 1984)

CL 5a)
Direct Finish (T4)
40ft Hard Severe 4b+
(FA R. Edwards and party 1979)

CL 6)
The Gingerbread Crack 165ft E2 5c, 4b, 3c
P1) 75ft P2) 80ft P3) 15ft
(FA R. Edwards, M. Edwards 1981)

CL 8)
Kittiwake (T4)
160ft Very Severe 4c, 3b, 3b ★★
P1) 100ft P2) 60ft
(FA M. Springett, J. Cooke 1968)

CL 9)
Seal Slab (T1)
180ft Very Severe 4c, 4b, 3b ★★
P1) 75ft P2) 75ft P3) 30ft
(FA G. Smith, J. Deacon alt 1955)

CL 11)
Watch Hunt (T4) 60ft Very Severe 4c **R**
This finishes at the belay of CL 13. Continue as for Seal Slab, CL 9.
(FA M. Edwards and party 1985)

CL 13)
West Face Direct (T4) ★★★
210ft E2 5c, 5b+, 5a, 4c **R**
P1) 60ft P2) 35ft P3) 75ft P4) 40ft
A little contrived, but very worthwhile and varied.
(FA R. Edwards, M. Edwards, alt. A. Shearder 1980)

Bulging Wall
First View Topo 3 (p224)

The best way up Bulging Wall for a HVS leader is to climb the initial crack of Pegasus to the roof and belay. Move left and continue up the corner of Seal Slab then finish up the last two pitches of West Face Direct (the third pitch of this combination is quite bold.)

CL 5)
Maureen (T4) 170ft Hard Severe 3b, 4b, 4a

Naked Edge E5 6b, Chair Ladder. Climber: Rowland Edwards

CL 13a)
Variation Finish
Hard Very Severe
5a
P3) Not depicted
on a topo. From
the ledge at the
base of the Peg-
asus slab climb
the steep crack on
the left.

CL 14)
**Rake's Progress
(T4)** 210ft Very
Difficult ★★
P1) 60ft P2) 30ft
P3) 70ft P4) 50ft
The first pitch is
the crux. Care
required to pro-
tect the second.
*(FA R. Handley, V.
Phillips, J. Hallam
1952)*

CL 15)
**Altered Images
(T4)** 190ft E1 **5b**,
4b, 4c, 3b **R**
P1) 50ft P2) 50ft
P3) 70ft P4) 20ft
*(FA R. Edwards,
M. Edwards alt
1983)*

CL 16)
Kaleidoscope
220ft Very Severe
4c, 4b, 4b, 4b, 4a **R** ★
P1) 45ft P2) 40ft P3) 40ft P4) 40ft P5) 55ft
Finish as for CL 13, West Face Direct.
(FA V. Stevenson, R. Todd 1961)

CL 17)
Medusa (T4) 170ft Very Severe 4b, 4b, 4b
P1) 50ft P2) 90ft P3) 30ft
(FA R. Edwards and party 1984)

**Topo 3
Bulging Wall
View One**

Bulging Wall
Second View Topo 4 (p225)

CL 5)
Maureen (T3) 170ft Hard Severe 3b, 4b, 4a

CL 5a)
Direct Finish (T3) 40ft Hard Severe 4b+

CL 7)
Overhanging Chimney (T1) 160ft Very
Severe 4c+, 3b, 3b

opo 4
ulging Wall
econd View

(line indicated by arrows) following slabs and chimneys to the top. Or continue as for Rake's Progress: CL 14, T3.
(FA J. Littlewood 1930s)

CL 11)
Watch Hunt (T3) 60ft Very Severe 4c **R**
This is a single pitch. Continue as for Seal Slab: CL 9, T3.
(FA M. Edwards 1985)

CL 12)
Pegasus (T1)
★★★
195ft Hard Severe 4b+, 4a, 4c (or 4a)
P1) 80ft P2) 70ft P3) 45ft
Enchanting. Good ropework required. Don't get too 'involved' in the initial crack which leads up to a small roof; pass this direct via a notch. The second pitch includes a short corner crack (hidden on the topo, shown by **?**) which leads to the slab. The start of the final pitch is a short hand traverse followed by a mantelshelf into a small scoop. (This can also be done as a foot traverse, which is easier.) Finish left and then up.
(FA P1 R. Handley, E. Phillips 1952. P2 & 3 J. Deacon 1955)

P1) 80ft P2) 60ft P3) 20ft
(FA J. Deacon 1955)

CL 8)
Kittiwake (T3) 160ft Very Severe 4c, 3b, 3b
★★

CL 10)
Great Slab Route 180ft Difficult+
The second belay shown (?) may help avoid rope-drag. Climb a short groove to the ledge. At the second belay climb up and leftwards

CL 13)
West Face Direct (T3) ★★★
210ft E2 5c+, 5b+, 5a, 4c **R**

225

Topo 5
Main Cliff
View One

GREAT
GULLY

CL 14)
Rake's progress (T3) 210ft Very Difficult
★★

226

CL 15)
Altered Images (T3) 190ft E1 **5b**, 4b, 4c, 3b **R**

CL 17)
Medusa (T3) 170ft Very Severe 4b, 4b, 4b

⤫ Main Cliff ⤫
View One Topo 5 (p226)

To get off the top of Main Cliff (which is a tower slightly detached from the cliff tops) move to the right-hand side (facing in), scramble to the rear and downclimb onto the large boulder at the back. It is worth top-roping novices down this as there is big fall potential into Ash Can Gully to the side. A scramble leads to the cliff top.

A popular nesting area, it is usually possible to climb around nests. Please make the effort to do so even if you have to pick and mix pitches.

CL 18)
Western Arête 160ft Hard Severe 2a, 2a, 4c, 4a
P1) 25ft P2) 25ft P3) 55ft P4) 60ft
To finish follow the arête.
(FA H. Banner, D. Bateman 1966)

CL 19)
The Great Western Arête 245ft Hard Very Severe 5b, 4a, 5a, 4a
P1) 20ft P2) 45ft P3) 70ft P4) 110ft
Climb the arête to the top; escape rightwards to descend from the back of the tower. On P4 traverse left into Great Gully and climb a steep, bubbly crack on the right side of the wall.
(FA R. Edwards, M. Edwards 1984)

CL 20)
Western Chimneys 160ft Difficult ★
A fairly obvious line. Think of the name. Finish as for Western Arête, CL 18.
P1) 30ft P2) 60ft P3) 40ft P4) 30ft
(FA W. Andrews climbed down them, J. Littlewood up them, both in 1910. No one knows which was first, both should share the honours)

CL 21)
The Thin Red Line (T6, T7) 150ft E2 5c, 3b
Finish as for Western Arête, CL 18.
P1) 80ft P2) 70ft
(FA M. Edwards, R. Edwards 1984)

CL 22)
Beaujolais 150ft E1 5b, 4c
Beaujolais and Scarlet Pimpernel cross at half height.

P1) 80ft P2) 70ft
(FA M. Edwards, R. Edwards 1984)

CL 23)
Scarlet Pimpernel (T6, T7) 165ft E3 5c, 4c
P1) 110ft P2) 55ft
(FA R. Edwards, M. Edwards 1984)

CL 24)
The Red Tower (T1, T6) 200ft E4 6a, 4c ★
P1) 50ft P2) 52ft P3) as for Scarlet Pimpernel
P1) 50ft scramble up large blocks to reach the start.
(FA P. Livesey, A. Evens 1976)

CL 28)
Central Buttress Chimneys (T6) 210ft Very Difficult R ★
P1) 60ft P2) 50ft P3) 30ft P4) 70ft
Start up the back of the hidden, steep, deep cleft to a ledge. A good second pitch follows the line of chimneys up to the right.
(FA L. Powell and party 1935)

CL 29)
Halfway House (T7) 60ft Very Severe 4c
A direct start to Excelsior, CL 30.
(FA R. Edwards solo 1987)

CL 30)
Excelsior (T6) 200ft E1 5a, 2a, 5a, **5b** R ★★★
P1) 50ft P2) 50ft P3) 30ft P4) 30ft
Tenacity and Friends very useful.
(FA V. Stevenson, J. Deacon 1959. Top pitch V. Stevenson, B. Wake 1961)

CL 30a)
Excelsior Variation Start (T6) Severe 4a.
Climb the short groove (hidden on topo).

CL 31)
The Shadows (T6) 175ft Very Severe 3a, 4b, 4a, 4b, 5a
P1) 20ft P2) 20ft P3) 40ft P4) 40ft P5) 55ft
(FA R. Edwards, M. Edwards 1983)

CL 38)
East Chimney (T6, T7) 120ft Difficult R

 Main Cliff

View Two Topo 6

The abseil point shown can be used to reach the starts of the second pitches of South Face Direct, Pendulum Chimney and Detergent Wall at high tide.

CL 21)
The Thin Red Line (T5, T7) 150ft E2 5c, 3b
A single pitch. Continue as for Western Arête: CL 18 (T5)

CL 23)
Scarlet Pimpernel (T5, T7) 165ft E3 5c, 4c, 4a

CL 24)
The Red Tower (T1, T5) 200ft E4 4b, 6a, 4c ★

CL 26)
Centre Piece 90ft E2 5c ★
Finish as for Scarlet Pimpernel - 4a. CL 23.
(FA R. Edwards, M. Edwards 1984)

CL 28)
Central Buttress Chimneys (T5) 210ft Very Difficult **R** ★
The start and final pitches.

CL 30)
Excelsior (T5) 200ft E1 5a, 2a, 5a, **5b** **R**
★★★

CL 30a)
Excelsior Variation Start (T6) Severe 4a
Climb the short groove.

CL 31)
The Shadows (T5) 175ft Very Severe 3a, 4b, 4a, 4b, 5a

CL 34)
Detergent Wall ☠ ★★
150ft Hard Very Severe 4b, 4c, **4c**+, 4a
P1) 50ft P2) 50ft P3) 35ft P4) 30ft
(FA J. Deacon, V. Stevenson 1959. Direct Finish V. Stevenson 1961)

CL 35)
South Face Direct ★★★★

170ft Very Severe 4a, 4c, 4c, 4a
P1) 35ft P2) 60ft P3) 45ft P4) 30ft
Good, tough, varied climbing. A joy to those who are competent at this grade.
(FA J. Courtlandt-Simpson, E. Stones 1948)

CL 38)
East Chimney (T5, T7) 120ft Difficult
P1) 30ft P2) 90ft
Start as for Cleft Route (CL 37, T7). Climb the wide chimney to the top.
(FA J. Littlewood 1930s)

CL 39)
South East Face Direct (T7) 50ft Hard Very Severe 5a
A single pitch.
(FA P. Littlejohn solo 1968)

CL 40)
Love 30 50ft E1 5a **R**
A single pitch.
(FA G. Gibson solo 1982)

CL 42)
Dexter Crack 100ft Severe 4a, 3c
P1) 40ft P2) 60ft
(FA L. Powell 1937)

CL 43)
Original Route (T1, T7) 80ft Very Difficult
To the right of Dexter Crack is a slab and crack leading to a ledge. Move left and stride over the gap. Continue as depicted.
(FA C. Kirkus and party 1938)

CL 44)
Nearly 100ft Hard Very Severe 4c, **5a** ★★
P1) 70ft P2) 30ft
This starts from Ash Can Gully. A wonderful, steep climb that anywhere else would be a classic trade route. Only the start is shown on the topo. On the left side of the tower is a prominent crack, climb this to a ledge and belay. Move right (facing in) and gain a crack, climb this to the top.
(FA J. M. Edwards, N. Morin, N. Albon 1953. P2 M. McDermott, D. Bateman 1962)

ASH
CAN
GULLY

🦅 Main Cliff 🦅

View Three Topo 7 (p230)

The abseil point shown, halfway down Ash
Can Gully, can be used to reach the starts of
the second pitches of South Face Direct,
Pendulum Chimney and Detergent Wall at
high tide.

*Red Wall Severe 4b, Chair Ladder.
Climber: Jeroen Bolluyt*

CL 21)
The Thin Red Line (T5, T6) 150ft
E2 5c, 3b
A single pitch. Continue as for
Western Arête (CL 18, T5).

CL 23)
Scarlet Pimpernel (T5, T6) 165ft
E3 5c, 4c

CL 25)
Red Wall 200ft Severe 2a, 4a, 4b,
4a ★★
*(FA J. Courtlandt-Simpson, E. Stones
1947)*

CL 27)
Central Route 135ft Hard Very
Severe 5b ★
P1) 75ft P2) 60ft
Finish as for Southern Arête (CL 36,
T6, T7) or the easiest line.
(FA P. Cullinan, A. Blackshaw 1959)

CL 29)
Halfway House (T5) 60ft Very Severe 4c

CL 32)
Pendulum Chimney (T1) R 🦅 ★★★
165ft Severe 4a, 4a, 4a, 4b, 4a
P1) 25ft P2) 40ft P3) 40ft P4) 40ft P5) 20ft
Energetic, varied climbing. Avoid during
spring and early summer nesting. The
pendulum referred to a chockstone, long gone,
which could be made to rock to and fro inside
the chimney.
*(FA P4 J. Littlewood 1930s. Lower pitches J.C.
Simpson, E. Stones 1947)*

CL 32a)
Pendulum Chimney Variation Start 30ft
Severe 4a

CL 33)
Digit Do It On Sight? 195ft E5 **6b/6c**, 5a, 6a,
5c 🌑 ★★★
P1) 40ft P2) 40ft P3) 80ft P4) 35ft
(FA M. Edwards, S. Rourke 1993)

CL 36)
Southern Arête 175ft E4 6a, 5a, 4c
P1) 40ft P2) 60ft P3) 75ft
(FA R. Edwards, C. Edwards 1985)

CL 37)
Cleft Route 180ft Difficult
A diagonal ramble across the main face. Start
from the sea ledges, as for South Face Direct.
Climb the chimney for 35ft and move left to a
ledge belay. Go left along ledges and up to a
ledge beside a pinnacle. Belay. Climb up
behind the pinnacle and squirm through the
cleft to a ledge and belay. Traverse left to
another ledge, climb a corner and go left along
a ledge to reach a crack running up the face.
Exit rightwards to descend from the back of
the tower.
(FA J. Littlewood 1930s)

CL 38)
East Chimney (T5, T6) 120ft Difficult **R**

CL 39)
South East Face Direct (T6) 50ft Hard Very Severe 5a

CL 41)
The Buccaneer 100ft Very Severe 4c, 4b ★
P1) 40ft P2) 60ft
(FA J. Deacon, J. Oakes 1956. P1 M. McDermott and party 1963)

CL 43)
Original Route (T1, T6) 80ft Very Difficult
(FA C. Kirkus and party 1938)

Wolf and Bishop Buttress
Topo 8 (p233)

CL 45)
Wolverine Chimney 180ft Very Difficult
P1) 35ft P2) 80ft P3) 25ft P4) 40ft
(FA Royal Marines 1946)

CL 46)
Giant Steps 210ft Severe 4a, 3c, 3c, 4a, 3c
P1) 35ft P2) 70ft P3) 40ft P4) 65ft
(FA M. Banks, J. Flint 1949)

CL 47)
Corporal's Route (T1) 175ft Hard Severe 4b, 3c, 4b, 4a ★
P1) 45ft P2) 50ft P3) 40ft P4) 40ft
(FA J. Deacon, M. Banks alt 1955)

CL 48)
Aerial (T1) 220ft Very Severe 4b, 4c, 4c, 3b ★
P1) 35ft P2) 65ft P3) 55ft P4) 65ft
(FA T. Peck, P. Biven 1956)

CL 49)
Animated Wall 70ft E5 6a **R** ★★
Small wires and micros useful. A single pitch.
(FA R. Edwards, M. Edwards 1987)

CL 50)
Caliban (T1) 50ft E4 6b ★★
A single pitch. Two PR.
(FA R. Abbas, N. Cotton 1975. FFA L. McGinley 1981)

CL 51)
The Tempest (T1) 70ft E5 6b ☀ ★★
A single pitch. Two PR.
(FA R. Edwards, M. Edwards 1987)

CL 52)
Rats In A Rage (T1) 50ft E6 7a ★
Fierce and livid, technical with controlled power. One BR (removed) replaced RURPS. Awaits an in situ protection free ascent.
(FA M. Edwards FFA M. Edwards 1996)

CL 53)
Laceration (T9) 185ft Hard Very Severe 5a, 4a, 4a, 4a
P1) 30ft P2) 65ft P3) 65ft P4) 25ft
(FA T. Peck, P. Biven 1956)

CL 55)
Flannel Avenue (T1, T9) ★★★★
185ft Severe 4b, 3c, 4a+, 4b
P1) 60ft P2) 30ft P3) 70ft P4) 25ft
Good varied climbing with enthralling exposure on the wall, above the roof of Diocese. The depicted start is the first pitch of Mine Climb which offers nicer climbing at the same grade; purists will insist on climbing the chimney before gaining the belay.
(FA Royal Marines 1949)

CL 57)
Diocese (T1, T9) ★★★
200ft Hard Very Severe 5a, 5a, 4a, 4b
P1) 65ft P2) 40ft P3) 70ft P4) 25ft
Interesting climbing on excellent rock and in good position combine to produce pure primal enjoyment. Large Friend useful, and smallish rocks! The traverse can be accomplished either as a foot traverse or by using the roof crack.
(FA M. Ridges, G. Lilly alt 1951)

CL 61)
The Steeple (T10) 170ft E3 5c, 4c **R** ★★
Stimulates the senses.
P1) 130ft P2) 70ft
(FA P. Livesey, A. Evans 1976)

Topo 8
Wolf and
Bishop Buttress

Topo 9
Bishop Buttress and
The Pinnacle
View One

PINNACLE GULLY

WHITE SLAB

Bishop Buttress and The Pinnacle
View One Topo 9 (p234)

CL 53)
Laceration (T8) 185ft Hard Very Severe 5a, 4a, 4a, 4a

CL 54)
Face Marks (T10) 70ft E4 6b ●⁑
This climbs the face and crack just right of Laceration to a good ledge. Finish as for Diocese.
(FA M. Edwards, R. Edwards 1995)

CL 55)
Flannel Avenue (T1, T8) ★★★★
185ft Severe 4b, 3c, 4a+, 4b

CL 57)
Diocese (T1, T8) ★★★★
200ft Hard Very Severe 5a, 5a, 4a, 4b

CL 59)
The Crusader 205ft Hard Very Severe 5a-, 4b, 4a ★
P1) 70ft P2) 60ft P3) 75ft
(FA R. Edwards, B. Cooper 1985)

CL 60)
Bishop's Arête 190ft Hard Very Severe 4b, 5a, 3a
P1) 45ft P2) 70ft P3) 70ft
(FA R. Edwards, M. Edwards, N. Wharton 1981)

CL 63)
Bishop's Rib (T1) 195ft E1 **5b**, 5a, 3a **R** ★★★
P1) 50ft P2) 70ft P3) 75ft
Outstanding and deservedly popular. Stimulating protection on P1, small rocks very useful.
(FA P1 M. McDermott and party 1963. P2 J. Deacon, J. Oakes, gained by a traverse from Dioceses 1956. Since substantially altered by rockfall on P1)

CL 63a)
Bishop's Rib Direct Start 25ft E2 5b+ ☠
Hard to protect, offset wedges useful.
(FA Unknown)

CL 66)
Left Edge 130ft Hard Severe 4b, 3c
P1) 70ft P2) 60ft
(FA R. Edwards and party 1982)

CL 69)
Expresso Bonzo 140ft E1 5b, 3a ★
P1) 70ft P2) 70ft
(FA P. Littlejohn, A.N. Other 1971)

CL 70)
Terrier's Tooth With A Direct Start (T1, T10) ☠ ★★★
140ft Hard Severe 4a, 3c, 3c.

CL 70a)
Terrier's Tooth (T1, T10) ☺ ★★★★
140ft Very Difficult 3c+

Bishop Buttress and The Pinnacle
View Two Topo 10 (p236)

CL 54)
Face Marks (T9) 70ft E4 6b ●⁑

CL 56)
Splash E4 5b, 6b, 6a
P1) 30ft P2) 70ft P3) 65ft
The crack to the right of the start is 5a.
(FA M. Edwards, R. Edwards alt 1995)

CL 58)
The Surfboard 190ft Hard Very Severe 5a, 5b
P1) 80ft P2) 110ft
(FA P1 Unknown P2 A. Pollitt and party 1981)

The roof right of Surfboard has been climbed starting from the Diocese stance; **Thruster**, E1 5a. *(FA M. Edwards, I. Blake 1986)*

CL 61)
The Steeple (T8) 170ft E3 5c, 4c **R** ★★

CL 62)
The Spire 170ft E3 5c, 4c ★★
P1) 70ft P2) 100ft
Steep, beautiful climbing.
(FA P. Littlejohn, W. Carver 1976)

Topo 10
Bishop Buttress
and The Pinnacle
View Two

PINNACLE GULLY

WHITE SLAB

CL 64)
Cardinal Sin 180ft E4 6b, 5a, 5b ★
P1) 45ft P2) 40ft P3) 70ft
(FA M. Edwards, R. Edwards alt 1985)

CL 65)
The Mitre 195ft Very Severe 4c+, 4c+, 3a **R**
★★
P1) 60ft P2) 60ft P3) 75ft
Snazzy. Ignoring the first pitch when wet is commonplace. P2 starts up the right wall of the gully heading towards the arête to find the traverse line shown on the topo. A sensation of sudden heightened spatial awareness is gained on this pitch.
(FA J. Deacon, J. Kinnaird 1954)

CL 67)
Fat City 70ft E1 6a
(FA M. Lyden, S. Fenwick, B. Craig 1985)

CL 68)
Blockbuster 70ft E4 5c 💣 ☠
(FA M. Edwards 1984)

CL 70)
Terrier's Tooth With A Direct Start (T1, T9)
☠ ★★★
140ft Hard Severe 4a, 3c, 3c+
P1) 60ft P2) 30ft P3) 50ft
Competence required. The first pitch boldly climbs up the obvious vein (there's a small rock placement on the obvious large handhold). Continue as for the parent route.
(Direct start J. Barford 1940. Ps 2 & 3 FA J. Mallory and party 1940)

CL 70a)
Terrier's Tooth (T1, T9) ☺ ★★★★
140ft Very Difficult 3c, 3c, 3c+
P1) 60ft P2) 30ft P3) 50ft
A good, varied, route building to a sensational climax on a real summit and justly one of the most famous and popular routes in the area. At half height on the first pitch it is also possible to move left and join the direct. A belay on the very top of the pinnacle is possible with a single sling around a flake. A slightly lower and more secure one is more popular. To descend either abseil off the large spike at the back of the pinnacle, arranging the rope so it can be 'flicked off' when you're down, or downclimb the right-hand (facing out) side to a ledge and the gully. Difficult, but serious if solo. Friends of all sizes useful. A good continuation climb is White Slab, Moderate, back up to the cliff top.
(FA J. Mallory and party 1940)

CL 71)
Masquerade 70ft E2 5c
(FA M. Edwards solo 1989)

CL 72)
Grit Exiles 140ft E2 5b, 3c
P1) 70ft P2) 70ft
The second pitch seeks the easiest way up the right-hand side (facing in) of the pinnacle.
(FA R. Fawcett, S. Foster 1978)

On the back of the pinnacle are two routes. These are not shown on a topo.

Terrier's Tooth Very Difficult,
Chair Ladder. Climber: Carl Edwards

237

PINNACLE GULLY

Topo 11
Coliseum Wall

CL 73)
Dracula The Undead 35ft E6 6b ☠ ★★
This takes a tenuous line up the cracks, up the back wall (facing the gully) of the pinnacle. The grade is for a lead but it is a good top rope problem. (Fix a sling round the prominent spike on the ledge.) **Toothmark**, E6 6c, climbs the rounded arête to the right of Dracula...
(FAs M. Edwards solo 1986 & 1995)

With your back to the pinnacle, standing at the base of the gully, a clean white wall can be seen on the right. This is **White Slab**, 60ft, Moderate, an enjoyable and less strenuous way back up to the cliff top.

Coliseum Wall
Topo 11 (p238)

Ravens nest in the vicinity.
To the left of Close To The Edge is a chimney, Difficult, which is a possible downclimb. Alternatively set up an abseil. All the following routes have a bold feel to them.

CL 74)
Close To The Edge 45ft Hard Very Severe 5a **R**
(FA M. Edwards, R. Edwards 1984)

CL 75)
La Spècialé 40ft Hard Very Severe 5a **R**
(FA M. Edwards, R. Edwards 1984)

CL 76)
Mini Minx Chimney 40ft Very Difficult **R**
The first chimney.
(FA M. Edwards, R. Edwards 1984)

CL 77)
Iron Maiden 165ft Very Severe 4c, 4c **R**
P1) 75ft P2) 60ft
P2 finishes up the second chimney.
(FA M. Edwards and party 1986)

CL 78)
Nautilus 140ft Hard Very Severe 4a, **4c** **R** ●⸚
P1) 75ft P2) 60ft
(FA M. Edwards, R. Edwards 1984)

CL 79)
Moon Dog 140ft Hard Very Severe **4c**, 5a **R** ●⸚
P1) 90ft P2) 50ft
(FA M. Edwards, R. Edwards 1984)

CL 80)
Softly Softly 150ft Hard Very Severe 4a, **4c** **R** ●⸚
P1) 50ft P2) 100ft
(FA M. Edwards, R. Edwards 1984)

CL 81)
The Great Divide 160ft E2 5a, **5c** **R** ★★
P1) 45ft P2) 115ft
(FA R. Edwards, M. Edwards 1984)

CL 82)
Private Performance 160ft HVS 4a, **5a** **R** ★★★★
P1) 45ft -4a P2) 115ft - 5a
One of many fine climbs at this grade. This offers pleasurable purity of movement on good rock in fine position.
(FA R. Edwards, M. Edwards 1984)

CL 83)
Midnight Runner 160ft E1 **5a**, **5b** **R** ★★★
P1) 45ft P2) 115ft
Both pitches require boldness.
(FA M. Edwards, R. Edwards 1984)

CL 84)
The Gladiator 160ft Hard Very Severe **4c**, 5a **R**
P1) 45ft P2) 115ft
(FA R. Edwards, M. Edwards 1984)

CL 85)
Rock Pilgrim 160ft Hard Very Severe **4c**, **4c** **R**
P1) 45ft P2) 115ft
(FA R. Edwards, M. Edwards 1984)

**Topo 12
Coliseum Buttress**

Coliseum Buttress
Topo 12 (p240)

CL 86)
Super Vision 170ft E3 <u>5c</u>, 5b **R** 💣☀ ★★
P1) 110ft P2) 60ft
(FA R. Edwards, M. Edwards 1984)

CL 87)
Fury Of Atlanta 180ft E4 5b, <u>6a</u>, 5a **R** 💣
P1) 80ft P2) 40ft P3) 60ft
(FA R. Edwards, M. Edwards 1984)

CL 88)
Master of Disaster 170ft E4 <u>6a</u>, 5b **R** 💣
P1) 80ft P2) 90ft
(FA M. Edwards, R. Edwards 1984)

*Midnight Runner E1 5b,
Chair Ladder.
Climber: Mark Edwards*

*West Face Direct E2 5c,
Chair Ladder.
Climber Rowland Edwards*

Porthgwarra Buttress
&
Hella Point

COASTGUARD IDENTITY: Hella Point & Porthgwarra.

NEAREST PHONE: ✆ Porthgwarra.

OS REFERENCE: 371 214.

TIDAL? Porthgwarra Buttress is partially tidal. The starts of Porthgwarra Chimney, Crack and Shawangunk can be reached at high tide. On Hella Point routes on the Panda Buttress and the Hella Wall are tidal and can be reached for two hours either side of low tide, if there is no swell running.

ASPECT: Southerly.

CHARACTER: A traditional cliff if ever there was one, the wearing of moleskin breeches and tweed jacket is optional. A good wet day crag, though a few climbs have a bold feel.

ROCK: Granite, a little gritty in places, but only a little.

TYPE OF CLIMBS: Chimneys, cracks and one Helluva Slab.

PROBLEMS: Tides on Hella Point. The rock is a little bit gritty in a few places.

ENVIRONMENTAL CONCERNS: ❀ SSSI ❀ Stick to existing paths, avoid nesting birds, remove little and climb considerately please.

PARKING: Porthgwarra car park.

APPROACH: Refer to maps for both Chair Ladder (p218) and the Porthgwarra area (p172). The cliffs are a 3-5 minute walk from the car park. Rather than walk via Chair Ladder, a shorter walk begins at the car park entrance. Follow the coastal path up a narrow pathway and along the coast edge, keeping to the left wherever the path forks, until three obvious buttresses come into view.

DESCENTS: A) To Porthgwarra Buttresses refer to topo one. Descend the obvious gully and scramble right (facing out) around to a platform. B) Hella Point is the most seaward (facing out) of the three small buttresses. Between the middle one and the most seaward an obvious jumble of boulders forms a narrow neck connecting the two. Cross this and scramble onto the top of Hella Point. From here set up an abseil down the seaward face or downclimb diagonally rightwards to sea level to gain a ledge. Traverse right (facing out) to reach Helluva Slab and Hella Wall.

Porthgwarra Buttress
Topo 1 (p243)

PB/HP 1)
Porthcrawl 130ft Very Difficult
P1) 40ft P2) 50ft P3) 40ft
Climb the chimney and the easiest line to the top.
(FA R. Bennet, J. Brennan alt 1971)

PB/HP 2)
Porthgwarra Face 110ft Very Difficult ★
P1) 50ft P2) 35ft P3) 25ft
(FA C. Kirkus, P. Fallows 1938)

PB/HP 3)
Porthgwarra Buttress 115ft Difficult
P1) 65ft P2) 50ft
(FKA R. Edwards, A.N. Other 1979)

PB/HP 4)
Porthgwarra Crack 115ft Very Difficult
(FA C. Kirkus, P. Fallows 1938)

PB/HP 5)
Shawangunk 120ft Hard Severe 4b, 3c R ★

P1) 40ft P2) 80ft
(FA Unknown; late 1960s, early 1970s)

PB/HP 6)
Shawangunk Direct 120ft Very Severe 4c
P1) 40ft P2) 80ft
(FKA R. Edwards, A.N. Other 1981)

PB/HP 6a)
Shawangunk Left Hand Finish 80ft Very
Severe 4c
(FKA R. Edwards, A.N. Other 1981)

PB/HP 7)
Porthgwarra Chimney 120ft Severe 4a **R**
★★
They don't teach you this on climbing walls!
(FA C. Noyce 1956)

PB/HP 8)
No Chatter 120ft Hard Severe 3c, 4b+
P1) 40ft P2) 80ft

Start right of the chimney by a wide crack.
(FKA R. Edwards and party 1979)

PB/HP 9)
Joshua Tree 90ft E2 5c
(FA M. Edwards, I. Blake 1985)

Hella Point
Panda Buttress Area
Topo 2 (p244)

PB/HP 10)
Panda Chimneys 40ft Severe 4a
(FA R. Edwards, A.N. Other 1978)

PB/HP 11)
Panda - Top Pitch 40ft Severe 4a, 4a
P1) 4a This starts in a wide gully behind the
buttress. Climb the wall left of a deep groove.
(FA V. Stevenson, J. Sheridan 1963)

APPROA

PB/HP 11a)
Left Paw 40ft Severe 4a
(FKA R. Edwards, A.N. Other 1978)

PB/HP 12)
Panda Wall 30ft Hard Very Severe 5a
(FKA M. Edwards solo 1981)

PB/HP 13)
Panda Crawl 30ft Severe 4a
(FKA R. Edwards, A.N. Other 1978)

PB/HP 14
Front Piece 30ft Difficult
(FKA R. Edwards, A. N. Other 1979)

PB/HP 17)
Sun Shadow (T3) 110ft Hard Very Severe <u>4c</u>, <u>4c</u> ★★
P1) 65ft P2) 45ft
(FKA M. Edwards, R. Edwards 1982)

PB/HP 18)
Finger Stretcher (T3) 105ft E3 6a, 5a
P1) 65ft P2) 40ft
P2) 5a Climb the crack on the left of the wall.
(FKA R. Edwards, M. Edwards 1982)

PB/HP 19)
Helluva Slab 135ft Severe 4a, 4b **R** ★★
P1) 55ft P2) 50ft P3) 30ft
(FA C. Fishwick, R. Fishwick 1956)

Hella Wall Area
Topo 3 (p245)

The first two routes are not depicted on the topos. To the left of **Ebony Crack** is a deep overhung cleft with a jammed boulder at the top.

PB/HP a)
Merde Del Buffolino 85ft Very Severe 4c, 4c
P1) 55ft P2) 30ft

Topo 3
Hella Point
Hella Wall

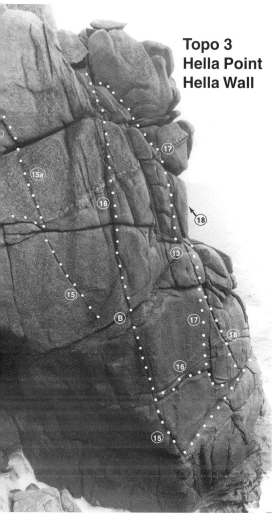

P1) Climb the rib to the jammed boulder and step beneath it across the cleft into a short groove. Climb this to a stance.
P2) Climb the painful crack passing a huge spike.
(FA D. Cook, P. Devine alt 1985)

PB/HP b)
Sandbag Variation 85ft Hard Very Severe 5a+
P2) Bridge out right to gain a steeper crack. Climb this to the top.
(FA B. Williams, A. Thompson 1985)

PB/HP 15)
Ebony Crack 160ft E2 5b, 5c
P1) 90ft P2) 70ft
(FKA R. Edwards, M. Edwards 1982)

PB/HP 15a)
Variation Finish 70ft E3 5c
(FKA R. Edwards, M. Edwards 1982)

PB/HP 16)
Fluid Connections 145ft Hard Very Severe 5a, 4b
P1) 90ft P2) 55ft
(FKA R. Edwards, M. Edwards 1982)

PB/HP 17)
Sun Shadow (T2) 110ft Hard Very Severe 4c, 4c ★★
P1) 65ft P2) 45ft
(FA R. Edwards, M. Edwards 1982)

PB/HP 18)
Finger Stretcher (T2) 105ft E3 6a, 5a
P1) 65ft P2) 40ft
(FA R. Edwards, M. Edwards 1982)

There are two other good routes in this area, not shown on the topo. Approach by traversing round the middle buttress from Porthgwarra Buttress; this wall faces Hella Point.

PB/HP c)
Child Of The Moon 45ft E3 6a
Climbs the very thin crack on the extreme seaward point of the buttress facing Helluva Wall. A good deep water solo.
(FA M. Edwards solo 1985)

PB/HP d)
Helluva Week 45ft Hard Severe 4b
Climb the broken crack in the obvious blunt arête finishing left with a mantelshelf onto the large ledge.
(FA E. Stone and party 1985)

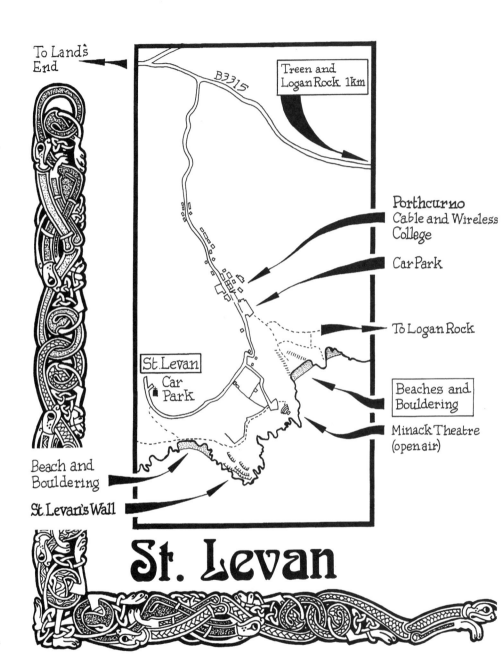

To Lands End

B3315

Treen and Logan Rock 1km

Porthcurno Cable and Wireless College

Car Park

To Logan Rock

St. Levan Car Park

Beaches and Bouldering

Minack Theatre (open air)

Beach and Bouldering

St. Levan's Wall

St. Levan

St Levan's Wall

COASTGUARD IDENTITY: Pedn-Mên-An-Mere.

NEAREST PHONE: ☎ At junction of B3315 with road to Porthcurno.

OS REFERENCE: 384 217.

TIDAL? Partially. The right-hand section from Geriatrics onwards is affected.

ASPECT: South-westerly, a good sun trap.

CHARACTER: The wall holds several test-pieces from HVS upwards. On a hot day there is a holiday atmosphere to this cliff; it is a very good place to leave non-climbers on the beach, whilst others go and play. It is also a good winter venue. Some skill required in protecting some of these climbs. The wall is part of a larger cliff and also known as the Bermuda Wall.

ROCK: Granite. Solid on the wall except for a little grittiness near the top.

TYPE OF CLIMBS: Technical crack and face climbs. We have only depicted one part of this cliff; many other good little pitches, problems and scrambles can be found.

PROBLEMS: Tides; it is best to time your visit to coincide with a falling spring tide. The approach from the beach is a lot more challenging at high tide, and not recommended at all if the sea is rough. The alternative is an approach from the top of the cliff and is not recommended unless with someone who has visited before, as it is complex and potentially serious. There is some gritty rock near the tops of a few of the depicted routes. The whole area is affected by rough seas and some cracks are slow drying. If it's very hot the rock feels greasy. A high chalk day.

ENVIRONMENTAL CONCERNS: Avoid any nesting birds and trampling vegetation in the gullies. Flowers look best in the ground rather than a vase. Tread lightly, please don't litter and leave the dog at home when you visit. Dogs must be kept on a lead and are not welcomed on the beach.

PARKING: Drive into Porthcurno and continue past the main car park and the Minack Theatre and park in the pay and display car park next to the St. Levan church.

APPROACH: Refer to the St. Levan map. On a falling tide take the path to the beach, going through a gate en route. Descend to the beach and bear leftwards to the start of the boulders. A 50m boulder hop and scramble leads to the start of routes on St. Levan's Wall. At low tide this is easy. If chased by the tide at the end of your visit, climb a pitch to the next platform and then pick the most enticing, easy line to the top, and the coast path back to the car. If at high tide, at the junction with the beach follow the coast path leftwards to the top of the headland, and then wind a way down the right-hand (facing out) side of the buttresses to the top of the Wall. Other ways down the cliff to the top of St. Levan's Wall are possible. Both hands need to be free and downclimbing is required and route-finding can be complex. Not recommended.

DESCENTS: Rig an abseil after your first route and collect it as you climb out as described above or walk leftwards (facing out) at lowish tide and carefully pick out a line down and around a jumble of large blocks and ledges that will bring you back around the base. Tricky. Care needed if wet and only possible during a lowish tide.

St. Levan's Wall

SLe 1)
Crack A Goo Goo 60ft E2 5b
(FA M. Edwards, R. Edwards 1985)

SLe 2)
Heaven's Snake E3 6a
(FA M. Edwards, R. Edwards 1985)

SLe 3)
Jamaica 70ft E3 6a
"No, she climbed it of her own free will." ©
Tommy Trinder 1933.
(FA R. Edwards, M. Edwards 1985)

SLe 4)
Bermuda Wall 70ft E3 5c **R ★★★**

A high side runner reduces the bite of the bold start; naughty but nice and only E2. A direct finish is E3 6a.
(FA M. Doyle, J. Hooper 1983. Direct Finish M. Edwards 1983)

SLe 5)
Frogs In A Frenzy 70ft E8 7a ● ☠ ★★
So thin it's positively anorexic, culminating in a leap for the break. Led with micros (E7) the runners left in situ have since ripped out with possible damage to the placements. Abseil inspection advised.
(FA M. Edwards unseconded 1992)

SLe 6)
Devil's Meridian 60ft E2 5c ★★
(FA A. Trevorrow, P. O'Sullivan 1984)

SLe 7)
Midnight Express 60ft E1 5b ★
(FA A. Trevorrow, D. Hannigan 1984)

SLe 8)
Geriatrics 40ft Severe 4a ★
(FA R. James, A. Skinner 1977)

SLe 9)
Layaway 40ft Severe 4a
(FA Unknown)

SLe 10)
The Sunne In Splendour E5 6b ●
(FA M. Edwards unseconded 1994)

SLe 11)
Fingerflinger 45ft E3 6a ★
(FA C. Nicholson unseconded 1984)

SLe 12)
Black Adder 45ft E5 6a ☠ ★
(FA M. Edwards, R. Edwards 1989)

SLe 13)
Falls The Shadow 45ft E3 6a
(FA M. Edwards, R. Edwards 1989)

SLe 14)
Zip 50ft Very Severe 4c+
(FA J. Hooper, A.N. Other 1981)

A few feet right of **Zip** is a line of weakness. This gives **Seamstress** 45ft E2 6a ★
(FA C. Nicholson unseconded 1984). The corner at the end of the channel gives **Redfish** 35ft Hard Very Severe 5a *(FA S. Salmon unseconded 1984)*.

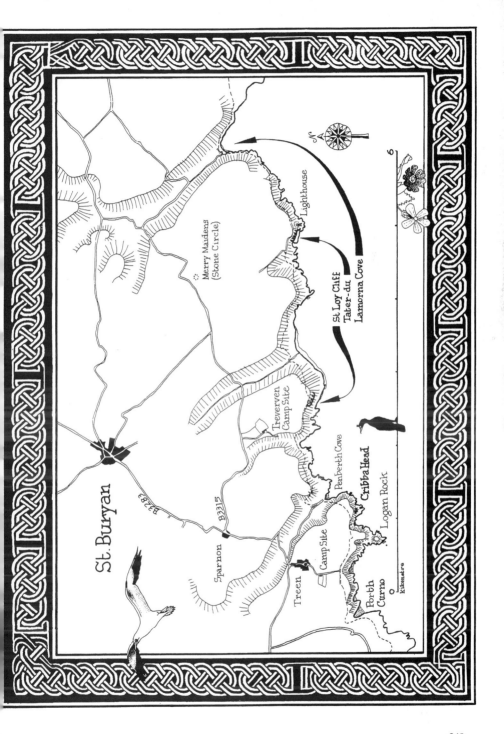

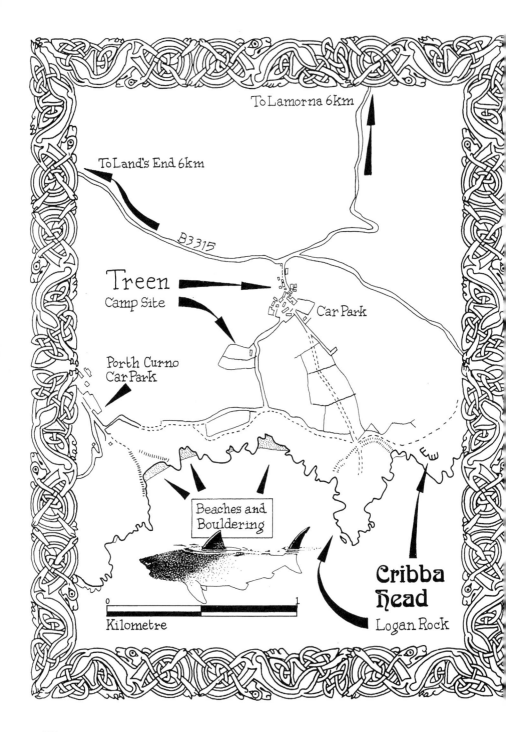

To Lamorna 6km

To Land's End 6km

B3315

Treen
Camp Site

Car Park

Porth Curno
Car Park

Beaches and
Bouldering

Cribba
Head

Logan Rock

0   1

Kilometre

Cribba Head

COASTGUARD IDENTITY: Cribba Head.

NEAREST PHONE: ☏ Penberth Cove.

OS REFERENCE: 404 223.

TIDAL? No.

ASPECT: South-westerly.

CHARACTER: The adepts' crag; you'll either love it or loathe it.

ROCK: Granite, very rough.

TYPE OF CLIMBS: Hard test-pieces, often very bold. If you like arêtes then this is your kind of place. Many other easier short pitches and problems can also be found on this headland.

PROBLEMS: Difficulty in getting bearings on first visit. Lack of protection on several routes. Rough rock, a bit 'crunchy' in places.

ENVIRONMENTAL CONCERNS: ❀ SSSI ❀ The maritime heath and scrubland on the headland is vulnerable to trampling. Please stick to paths and act considerately. Please also avoid any nests as jackdaws etc. nest in cracks, and take your litter home. This includes finger tape and chalk wrappers etc. Handle lichen with care.

PARKING: A pay and display car park is at Treen; quite cheap for the day.

APPROACH: Refer also to the St. Buryan area map (p249). Park in the car park at Treen. Walk out of the entrance and turn left. Opposite the little Methodist chapel follow a signed path over a stile to the main track, which goes over fields to join the coast path. At this take the first left-hand fork and follow the coast path, going past the obvious promontory of Logan Rock (a good view of the main section of Cribba Head is found from the Logan Rock promontory itself) and continue for 300m past dense gorse thickets. Where they thin out on the right, walk seawards and reach the tops of a number of small buttresses. Bear right and descend to a rock gully that drops to the sea. Skirt the right hand side of the gully; a scramble round the buttress leads to a rock platform. The climbs depicted are on the north-western side and face Logan Rock.

DESCENTS: After an ascent scramble and walk down and back round to the terrace.

Cribba Head
Topo 1

CH 1)
Back To The Grind 50ft E3 6a ★★
(*FA A. Grieve, N. Hancock 1989, also claimed by M. Edwards 1989*)

CH 1a)
Direct Start E4/5 6a
(*FA M. Edwards solo 1989*)

CH 2)
Chimney Climb 50ft Difficult
Easiest way to the top.
(*FA Unknown*)

CH 3)
New Sensation 50ft Hard Very Severe 5a
(*FA N. Mooney and party 1989*)

CH 4)
Pass The Pigs (T2) 50ft E4 6a ★★
Get your motor running! It may be worth taping up your hands for this one.
(*FA A. Grieve, N. Hancock 1988*)

CH 5)
Lovely, Lovely, Lovely (T2) 50ft E5 6b **R** ☀
★★★
Good rock, dynamic movement, tenuous moves and thought provoking protection make this a really unforgettable challenge. A size 7 Tricam, two size 4 Friends and a size 1 Friend were used on the FA. As were three

ropes and 2 belayers.
(FA N. Hancock, A. Grieve, G. Butler 1989)

CH 6)
Question Mark (T2) 50ft E9 7a+ 💣 ☠
★★★

CH 7)
Kernyck (T2) 50ft Hard Severe 4b ☺ ★★

CH 8)
Kernack (T2) 50ft E1 5a ☠ ★
A bold, balding slab.
(FA S. Salmon unseconded 1985)

CH 9)
Boysen's Groove (T2) 50ft E3 5c ★★

CH 10)
Pre-Marital Tension (T2) 50ft E8 7a ☠
★★★★
E6 if led with a side runner

Cribba Head
Topo 2

CH 4)
Pass The Pigs (T1) 50ft E4 6a ★★

CH 5)
Lovely, Lovely, Lovely (T1) 50ft E5 6b 💣
★★★

CH 6)
Question Mark (T1) 50ft E9 7a+ 💣 ☠
★★★
Extreme technicality in an obscenely terminal position. One for the anally retentive! A provocative little pitch, and grade. E9 - question mark (?). Repeats please. A skyhook use on the FA with a Quadcam for the uppermost break after the crux sequence.
(FA M. Edwards unseconded 1994)

CH 7)
Kernyck (T1) 50ft Hard Severe 4b ☺ ★★
(FA M. McDermott, D. Bateman, V. Stevenson 1965)

Question Mark E9 7a, Cribba Head.
Climber: Mark Edwards

**Topo 2
Cribba Head**

CH 8)
Kernack (T1) 50ft E1 5a ☠ ★

CH 9)
Boysen's Groove (T1) 50ft E3 5c ★★
Generally good protection, awkward to place at times. Large Friend useful.
(FA M. Boysen, A. Hubbard 1981)

CH 10)
Pre-Marital Tension (T1) 50ft E8 7a ☠ ★★★★
E6 if led with a side runner. Exquisitely technical. An ultra modern test-piece that will either delight or frustrate. E6 if led with a side runner. The other side of the arête was first led with a BR (two holes) but left unclaimed. It has since been led without (E7 6c+) past a PR (removed) in the upper break but both routes still await an on-sight ascent.

---

*Pegasus Hard Severe 4c, Chair Ladder.
Climber Jane Fisher*

*(FA N. Dixon, T. Reseigh 1989. FFA M. Edwards 1990. Right side, 1BR M. Edwards.
FFA M. Edwards 1994)*

CH 11)
Harder 40ft Very Severe 5c ☺
(FA M. McDermott, D. Bateman, V. Stevenson 1965)

CH 12)
Storms Over Africa 40ft E6+ 6b/c ☠ ★★
A rope is optional. A conventionally placed peg was placed at half height for an on-sight ascent. Led without since; first moving into Boysen's Crack on the right and then finally direct. On-sight. A very bold effort.
(FA M. Edwards unseconded 1989. FFA variation C. Waddy 1994. FFA direct S. Ohly solo 1995)

CH 13)
Boysen's Cracks 40ft E1 5c ☺
Climb the cracks in the south face.
(FA M. Boysen, A. Hubbard 1981)

253

St Loy

COASTGUARD IDENTITY: Merthen Point.

NEAREST PHONE: 📞 Treverven campsite (farm) or in Penberth.

OS REFERENCE: 414 228.

TIDAL? No, a land locked cliff.

ASPECT: Southern.

CHARACTER: A baby Bosigran, perhaps it'll grow? Or a stray tor from Dartmoor? A visit here is reminiscent of climbing on both.

ROCK: Solid, rough granite.

TYPE OF CLIMBS: Corners, grooves and wide cracks or bold, bare slabs.

PROBLEMS: A long walk in. Lack of protection on the slab routes. The descent path is showing signs of wear. Some steps would help remedy this.

ENVIRONMENTAL CONCERNS: ❀ SSSI ❀ NB: At the time of writing (1995) SSSI status has been applied for. There is lush vegetation at the base and on the top. Cliff bluebells grow here and should not be disturbed. It is heavily lichenous in parts. Please follow paths, don't stray from the cliff base and don't garden or litter. There are nesting birds in the vicinity.

PARKING: A pay and display car park is at Treen (south). Quite a reasonable price for the day.

APPROACH: Refer to the St. Buryan area map (p249). A stiff 40 minute walk, but a scenic one. Walk out of the entrance of the car park and turn left by a little Methodist chapel. Opposite the little Methodist chapel follow a signed path over a stile to the main track, which goes over fields to join the coast path. At this take the first left-hand fork and follow the coast path, going past the obvious promontory of Logan Rock, and continue to the little fishing cove of Penberth. Follow the coast path south-east; the tiers of the cliffs of Porthguarnon East (Old England) are clearly visible once the next cove is reached along with a steep path and a walk up a long flight of steps. At the top turn right at the junction and walk along the coast path for about 1km until St. Loy comes into clear view. It is the last major area of rock on the headland it stands on and the slab of The Baldest is obvious. If you reach a gate in a stone wall then you've gone too far. A steep, faint path drops down the right-hand (facing out) side of the cliff and leads to the starts of the climbs.

DESCENTS: Walk off and around to the left (facing in), keeping well back, and follow the steep, faint approach path back down to the starts of climbs.

SLo 1)
Ivy Incorporated 90ft Very Difficult
(FA D. Brown, J. Atherton 1969)

SLo 2)
Chicory Chock 75ft Hard Severe 4b
(FA D. Brown and party 1969)

SLo 3)
Chicory Check 75ft Very Severe 4b
A gauche climb.
(FA D. Brown and party 1969)

SLo 4)
Harmony 100ft Hard Very Severe 5b
(FA I. Lonsdale, A. Hartnett 1979)

SLo 5)
The Hairiest 100ft E2 5b, 5c
P1) 50ft P2) 50ft
(FA C. Nicholson, S. Salmon 1981)

SLo 6)
Old Fools 100ft E3 5b, 5c **R** ★
P1) 50ft P2) 50ft
Nothing foolish about their eye for a line.
(FA P. O'Sullivan, D. Hannigan 1990)

SLo 7)
Cress Cendo 100ft Hard Very Severe 4c, **5a**
★★
P1) 45ft P2) 55ft
The upper groove is awkward. Large Friend

St Loy

useful.
(FA P. Gordon, G. Morgan 1970)

SLo 8)
Chlorophyll Cluster 100ft E1 5b+ **R** ★★★
P1) 45ft P2) 55ft
A testing upper section. A good introduction to the slab. Small rocks useful.
(FA P. Gordon 1970. Later claimed by P. Littlejohn, S. Jones 1974)

SLo 9)
The Baldest 100ft E4 5c+ ☠ ★★★
Courage, mon brave, or it may deliver a coup de grâce.
(FA P. Littlejohn, S. Jones 1974)

SLo 10)
The Damned 100ft E5 5c ☠ ★★
Pièce de résistance. Essentially a direct start to The Barber. A long, lonely lead with little room for second thoughts, though protection can be gained by traversing to the flake of The Baldest (micros) and also about 20ft from the top. Allez, Allez.
(FA Claimed by both M. Edwards solo 1987 and P. O'Sullivan and party 1990)

SLo 11)
Finesse 120ft E4+ 5c, **5c** ☠ ★★★
P1) 60ft P2) 60ft
A risqué pitch. Bonne chance!
(FA P. Littlejohn, S. Jones 1974)

SLo 12)
The Barber 120ft E4 5b, **5c** ☠ ★★
P1) 60ft P2) 60ft
A certain sang-froid is required. In its upper section this route leaves the wide crack and takes a rising right to left traverse line to join and finish as for Chlorophyll Cluster: SL 8.
(FA M. Edwards, R. Edwards 1982)

SLo 13)
Sloe Steel 40ft Very Severe 4c+ ★
(FA D. Steel, I. Duckworth 1970

SLo 14)
Monochrome Men 65ft E1 5b+ ★★★
Radiant climbing.
(FA P. O'Sullivan, K. Hosie, M. Dunning 1990)

SLo 15)
Scarlet Woman 65ft E1 5c ★
(FA P. O'Sullivan, S. Elliot 1990)

255

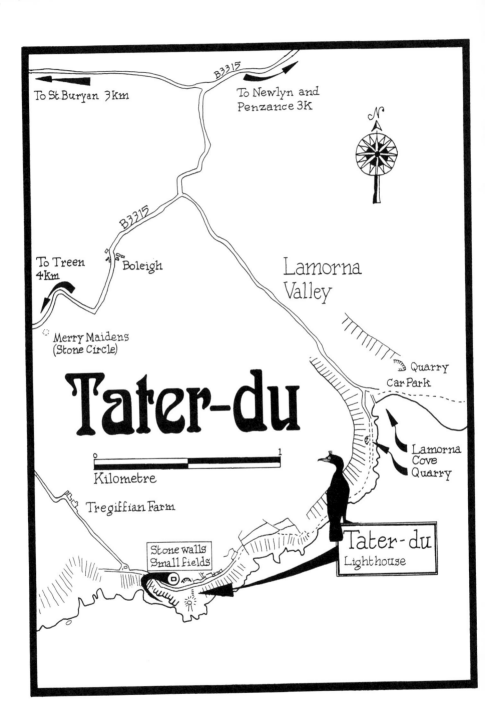

To St.Buryan 3km

B3315

To Newlyn and
Penzance 3K

N

To Treen
4km

B3315

Boleigh

Lamorna
Valley

Merry Maidens
(Stone Circle)

Quarry
Car Park

Tater-du

0   1

Kilometre

Lamorna
Cove
Quarry

Tregiffian Farm

Stone walls
Small fields

Tater-du
Lighthouse

Tater du

COASTGUARD IDENTITY: Tater du.

NEAREST PHONE: ℭ Lamorna Cove.

OS REFERENCE: 439 231

TIDAL? Yes, partly. Martell Slab is tidal and can only be started two hours either side of low tide. The routes from Knight's Pillar to Commando Special are non-tidal. The starts of routes on Marine Parade are tidal but ledges can be reached by abseil at high tide, enabling a pitch to be climbed.

ASPECT: Southerly, a sun trap away from the crowds.

CHARACTER: The greenstone joker in the southern granite pack. Amiable, friendly and with a classic route to trump its near neighbours with.

ROCK: Greenstone (Pillow Lava) very slippery if wet. Generously supplied with cracks, sharp ncuts, small pockets, hidden holds and huge flatties.

TYPE OF CLIMBS: Bold slabs but also well protected cracklines and nervy overhangs. Friends very useful.

PROBLEMS: Tides, and the area is restricted until early summer. It's owned privately; the owner lives locally and takes an interest in what goes on. Please do follow the described approach along the coast path. Local residents are sensitive about people attempting to take short cuts across their lands. Observe the nesting restrictions and do not leave litter.

ENVIRONMENTAL CONCERNS: ✿ SSSI ✿ It is an important, sensitive, popular nesting site and the owner has asked climbers to observe nesting restrictions between March 1st and July 1st. It is important you do so. Please avoid any chicks after this date. Some of the upper parts of the cliff are covered in a heavy coating of lichen and turf is found on some ledges and on the top, so please handle this carefully, take litter home and act considerately. Large groups may wish to think of avoiding this very unspoilt cliff which is in an area of outstanding natural beauty.

PARKING: A pay as you enter car park is at Lamorna Cove; park early in the tourist season, as it is small and parking anywhere else is very tricky.

APPROACH: Refer also to the St. Buryan area map (p249). A stiff half hour walk. From the Lamorna Cove car park, and an obvious small disused quarry on the north side, follow the coast path northwards to a steep flight of steps on the first headland. From the top of this a small lighthouse comes into view on the next headland. Continue towards this, and some small stands of trees, until another small quarry is reached, opposite a gate and long flight of steps leading down to the unmanned lighthouse. Just to help you keep your bearings the cliffs are around 40m to the right of this, but Trinity House don't like trespassers. Continue up the track for 100m, past dense undergrowth, to reach a telegraph pole on the left. Here the undergrowth thins out. Branch left and cross a low wall to reach a number of small bluffs of rock. Begin descending these and the slopes to pick a line (some downclimbing) leading to the cliff base. Skirt this leftwards (facing out) to reach the main cliff area. Refer to topo one.

It is worth reversing this to get back to the path as attempting to plough through the abandoned fields covered in bracken, fern, bramble and thornbush is the kind of jungle bashing that could give Steven Spielberg enough ideas to inspire several films. It is also damaging.

DESCENTS: As well as the approach path that can be used to descend from The Martell Slab area routes it is also possible to climb or abseil down the gully next to Eric's Route or scramble down the left-hand (facing out) side of the Dorna area.

NB: In some parts it is possible to wander at will and many variations have certainly been climbed over the years and left unrecorded. Other lines have doubtless been claimed and claimed again. Unknown climbers have been seen on Lighthouse Arête, for example, before the FKA here. The Marines probably climbed other, unreported, routes. We've taken liberties with Tater Du: rationalising some lines, combining others to produce the best climbing at a grade, adding some new ones and looking for probable original lines where lines are in doubt, etc. We hope you enjoy them.

Martell Slab Area
Topo 1

Td 1)
Knight's Pillar 75ft Very Severe 4c
A variation moves left at half height and tends diagonally up the left wall at Hard Severe 4b

Topo 1
Tater du
Martell Slab Area

standard.
(FA J. Deacon, D. Knights 1960. Variation FKA J. Frankiss, T. Dennell 1988)

Td 1a)
Knight's Pillar Direct Finish 75ft Very Severe 4c
(FKA R. Smart, I. Brazier 1988)

Td 2)
Check Mate 75ft Hard Very Severe 5a
(FKA R. Edwards solo 1995)

Td a)
Just Du It 75ft Hard Very Severe 5a
This climbs the wall between Knight's Pillar and Pericles.
(FA A. Grieve, A.N. Other 1985)

Td 3)
Pericles 70ft Hard Very Severe 5a
(FA P. O'Sullivan, C. Woodhead 1978)

Td 4)
Lysander 140ft E1 5b
This finishes up the leaning headwall on huge holds. The lichen on the final few feet should be treated with care.
(FA P. O'Sullivan, C. Woodhead 1978)

Td 5)
Crows Nest Direct 115ft Hard Very Severe 5b, 4b **R**
P1) 65ft P2) 50ft
The lichen on the final few feet should be treated with care.
(FA V. Stevenson, G. Wilson 1962)

Td 6)
Rooks Folly 65ft Hard Very Severe 5a
(FKA R. Edwards and party 1979)

Td 7)
Crows Nest Ordinary 130ft Hard Severe 4b
The lichen on the final few feet should be treated with care.
(FA Royal Marines 1950s)

Td 8)
Commando Special 130ft Very Severe 4c
(FA Royal Marines 1950s)

Td 9)
Gully Route 130ft Severe 4b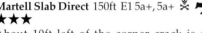
P1) 70ft P2) 60ft
This follows a slabby ramp to the broad
corner/chimney. Follow this to the top.
Indicated by arrows on the topo.
(FA Royal Marines 1950s)

The following routes start from a tidal
platform. The Martell Slab rises above and to
the left of a deep recess behind a large pool, in
which sits a large boulder, and bounded on
its right (facing in) by the steep, smooth
Lamorna Wall.

Td 10)
Martell Super Direct 65ft E1 5a+ ☠ 🪶
Useful as a high tide variation start to Martell
Slab. A single pitch.
(FA Unknown 1970s)

Td 11)
Martell Slab Direct 150ft E1 5a+, 5a+ ☠ 🪶
★★★
About 10ft left of the corner crack is an
undercut scoop (often wet). Pull directly into
this and climb a tiny slab, step left and move
up to join Martell Variation Start to the belay.
Continue as depicted. Td 11a.
(FA P1 J. Deacon, D. Holdroyd 1957)

Td 11a)
Variation Finish 60ft E1 5a
(P2 P. O'Sullivan, C. Woodhead 1979)

Td 12)
Martell Slab With A Variation Start 🪶
★★★
155ft Hard Very Severe 4c+, 4c **R**
P1) 65ft P2) 90ft
Surprisingly exacting and exercises the mind
far more than the arms. Various sized rocks,
small to medium Friends and even the odd
micro could be useful. Start below a short
corner crack at the back of the recess. Climb
the crack and move left and up before a long
step left brings you to a position beneath a
diagonal crack. Move up with difficulty to gain
this (holds and protection improve near its
top) then leave it to step anxiously up left to
gain a belay ledge. Continue as depicted.
(FA J. Deacon, D. Holdroyd 1957)

Td 13)
Martell Groove 70ft Hard Very Severe 4c+
R 🪶
A single pitch.
(FA Unknown. Lower part by P. Livesey 1976)

Td 14)
The Water Margin 130ft E4 6a, 4c **R** 🪶 ●
★
P1) 50ft P2) 80ft
Combined with a variation to Lamorna Wall
and the original finish of Martell Slab to
produce an independent line.
*(FA K. Palmer, A. Grieve, P. Saunders 1987.
Variation P. Livesey 1976. P2 J. Deacon, D.
Holdroyd 1957)*

Td 15)
Lighthouse Arête 130ft E2 5c, 4c 🪶 ★
P1) 50ft P2) 80ft
*(FKA R. Edwards, M. Edwards 1978. Also claimed
by J. Ford, S. Elliott 1991)*

Td 16)
Lamorna Wall 120ft E3 5c **R** ★★
There are a number of variations to this route.
This follows the strongest natural line.
*(FA J. Deacon, M. McDermott 1959. FFA R.
Edwards 1978)*

Td 17)
The Veil 130ft E1 5b, 4b **R** 🪶 ★
A direct start climbs from the platform to join
it at E2 5b standard.
*(FA J. Deacon, D. Knights 1960. Direct Start M.
Edwards solo 1984)*

Td 18)
Eric's Route (T2) 125ft Very Difficult 🪶
P1) 30ft P2) 40ft P3) 55ft
Climb the obvious wide corner crack finishing
up the wall above.
(FA Royal Marines 1950s)

Marine Parade Area
Topo 2

Td 18)
Eric's Route (T1) 125ft Very Difficult
The upper section.

Td 19)
Fat Panda 70ft Severe 4a
(FA S. Salmon, D. Hannigan 1981)

Td 20)
The Ramble 110ft Very Difficult
The gully can also be downclimbed or
abseiled.
(FA Royal Marines 1950s)

Td 21)
Willie's Way 100ft Hard Very Severe 4a, 5a
★★
P1) 75ft P2) 25ft
(FA W. Morrow 1960)

Td 22)
Bus Route 100ft Very Difficult
P1) 75ft P2) 25ft
(FA Royal Marines 1950s)

Td 23)
Flaky Wall 100ft Very Severe 4a, 4c ★
P1) 55ft P2) 60ft
(FKA R. Edwards solo 1995)

Td 24)
Raven's Nest Direct E1 3c, 5b
P1) 60ft P2) 65ft
(FKA R. Edwards solo 1995)

Td 25)
Marine Parade 100ft Very Difficult
(FA Royal Marines 1950s)

Td 26)
Final Touch 90ft Hard Very Severe 5a
★
(FKA R. Edwards solo 1995)

Td 27)
The Sentry Box 80ft Severe 4a  ★
(FA Royal Marines 1950s)

Td 28)
Pregnant Pause 70ft Severe ★
Deceptively pleasant. Climb the gully to a roof. Traverse leftwards to a slightly overhanging groove in the wall. Climb this to the top.
(FA S. Salmon, D. Hannigan 1980)

Td 29)
Dorna 60ft Hard Severe 4b ★
(FA Royal Marines 1950s)

Td 29a)
Dorna Direct 60ft Hard Severe 4b
(FA M. Edwards and party 1980)

Td 30)
Head Hunter 60ft E1 5a
(FA M. Edwards and party 1984)

Td 31)
Kalahari 60ft Hard Very Severe 4c
(FA M. Edwards, the Peplow brothers 1980. Also claimed by A. Trevorrow 1981)

Looking north across Carn Barra

AFTERWORD

The introduction somewhat blithely states that the topos and maps are at the heart of this guide. Those who are interested in photography or the technicalities of guide production may wish to know more about how they were achieved.

Photographing a cliff well may seem to be a simple exercise; it is after all a stationary object. But each cliff, particularly sea cliffs, offer their own individual challenge. The light and time of day are the most crucial considerations. To come out well it is important that there is strong contrast; that features such as cracks, flakes and the rock's texture, etc. are clearly visible and not hidden in shadow. This can mean that the optimum time to capture a cliff may last only a few minutes whilst the sun moves across the sky. You can imagine the frustration if a cloud obscures it during that time.

Some of the cliffs in this guide were photographed in the hour after sunrise, others when the sun was low on the horizon in the evening in order to achieve the desired effect. The 'black' cliffs of greenstone and slate are particularly difficult, those that cast their own shadow by overhanging doubly so. It took many attempts to finally capture Tater du; one of the most camera shy cliffs on the coast.

Then there's the matter of being in the right place to get the best shot. Many cliffs were photographed from canoe. This may seem a simple operation until you realise that framing a shot and operating shutter speeds of up to one thousandth of a second whilst bobbing up and down presents its own difficulties. A large number of expeditions were mounted to capture some cliffs as camera shake, shadow or having missed a route out only show up in the darkroom and the only thing to do then is to attempt the exercise again.

Canoes, however, are not the whole answer, particularly with cliffs raised some height above the sea. The lack of a suitable alternative vantage point can mean recourse to some creative solutions. The Raven Wall area of Bosigran, for example, was eventually photographed from the lowest point of Rosemergy Ridge, a kilometre away, using a 200mm lens, after attempts from other points, including swimming to the island uncovered at low tide off Seaward face, proved unsatisfactory.

For other shots the best results came from aerial photography. Our thanks to the crews from RNAS Culdrose who have attempted this, and in particular to Peter Kaye, then with the Royal Marines, for capturing Chair Ladder's Main Cliff, Bosigran's Great Zawn and The Hayloft Area of Sennen. When all else failed montage proved the only solution. This was used for the West Face of Great Zawn, the photographs being taken from various points on Xanadu and Cribba Head which presented its own peculiar difficulties involving perspective.

Photographers may be interested to know that the bulk of the shots in this book were taken using a Tamron wide angle 24mm-45mm lens on Cannon T90 and A1 bodies. The other principal lenses used were Cannon 28mm, 50mm and 80mm fixed focal length. All developing was onto Illford FP4. Although over half of the photographs for topos were taken specifically for this guide, the photographs in this book represent fifteen years' work. Many cliffs were photographed when out climbing both as a memento and as an aid to spotting unclimbed lines. Thus a collection was slowly built up over the years.

After photographing comes developing. When developing a crag shot it is always worth playing with exposures to see which produces the best effect. The topos of Chair Ladder's Main Cliff and Fox Promontory are also photomontages: superimposing a cut-out photograph of the cliff onto a slightly underexposed version of the background. We hope this brings out the fact that they are standing proud of the cliffs in the background. Then came route checking which involved just about everyone, though the bulk was done by Rowland. For many routes this guide shows clearly for the first time where routes go, particularly in the case of some of the more obscure routes that are a few decades old. The design concept for the guide was hammered out in the summer of 1994. The dot to dot route lines were all marked by hand onto plastic overlaying sheets. Over this was a final sheet on which were added the numbers and information to be inserted at the layout stage. Each topo is made up of at least three separate components superimposed onto each other.

The maps were all drawn by hand and it took around a year to produce all the maps and borders in this book. Our thanks to Courtney Davis and Cassell PLC for agreeing to supply five of the borders. The text was produced on a 486 desktop computer using Lotus AmiPro 3 for Windows software. Layout on an Apple Power Macintosh using Pagemaker 6. Although a collaborative effort, production often has been undertaken independently, spread out across the country and, for nine months, Europe. It took fourteen months in all. As an exercise in kinetic energy and problem solving it has been instructive. Periodically we would meet to pull the strands together and bounce ideas around and, if nothing else, we have demonstrated that order can come out of chaos! Given that collaborations can end up with people working at cross purposes this is no mean feat.

We hope this guide helps you enjoy Penwith climbing as much as we have and that you like the guide as much as we have enjoyed producing it. We also hope that it may even inspire! If it does move you to look away from the popular cliffs, or for new routes, please heed our advice in the Green Pages.

Nut Route Severe 4a,
Pordenack Point.
Climber: Carl Edwards

SYMBOLS, ABBREVIATIONS & TERMS

❀ SSSI ❀ = Site of Special Scientific Interest.

❀ = Environmentally Sensitive - refer to appropriate text for that route or cliff.

🦅 = Known nesting site. check visually prior to an ascent or avoid during spring and summer.

☠ = Very Bold. Route noted for lack of protection possibilities.

💣 = Approach warily as the grade may be unconfirmed or the route may have in situ protection missing.

R = Route may be run out in places or the first protection may be some way above the ground.

☺ = Well protected, makes a good 'gradebreaker'.

⚑ = Rock particularly loose on this route.

✝ ☹ = Bolts cut or removed from this sports route.

(T) = Also shown on other topo(s). The number is also given.

A + (plus) or - (minus) sign next to the grade indicates whether a route is thought to be a hard or soft touch within its grade. If a technical grade is highlighted by being both in bold and underlined then it is this grade that the descriptive grade primarily applies to, e.g. HVS **4c**, 5a (1st pitch bold) E2 5a, **5b** etc.

FA ~ First Ascent with aid or in situ protection if followed by

FFA ~ First Free Ascent.

FKA ~ First Known Ascent.

FKFA ~ First Known Free Ascent.

alt/var ~ Alternate/Various leads.

TR ~ Top Rope.

A ~ Abseil Point.

B ~ Belay.

D ~ Descent or Downclimb.

P ~ Pitch.

PR ~ Peg Runner - the presence or quality of which cannot be guaranteed.

PB ~ Peg Belay - the presence or quality of which cannot be guaranteed.

BR ~ Bolt Runner - the presence or quality of which cannot be guaranteed.

BB ~ Bolt Belay - the presence or quality of which cannot be guaranteed.

SS ~ Stainless Steel.

XS ~ Extremely Severe.

Friends ~ Friends, Quadcams, Camalots and other comparable camming devices.

TCUs ~ Triple Camming Units including Friends 0.5 and .00.

Rocks ~ Rocks, Wallnuts, Gems, Stones etc. on both wire and tape.

Micros ~ Smallest rocks, Wallnuts etc. and RPs, HBs etc.

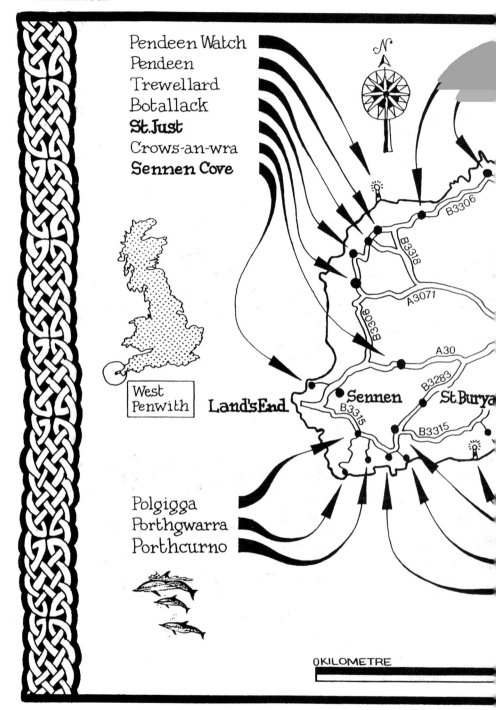

Pendeen Watch
Pendeen
Trewellard
Botallack
St.Just
Crows-an-wra
Sennen Cove

West Penwith

Land'sEnd

Polgigga
Porthgwarra
Porthcurno

Sennen

St.Burya

B3306
B3318
A3071
B3306
A30
B3283
B3315
B3315

0 KILOMETRE